Connecting Virtues

T0385525

METAPHILOSOPHY

METAPHILOSOPHY SERIES IN PHILOSOPHY

Series Editors: Armen T. Marsoobian and Eric Cavallero

The Philosophy of Interpretation, edited by Joseph Margolis and Tom Rockmore (2000)

Global Justice, edited by Thomas W. Pogge (2001)

Cyberphilosophy: The Intersection of Computing and Philosophy, edited by James H. Moor and Terrell Ward Bynum (2002)

Moral and Epistemic Virtues, edited by Michael Brady and Duncan Pritchard (2003)

The Range of Pragmatism and the Limits of Philosophy, edited by Richard Shusterman (2004)

The Philosophical Challenge of September 11, edited by Tom Rockmore, Joseph Margolis, and Armen T. Marsoobian (2005)

Global Institutions and Responsibilities: Achieving Global Justice, edited by Christian Barry and Thomas W. Pogge (2005)

Genocide's Aftermath: Responsibility and Repair, edited by Claudia Card and Armen T. Marsoobian (2007)

Stem Cell Research: The Ethical Issues, edited by Lori Gruen, Laura Gravel, and Peter Singer (2008)

Cognitive Disability and Its Challenge to Moral Philosophy, edited by Eva Feder Kittay and Licia Carlson (2010)

Virtue and Vice, Moral and Epistemic, edited by Heather Battaly (2010)

Global Democracy and Exclusion, edited by Ronald Tinnevelt and Helder De Schutter (2010)

Putting Information First: Luciano Floridi and the Philosophy of Information, edited by Patrick Allo (2011)

The Pursuit of Philosophy: Some Cambridge Perspectives, edited by Alexis Papazoglou (2012)

Philosophical Engineering: Toward a Philosophy of the Web, edited by Harry Halpin and Alexandre Monnin (2014)

The Philosophy of Luck, edited by Duncan Pritchard and Lee John Whittington (2015)

Criticism and Compassion: The Ethics and Politics of Claudia Card, edited by Robin S. Dillon and Armen T. Marsoobian (2018)

Connecting Virtues: Advances in Ethics, Epistemology, and Political Philosophy, edited by Michel Croce and Maria Silvia Vaccarezza (2018)

Connecting Virtues

Advances in Ethics, Epistemology, and Political Philosophy

Edited by

Michel Croce and Maria Silvia Vaccarezza

This edition first published 2018.

Chapters and book compilation © 2018 Metaphilosophy LLC and John Wiley & Sons Ltd.

First published as *Metaphilosophy* volume 49, no. 3 (April 2018).

Registered Offices
John Wiley & Sons, Inc., 111 River Street, Hoboken, NJ 07030, USA
John Wiley & Sons Ltd, The Atrium, Southern Gate, Chichester, West Sussex, PO19 8SQ, UK

Editorial Office
9600 Garsington Road, Oxford, OX4 2DQ, UK

For details of our global editorial offices, for customer services, and for information about how to apply for permission to reuse the copyright material in this book please see our website at www.wiley.com.

The rights of Michel Croce and Maria Silvia Vaccarezza to be identified as the authors of the editorial material in this work have been asserted in accordance with the UK Copyright, Designs and Patents Act 1988.

All rights reserved. No part of this publication may be reproduced, stored in a retrieval system, or transmitted, in any form or by any means, electronic, mechanical, photocopying, recording or otherwise, except as permitted by the UK Copyright, Designs and Patents Act 1988, without the prior permission of the publisher.

Wiley also publishes its books in a variety of electronic formats. Some content that appears in print may not be available in electronic books.

Designations used by companies to distinguish their products are often claimed as trademarks. All brand names and product names used in this book are trade names, service marks, trademarks or registered trademarks of their respective owners. The publisher is not associated with any product or vendor mentioned in this book.

Limit of Liability/Disclaimer of Warranty: While the publisher and editors have used their best efforts in preparing this book, they make no representations or warranties with respect to the accuracy or completeness of the contents of this book and specifically disclaim any implied warranties of merchantability or fitness for a particular purpose. It is sold on the understanding that the publisher is not engaged in rendering professional services and neither the publisher nor the author shall be liable for damages arising herefrom. If professional advice or other expert assistance is required, the services of a competent professional should be sought.

Library of Congress Cataloging-in-Publication Data

Names: Croce, Michel, 1988- editor. | Vaccarezza, Maria Silvia, editor.
Title: Connecting virtues : advances in ethics, epistemology, and political philosophy / edited by
    Michel Croce and Maria Silvia Vaccarezza.
Description: Hoboken, NJ : John Wiley & Sons, 2018. | Series: Metaphilosophy series in philosophy |
    "First published as Metaphilosophy volume 49, no. 3 (April 2018)." | Includes bibliographical
    references and index. |
Identifiers: LCCN 2018028786 (print) | LCCN 2018035284 (ebook) | ISBN 9781119525745 (Adobe PDF) |
    ISBN 9781119525691 (ePub) | ISBN 9781119525738 (pbk.)
Subjects: LCSH: Virtues. | Knowledge, Theory of. | Political science–Philosophy.
Classification: LCC BJ1521 (ebook) | LCC BJ1521 .C67 2018 (print) | DDC 179/.9–dc23
LC record available at https://lccn.loc.gov/2018028786

A catalogue record for this book is available from the British Library.

Cover Design: Wiley
Cover Image: © Lidia Puica/EyeEm/Getty Images

Set in 10/11pt TimesNewRomanMTStd by Aptara Inc., New Delhi, India
Printed in Singapore by C.O.S. Printers Pte Ltd

10 9 8 7 6 5 4 3 2 1

CONTENTS

NOTES ON CONTRIBUTORS

J. Adam Carter is a lecturer in philosophy at the University of Glasgow. He works mainly in epistemology, and his publications have appeared in such journals as *Noûs, Philosophy and Phenomenological Research, Australasian Journal of Philosophy, Philosophical Studies,* and *Analysis.* His book *Metaepistemology and Relativism* was published by Palgrave Macmillan in 2016.

Sophie Grace Chappell is a professor of philosophy at the Open University. She was educated at Magdalen College, Oxford, and the University of Edinburgh. She has published widely on ethics, moral psychology, epistemology, ancient philosophy, and philosophy of religion. Her main current research is about epiphanies, immediate and revelatory encounters with value. She lives with her family in the northeast of Scotland.

Michel Croce is Early Stage Marie Curie Fellow in the Department of Philosophy at the University of Edinburgh and a junior researcher at the Aretai Center on Virtues, Genoa. His research interests lie at the intersection of epistemology, ethics, and the philosophy of education. He has published several articles in these fields. He also coauthored *Etica delle virtù: Un'introduzione,* the first critical introduction to virtue ethics published in Italian (2017, Carocci).

Phillip Deen is a senior lecturer in philosophy and humanities at the University of New Hampshire and the editor of John Dewey's *Unmodern Philosophy and Modern Philosophy.* His work on the history of American philosophy, the climate debate, civic education, and aesthetics has appeared in *History of Political Thought, Public Affairs Quarterly,* and the *Journal of Value Inquiry,* among other venues. He is currently writing a book on the ethics of stand-up comedy.

Christian B. Miller is the A. C. Reid Professor of Philosophy at Wake Forest University. Recent popular writings have appeared in the *Wall Street*

Journal, Dallas Morning News, and *Slate.* He is the author of more than seventy-five academic papers as well as three books with Oxford University Press, *Moral Character: An Empirical Theory* (2013), *Character and Moral Psychology* (2014), and *The Character Gap: How Good Are We?* (2017).

Valeria Ottonelli is an associate professor of political philosophy at the University of Genoa. Her main research interests are in the normative theory of democracy and in the theory of justice in migration. Her work has appeared in *Political Studies, Journal of Political Philosophy, Critical Review of Social and Political Philosophy, International Migration Review,* and *Politics, Philosophy and Economics.*

Duncan Pritchard is Chancellor's Professor of Philosophy at the University of Irvine, California, and chair in Epistemology at the University of Edinburgh. His monographs include *Epistemic Luck* (Oxford, 2005), *The Nature and Value of Knowledge* (coauthored, Oxford, 2010), *Epistemological Disjunctivism* (Oxford, 2012), and *Epistemic Angst: Radical Skepticism and the Groundlessness of Our Believing* (Princeton, 2015).

Nancy E. Snow is a professor of philosophy and director of the Institute for the Study of Human Flourishing at the University of Oklahoma. She is the author of *Virtue as Social Intelligence: An Empirically Grounded Theory* (Routledge, 2009) and more than forty papers on virtue and ethics more broadly. She has also edited or coedited six volumes, including *The Oxford Handbook of Virtue* (2018). She is currently cowriting a book on virtue measurement.

Alessandra Tanesini is a professor of philosophy at Cardiff University. She is the author of *An Introduction to Feminist Epistemologies* (Blackwell, 1999), of *Wittgenstein: A Feminist Interpretation* (Polity, 2004), and of several articles on epistemology, feminist philosophy, the philosophy of mind and language, and Nietzsche. Her current work lies at the intersection of ethics, the philosophy of language, and epistemology, with a focus on epistemic vice, silencing, prejudice, and ignorance.

Maria Silvia Vaccarezza is a lecturer in ethics at the University of Genoa and a junior researcher at the Aretai Center on Virtues. Her research focuses on classical and contemporary Aristotelian virtue theory. Among her latest publications are "The Unity of the Virtues Reconsidered: Competing Accounts in Philosophy and Positive Psychology," *Review of Philosophy and Psychology* 8 (2017), and (with Michel Croce) "Educating Through Exemplars: Alternative Paths to Virtue," *Theory and Research in Education* 15 (2017).

Alan T. Wilson is a lecturer in ethics in the Department of Philosophy at the University of Bristol. His work mainly focuses on virtue theory within ethics and epistemology, and he has additional research interests in applied ethics and political philosophy. He is currently working on issues relating to the development of virtue and on the connection between virtue and well-being.

INTRODUCTION

MICHEL CROCE AND MARIA SILVIA VACCAREZZA

The literature on the virtues has seen several shifts and turns in its relatively short history. The first landmark was the renewed interest in the moral virtues urged by proponents of virtue ethics, who, starting in the late 1950s, proclaimed their dissatisfaction with deontologist and consequentialist views in moral theory. Despite a number of divergences among various figures of virtue ethics, their core and shared move was shifting the focus of normative moral theory from mere acts (including the consequences of an act and the normative requirements that make an act right or wrong) to the agents performing those acts. In particular, virtue ethicists shed light on the character traits—that is, the virtues—that allow a moral agent to act well. Thus, virtue ethics led to a renewed discussion of many themes that lay at the centre of the debate in ancient and medieval philosophy, among which we would mention the problem of the unity/disunity of the virtues, the role of practical wisdom as the key to living virtuously and avoiding akratic behaviour, the relationship between virtue, happiness, and flourishing, and the relationship between the good and the right. In so far as moral philosophers interested in the virtues are still discussing these topics, we can think of their work as a contribution to the original approach to the virtue-theoretic discourse.

Then, in the 1980s, the interest in the virtues reached the domain of epistemology, where at the time a lot of discussion was devoted to solving the Gettier problem—that is, to finding plausible ways to back up the tripartite analysis of knowledge with some extra conditions. The debate about moral virtues offered to epistemologists the possibility of leaving behind neutral and individualistic approaches to the analysis of knowledge, to endorse an agent-centred epistemological perspective. Ernest Sosa's first attempt

Connecting Virtues: Advances in Ethics, Epistemology, and Political Philosophy.
Edited by Michel Croce and Maria Silvia Vaccarezza.
Chapters and book compilation © 2018 Metaphilosophy LLC and John Wiley & Sons Ltd.

to propose a virtue epistemology was grounded in Aristotle's idea that the virtues require reliable success and in Aristotle's account of intellectual virtues as dispositions that lead the rational soul to the truth (virtue reliabilism) (see Aristotle *Nicomachean Ethics* VI, 2, 1139b12–13). Following these Aristotelian principles, Sosa developed his virtue epistemology around the notion of virtues as cognitive faculties (for example, visual perception, memory, and introspection) that allow an epistemic subject to perform well in the epistemic domain (that is, in acquiring knowledge) (see, e.g., Sosa 2007; 2015). For others, however, a virtue epistemology must capture another Aristotelian principle: namely, the idea that a virtue is an acquired character trait for which an agent is somehow responsible—at least in the relevant sense according to which she cannot be responsible for, say, the limits and the deterioration of her visual capacities—and which can be cultivated through education (virtue responsibilism) (see Code 1984; Montmarquet 1992; and Zagzebski 1996). Accordingly, these virtue epistemologists focused on the role that specific intellectual virtues such as intellectual courage, open-mindedness, intellectual humility, intellectual honesty, and epistemic justice play in our intellectual inquiry.

There is no need for us to go into much detail, as the important point we want to stress is the turn currently taking place within the virtue-theoretic panorama, along with the fundamental contribution of virtue ethics and virtue epistemology to the current philosophical discussion. Several virtue theorists have started developing a genuine interest in questions related to the links among various approaches to the virtue-theoretic discourse, as well as to the possibility of extending this framework to other philosophical domains. Most works on the virtues in epistemology, ethics, or other areas are frequently isolated from each other, yet they would benefit enormously from being brought into a conversation. The main thrust of this collection of essays is to offer a plausible remedy to bridge this gap. In particular, its aim is to break down barriers between different philosophical perspectives on the study of the virtues—both to highlight the interplay and overlap among virtues pertaining to different philosophical areas and to stress the peculiarity of specific virtues within their own fields.

The goals of this project are rooted in recent advances within virtue theory and, in particular, in the core idea that a serious concern for the agent and his character traits can be extremely helpful for addressing urgent philosophical issues. A few important manifestations of this assumption in the current debate need to be mentioned here (without any claim to be exhaustive), as this collection purports to share their spirit and possibly bring such spirit to further domains of inquiry. First, the serious challenge posed by situationism, which threatened the very idea of a character trait (see, e.g., Harman 1999; Appiah 2008; Doris 2010), eventually helped virtue ethicists to take an empirical approach to character more seriously, and therefore to elaborate more plausible versions of traditional views of what counts as a character trait.[1] Secondly, and partly along the same lines, virtue theorists are now more inclined than ever to work jointly with different kinds of psychologists, especially within the positive-psychology movement (see, e.g., Peterson and Seligman 2004; Park 2009; Peterson 2006), to sketch out a plausible account of human happiness and flourishing, and to find joint strategies to foster character development and human well-being. Even if some divergences endure (see Schwartz and Sharpe 2006; Kristjánsson 2013; Vaccarezza 2016), the synergy between the two movements is surely a healthy and mutually enriching one whose results are increasingly benefitting reflection on both sides.

Thirdly, both virtue ethics and virtue epistemology are currently raising their voices about the impact of virtue-theoretic approaches on the philosophy of education, with a particular interest in the role of virtue formation in traditional school curricula. Since David Carr and Jan Steutel's work in *Virtue Ethics and Moral Education* (1999), several other moral philosophers have already addressed this important issue (e.g., Kristjánnson [2014]; Russell [2015]), and further research is going to appear in the coming years as a response to Linda Zagzebski's recent work *Exemplarist Moral Theory* (2017), which approaches the topic of virtue and education from an exemplarist perspective.[2] It is also a pleasure to notice that the past few years have seen the rise of several research centres working on these topics all over the world: after the founding of the Jubilee Centre for Character and Virtues based at the University of Birmingham (which hosted David Carr and Tom Harrison's Knightly Virtues Programme, a remarkable attempt to bring character education to British schools [2015]), further centres have been founded in the United States (the Institute for the Study of Human Flourishing at the University of Oklahoma) and in Italy (the Aretai Center on Virtues at the University of Genoa).

As regards the interest of virtue epistemologists in the philosophy of education, the brightest and most concrete witness is offered by Jason Baehr's research (e.g., 2011; 2016) and commitment to help found a new charter middle school in Long Beach, California, named Intellectual Virtues Academy of Long Beach. This institution takes the view that a school is a place that fosters growth in intellectual character virtues in a supportive academic environment and equips students to "engage the world with curiosity and thoughtfulness, to know themselves, and to live well."[3] Besides Baehr's seminal work, recent research in this area has addressed several main topics, including the following: (i) the importance of specific intellectual virtues in the context of education, such as intellectual

---

[1] See, e.g., Russell 2009; Annas 2011; Alfano 2013; Kristjánnson 2013; Miller 2017.

[2] See, e.g., Kristjánsson 2006; Sanderse 2013; Carr and Harrison 2015; Croce and Vaccarezza 2017.

[3] From the Mission and Vision page on the website of the Intellectual Virtues Academy (consulted on January 4, 2018, at http://www.ivalongbeach.org/about/mission-and-vision).

humility, inquisitiveness, and open-mindedness;[4] and (ii) the epistemic aims of education and the variety of educational strategies that allow us to achieve those aims.[5]

Another area that both virtue ethicists and virtue epistemologists have recently started to (re)investigate is the relationship between virtues and vices. The debate on the interconnection of the virtues—whether having a virtue requires having them all; whether one can be genuinely virtuous in some respects while lacking other virtues—has contributed to casting light on the need for a more detailed framework for understanding how virtues relate to their vices, as it has shown that there might be cases in which, for example, displaying benevolence is overtly in contrast with being just, to the extent that a profound benevolence might appear as a vice rather than a virtuous trait. Recent work in this area includes the important collection *Virtues and Their Vices* (Timpe and Boyd 2014), several projects on the role of intellectual vices in epistemology (e.g., Cassam 2016; Kidd 2016b; Tanesini 2016b), and well-known research on epistemic injustice and its corrective virtues (e.g., Fricker 2007; Battaly 2017).

As a final important instance of how virtue theory is benefitting current philosophical discussion, a new wave of interest in the virtues and their role in public life has arisen from current research in political philosophy. A few remarks are needed in this regard. Within the classical republican tradition, interest in civic virtues, aimed at ensuring stability in a well-ordered republic, has never faded.[6] This tradition, rooted in Machiavelli's writings and ending with both modern civic humanism and civic republicanism, has always grounded the maintenance of a stable republic not only in the existence of just laws but also—and foremost—in the creation of good customs among citizens. This means, practically speaking, carrying out three strategies: first, "[one might select] institutions that inspire virtue; second, one might design institutions to economize on the stock of virtue readily available; third and finally, one might attempt to inculcate virtue (through education, religion, public mythology, etc.) so as to bridge any gap left by the former" (Lovett 2014, 512). In contrast, rival approaches to political theory seem to have long underestimated (and therefore insufficiently theorized about) the political significance of virtues broadly conceived. Even those scholars we may call "republican liberals"—despite criticizing the main tenets of both civic humanism and civic republicanism—are, however, increasingly trying to reconcile the language of rights and that of virtues, provided these liberal virtues are taken in a merely instrumental sense and not as part of a controversial conception of human flourishing (see Lovett 2014, 516).

[4] See, e.g., Kidd 2016a; Watson 2015; Riggs 2016; Tanesini 2016a.
[5] See, e.g., Kotzee 2014; Porter 2016; Pritchard 2013, 2016; Siegel 2017.
[6] See, e.g., Pettit 1997; Dagger 1997; Honohan 2002; Brennan and Pettit 2003.

This collection covers several of these key themes within virtue theory. It includes ground-breaking articles offering original solutions to long-standing issues in virtue theory, such as the plausibility of different lists of virtues, the relationship between virtues and the vices that oppose them, and the connection between moral and intellectual virtues. In addition, the collection offers insights into cutting-edge fields of application of the topic of virtue, such as the role of intellectual virtues in an age of neuromedia, virtuous dispositions related to social epistemology, and the role of some neglected virtues for political philosophy.

The collection has three parts: (i) "Moral Philosophy," (ii) "Epistemology," and (iii) "Political Philosophy." The first part tackles long-debated issues concerning virtue theory within the moral-philosophical field, such as the plausibility of drawing a single list of virtues and the stance to be taken in the debate on generalism versus particularism. It also offers novel accounts of particular virtues, thus providing new solutions to vexed questions and showing how advances in virtue research can improve our understanding of single virtuous traits.

The first part opens with Sophie Grace Chappell's fascinating contribution, "Utrum sit una tantum vera enumeratio virtutum moralium" (It seems that there cannot be a single correct list of the virtues of character). By making use of an original style, which is a tribute to Thomas Aquinas and mimics the structure of a *quaestio disputata*, Chappell offers a positive answer to the old question of the possibility of drawing a single correct list of the virtues. Having defined the virtues of character as "permanently admirable and reliably beneficial dispositions of the will that always express our attachment and orientation to the good," and having established their principle of individuation in the need to face all sorts of difficulties, Chappell is in a position to list seven virtues that fit such a description and will always be part of a single correct list: faith, hope, love, justice, self-control, courage, and wisdom.

In the second contribution, drawing both on a philosophical analysis and on the available psychological literature, Christian B. Miller in "Generosity" casts light on the extremely neglected virtue of generosity in order to spell out the necessary conditions for possessing it and to reveal its surprising complexity. A generous action, in Miller's account, is one (i) involving the giving of a gift that is valuable in the eyes of the giver, (ii) ultimately motivated by an altruistic desire to benefit the recipient, (iii) morally optional or supererogatory, and proving to be (iv) cross-situationally consistent and (v) stable. Miller defends an ultimately "subjective" approach to generosity, according to which for someone to be generous it is enough that she thinks she is benefitting others, even if it is objectively not the case. Then Miller considers three other plausible candidates for necessary conditions of generosity: reliable success, a specific manner to donate, and lack of presumptuousness. Finally, he briefly maps the relevant moral field and argues that both compassion and generosity are types of benevolence, and that they partly overlap.

Maria Silvia Vaccarezza's aim in "An Eye on Particulars with the End in Sight" is to take a stance on the debate within Aristotelian scholarship on moral particularism versus generalism so as to get a fuller grasp of the master virtue of *phronesis*, or practical wisdom. Vaccarezza starts by sketching a portrait of what she labels "radical Particularistic Reading (PR)" and contrasts it with the view she favours: the "Priority of Particulars Reading (PPR)." In particular, she argues that PPR succeeds in accounting for the priority Aristotle assigns to practical perception while at the same time counterbalancing that priority by means of two interpretive strategies and of a novel reading of some neglected passages of Aristotle's works. These passages, Vaccarezza argues, offer plenty of insight to support a moderate particularistic (or "qualified generalistic") reading. Finally, she applies such reading to educational practice, claiming that qualified generalism holds true also at an applied-educational level.

In the final contribution to the moral philosophy section, Alan T. Wilson in "Honesty as a Virtue" offers a framework for a novel understanding of another neglected virtue: honesty. In particular, he draws on Christian Miller's recent work on the topic to propose "success criteria that ... need to be met by any plausible account of honesty": namely, the following: (i) meeting the "unification challenge"—that is, explaining "why the trait is thought to be manifest in a range of seemingly distinct behaviours," including truthfulness, respect for property, proper compliance, fidelity to promises, and forthrightness; (ii) generating plausible verdicts "concerning who should (or should not) be classed as an honest agent"; (iii) being compatible with a corresponding account of dishonesty; and (iv) providing an explanation for why honesty is valuable and constitutes a moral virtue. Then Wilson defends a motivational account of honesty, which, as opposed to views focused on reliable behaviour or a tendency to produce certain outcomes, has as its core claim that honesty "centrally involves a deep motivation to avoid deception."

The second part of the collection, "Epistemology," introduces four original ways virtue epistemology successfully applies to other domains—some within, others outside, mainstream epistemology—by providing novel responses to old questions as well as by addressing more recent issues. In particular, this part explores topics such as the relationship between virtue epistemology and enhanced performances, the role of intellectual virtues in social epistemology, the importance of having an epistemology of education informed by virtue epistemology in order to face an upcoming technological revolution such as neuromedia, and the relationship between epistemic vices and motives in vice epistemology.

In his contribution, "Virtue Epistemology, Enhancement, and Control," J. Adam Carter evaluates the place of enhanced performances—the performance of athletes under the effect of a performance-enhancing drug—within Sosa's virtue epistemology. In particular, Carter tackles Sosa's recent idea that such performances fall short of aptness because they do not arise out of an agent's genuine competence. Carter shows how that idea leaves Sosa with an uncomfortable dilemma to deal with whenever we take into consideration cases of cognitive enhancement—cases in which one's cognitive performances are boosted by some kind of drug. Carter's suggested way out of the puzzle highlights the connections between virtue epistemology and the fields of ethics and the philosophy of mind and cognitive science. Specifically, he draws insights from Fischer and Ravizza's guidance-control thesis in the debate on moral responsibility to set up a parallel argument for epistemic responsibility, while he refers to Pritchard's take on cognitive integration—which reconciles virtue epistemology and extended cognition—to split the horns of the dilemma and avoid Sosa's conclusion.

Michel Croce's aim in "Epistemic Paternalism and the Service Conception of Epistemic Authority" is to apply virtue epistemology to a recent issue in social epistemology: the problem of evaluating whether epistemic paternalism can be an epistemically justified practice. Specifically, Croce tackles the issue from a novel perspective: namely, by asking *who* can be rationally entitled to undertake epistemically paternalistic interferences for the benefit of another. He argues that experts, when defined along Goldman's lines, are not the best candidates to provide that service. Virtue epistemology plays a crucial role in Croce's account because it provides the tools for introducing a virtue-based framework that distinguishes various kinds of epistemically privileged subjects (for example, experts and epistemic authorities). Thus, it makes room for individuating the key features of a *virtuous paternalist interferer*: a subject who relies on a specific set of intellectual virtues—which Croce calls novice-oriented abilities—to interfere with someone's inquiry for their own epistemic good. The essay focuses on situations where the interferer is an epistemic subject, but the last section broadens the argument to account for circumstances in which collective agents such as groups and institutions undertake epistemically paternalistic interferences.

The ground-breaking topic of educating in a futuristic age of technological development is tackled by Duncan Pritchard in "Neuromedia and the Epistemology of Education." Pritchard depicts neuromedia as a technological revolution that will make information-processing technology so integrated with our cognitive processes that we will not be able to distinguish between on-board processes and the technology itself. If it becomes real, this particular kind of extended cognition will have a strong impact on education: any concern with, for example, helping the young make good use of their memory and learn a language would become unnecessary, as they could count on their extended memory and rely on the technology to speak any language they want. In such a scenario, it becomes even more fundamental to select the most apt epistemic aim of education, which

Pritchard individuates in helping the young build their intellectual character. For while technology will help us, it will not be able to make us intellectually virtuous, as intellectual virtues cannot be offloaded onto technology. Thus, Pritchard explores several ways an epistemic agent can be intellectually virtuous in her interaction with the new technology, but he also sheds light on how technology can aid the development of our intellectual character.

The "Epistemology" part concludes with Alessandra Tanesini's "Epistemic Vice and Motivation," on vice epistemology, one of the most recent advances in virtue epistemology. Tanesini defends from recent attacks the view that intellectual character vices involve a motivation to actively turn away from the epistemic good. After introducing some counterexamples to the thesis—according to which, intellectual character vices require epistemically bad motives or, at least, the absence of good motives—Tanesini argues that all the examples feature what she calls a non-instrumental aversion to epistemic good, which undermines the force of the counterexamples and shows that they are in fact compatible with the motivational account of epistemic vices. To provide a successful defence of such a view, Tanesini appeals to the distinction between justifications of, rationalisations of, and explanations for acts and beliefs, and she argues that the distinction supports the motivational account of epistemic vices. For the fact that vice attribution is a genuinely explanatory practice entails that we consider vices to have a psychological component explaining someone's actions and/or beliefs, which on Tanesini's view is exactly what is required for having a motivation.

The final part of the collection is devoted to political philosophy and aims at applying the framework of the virtues to fields traditionally analysed with other conceptual tools. More specifically, it inquires into whether it is legitimate to complement traditional accounts of democratic agency—focused on rationality and reasonableness—with a picture of the moral and intellectual traits needed by citizens. In particular, contributions in this part investigate which of the traditional virtues might best serve the purpose of enabling full democratic agency, and whether Aristotelian-type civic virtues can be complemented by traits found in different traditions, such as American pragmatism.

In Philip Deen's contribution, "Senses of Humor as Political Virtues," the central claim is that a sense of humour amounts to a secondary virtue conducive to the cardinal political virtues of sociability, prudence, and justice. In particular, Deen defends the view that humour is instrumental to political virtue rather than a virtue in itself. The argument is developed through a critical analysis of the current debate over a sense of humour as an excellent trait, where Deen draws from recent findings in psychology to stress the idea that humour can, and in fact should, be connected to political virtues in various ways. Then, after introducing the case of Donald Trump as an exemplar of a sense of humour as a vicious trait,

Deen explores in detail three ways a sense of humour can be politically virtuous. A sense of humour can be virtuous in its relationship with sociability when it fosters a sense of equality and mutual affection among the citizenry. It can be virtuous in so far as it is a way of expressing the virtues of humility and transcendence to the extent that they are conducive to prudence. Finally, a sense of humour, unlike wit, can be virtuous in its relationship with justice whenever it fosters respect for institutions and social bonds.

In her essay "Citizens' Political Prudence as a Democratic Virtue," Valeria Ottonelli vindicates by means of a reconstructive method the importance of this neglected and undertheorized virtue in a democratic society. Despite a long tradition of thought that makes political prudence the key political virtue of the enlightened statesman, contemporary theories of democratic prudence tend to be exclusively concerned with the behaviour and responsibilities of professional politicians, rather than those of ordinary citizens, both out of a concern for feasibility and as an attempt to avoid having substantial conceptions of the good life play any role in the democratic process. To reverse such an attitude, Ottonelli starts by offering a Weberian analysis of the virtuous traits of a prudent politician: political passion, sense of proportion, and responsibility. All of these traits, Ottonelli argues, can be recognized in the political action of ordinary citizens. In the next two sections, she shows the relevance of citizens' political prudence for democratic theory, and the ways it can fail to be properly exercised. Finally, she concludes by contending that, potential ill uses of political prudence notwithstanding, the importance and value of its exercise should be protected and secured by means of adequate institutional devices.

In the final contribution, "Hope as a Democratic Civic Virtue," Nancy E. Snow sketches an account of hope as a democratic civic virtue. Against the backdrop of the current political scenario, dominated by the resurgence of populism in several countries, including the United States, Snow points to hope as an especially valuable civic virtue, which could help democracies facing current challenges. After offering her account of hope, she contends that the United States' becoming a nation of worriers, as opposed to one of carers (see Hage 2003), is partly due to a lack of social hope. "Paranoid nationalism," she contends, results from a scarcity of hope. Then, against the background of such a fragmented and divided political context, she provides examples of what hope as a democratic civic virtue looks like in the United States today. Drawing upon a distinction between pure and impure virtues, she is then in a position to define conclusively hope both as a pure and as an impure democratic civic virtue as the "disposition of openness to the political possibilities a democratic government can provide." In her conclusion, Snow suggests that her conception of hope is best theorized within a modified pragmatist account—that is, one fortified with empirical psychological evidence.

Acknowledgments

Several contributions to this collection were presented in an earlier form at the first annual conference of the Aretai Center on Virtues, held at the University of Genoa in 2016. We are extremely grateful to Angelo Campodonico for setting up and leading the Aretai Center, as well as to the following organizations for their financial support of the conference: the Department of Classics, Philosophy, and History at the University of Genoa, the FINO (Northwestern Italian Philosophy Consortium), and the SIFM (Italian Society for Moral Philosophy). We would also like to thank the editor in chief of *Metaphilosophy*, Armen T. Marsoobian, for hosting the collection, and the managing editor, Otto Bohlmann, for his help in every phase of its preparation.

Bibliography

Alfano, Mark. 2013. "Identifying and Defending the Hard Core of Virtue Ethics." *Journal of Philosophical Research* 38:233–60.

Annas, Julia. 2011. *Intelligent Virtue*. Oxford: Oxford University Press.

Appiah, Anthony. 2008. *Experiments in Ethics*. Cambridge, Mass.: Harvard University Press.

Baehr, Jason. 2011. *The Inquiring Mind: On Intellectual Virtues and Virtue Epistemology*. New York: Oxford University Press.

——, ed. 2016. *Intellectual Virtues and Education: Essays in Applied Virtue Epistemology*. New York: Routledge.

Battaly, Heather. 2017. "Testimonial Injustice, Epistemic Vice, and Vice Epistemology." In *The Routledge Handbook of Epistemic Injustice*, edited by Ian James Kidd, Gaile Polhaus Jr., and José Medina, 506–25. New York: Routledge.

Brennan, Geoffrey, and Philip Pettit. 2003. *The Economy of Esteem*. Oxford: Oxford University Press.

Carr, David, and Tom Harrison. 2015. *Educating Character Through Stories*. Exeter: Imprint Academic.

Carr, David, and Jan W. Steutel, eds. 1999. *Virtue Ethics and Moral Education*. London: Routledge.

Cassam, Quassim. 2016. "Vice Epistemology." *Monist* 99, no. 2:159–80.

Code, Lorraine. 1984. "Toward a 'Responsibilist' Epistemology." *Philosophy and Phenomenological Research* 45, no. 1:29–50.

Croce, Michel, and Maria Silvia Vaccarezza. 2017. "Educating Through Exemplars: Alternative Paths to Virtue." *Theory and Research in Education* 15, no. 1:1–15.

Dagger, Richard 1997. *Civic Virtues: Rights, Citizenship, and Republican Liberalism*. Oxford: Oxford University Press.

Doris, John M. 2010. *The Moral Psychology Handbook*. Oxford: Oxford University Press.

Fricker, Miranda. 2007. *Epistemic Injustice: Power and the Ethics of Knowing*. Oxford: Oxford University Press.

Hage, Ghassan. 2003. *Against Paranoid Nationalism: Searching for Hope in a Shrinking Society*. Annandale, Australia: Pluto Press.

Harman, Gilbert 1999. "Moral Philosophy Meets Social Psychology: Virtue Ethics and the Fundamental Attribution Error." *Proceedings of the Aristotelian Society* 99:315–31.

Honohan, Iseult. 2002. *Civic Republicanism*. London: Routledge.

Kidd, Ian James. 2016a. "Educating for Intellectual Humility." In *Intellectual Virtues and Education: Essays in Applied Virtue Epistemology*, edited by Jason Baehr, 54–70. New York: Routledge.

———. 2016b. "Charging Others with Epistemic Vice." *Monist* 99, no. 3: 181–97.

———. 2017. "Capital Epistemic Vices." *Social Epistemology Review and Reply Collective* 6, no. 8:11–16.

Kristjánsson, Kristján. 2006. "Emulation and the Use of Role Models in Moral Education." *Journal of Moral Education* 35, no. 1:37–49.

———. 2013. *Virtues and Vices in Positive Psychology*. Cambridge, Mass.: Cambridge University Press.

———. 2014. "There Is Something About Aristotle: The Pros and Cons of Aristotelianism in Contemporary Moral Education." *Journal of Philosophy of Education* 48, no. 1:48–68.

Kotzee, Ben, ed. 2014. *Education and the Growth of Knowledge: Perspectives from Social and Virtue Epistemology*. Malden, Mass.: Wiley-Blackwell.

Lovett, Frank 2014. "Civic Virtue." In *The Encyclopedia of Political Thought*, edited by Michael T. Gibbons, 509–18. Malden, Mass.: Wiley-Blackwell.

Miller, Christian B. 2017. *The Character Gap: How Good Are We?* New York: Oxford University Press.

Montmarquet, James. 1992. "Epistemic Virtue and Doxastic Responsibility." *American Philosophical Quarterly* 29, no. 4:331–41.

Park, Nansoon 2009. "Character Strengths (VIA)." In *The Encyclopedia of Positive Psychology*, edited by S. J. Lopez, 135–41. Malden, Mass.: Blackwell.

Peterson, Christopher. 2006. *A Primer in Positive Psychology*. Oxford: Oxford University Press.

Peterson, Christopher, and Martin Seligman. 2004. *Character Strengths and Virtues: A Handbook and Classification*. New York: Oxford University Press.

Pettit, Philip. 1997. *Republicanism*. Oxford: Oxford University Press.

Porter, Steven. 2016. "A Therapeutic Approach to Intellectual Virtue Formation in the Classroom." In *Intellectual Virtues and Education: Essays in Applied Virtue Epistemology*, edited by Jason Baehr, 221–39. New York: Routledge.

Pritchard, Duncan. 2013. "Epistemic Virtue and the Epistemology of Education." *Journal of Philosophy of Education* 47:236–47.

——. 2016. "Intellectual Virtue, Extended Cognition, and the Epistemology of Education." In *Intellectual Virtues and Education: Essays in Applied Virtue Epistemology*, edited by Jason Baehr, 113–27. New York: Routledge.

Riggs, Wayne. 2016. "Open-Mindedness, Insight, and Understanding." In *Intellectual Virtues and Education: Essays in Applied Virtue Epistemology*, edited by Jason Baehr, 18–37. New York: Routledge.

Russell, Daniel. 2009. *Practical Intelligence and the Virtues*. Oxford: Oxford University Press.

——. 2015. "From Personality to Character to Virtue." In *Current Controversies in Virtue Theory*, edited by Mark Alfano, 92–105. London: Routledge.

Sanderse, Wouter. 2013. "The Meaning of Role Modelling in Moral and Character Education." *Journal of Moral Education* 42, no. 1:28–42.

Schwartz, Barry, and Kenneth Sharpe 2006. "Practical Wisdom: Aristotle Meets Positive Psychology." *Journal of Happiness Studies* 7, no. 3:377–95.

Siegel, Harvey. 2017. *Education's Epistemology: Rationality, Diversity, and Critical Thinking*. Oxford: Oxford University Press.

Sosa, Ernest. 2007. *A Virtue Epistemology: Apt Belief and Reflective Knowledge*, Volume 1. Oxford: Oxford University Press.

——. 2015. *Judgment and Agency*. New York: Oxford University Press.

Tanesini, Alessandra. 2016a. "Intellectual Humility as Attitude." *Philosophy and Phenomenological Research*. doi: 10.1111/phpr.12326.

——. 2016b. "'Calm Down Dear': Intellectual Arrogance, Silencing, and Ignorance." *Aristotelian Society* suppl. 90, no. 1:71–92.

Timpe, Kevin, and Craig A. Boyd, eds. 2014. *Virtues and Their Vices*. Oxford: Oxford University Press.

Vaccarezza, Maria Silvia 2016. "The Unity of the Virtues Reconsidered: Competing Accounts in Philosophy and Positive Psychology." *Review of Philosophy and Psychology* 8:637–51.

Watson, Lani. 2015. "What Is Inquisitiveness?" *American Philosophical Quarterly* 52, no. 3:273–88.

Zagzebski, Linda. 1996. *Virtues of the Mind: An Inquiry into the Nature of Virtue and the Ethical Foundations of Knowledge*. Cambridge, Mass.: Cambridge University Press.

——. 2017. *Exemplarist Moral Theory*. Oxford: Oxford University Press.

PART 1

MORAL PHILOSOPHY

CHAPTER 1

UTRUM SIT UNA TANTUM VERA ENUMERATIO VIRTUTUM MORALIUM

SOPHIE GRACE CHAPPELL

(Readers should feel at liberty, if they wish, to translate this into thirteenth-century Latin, as well as the title.)

It seems that there cannot be a single correct list of the virtues of character.

Objection 1. For any counting of items presupposes that we have a principle of individuation applicable to those items. But there is no one correct principle of individuation for the virtues of character. And so, no single correct list.

Objection 2. For what is true in ethics is "what everyone or most of us or the wisest have always thought is true," as Aristotle (*Topics* 100b23–25) and the Catholic Catechism both incline us to agree. But there is no single list of the virtues that has been accepted *semper ubique ab omnibus* [always, everywhere, by everyone]: different lists are found in Plato and Aristotle and St. Paul and Buddhism and Islam and Confucianism and (implicitly) the Lonely Hearts columns and in many other places too. Therefore there cannot be a single correct list of the virtues of character.

Objection 3. Moreover, if there were a single correct list of virtues of character then Aristotle or Plato or St. Paul would already have discovered it. But Plato and Aristotle and St. Paul all give different lists in different places; and Aristotle and St. Paul present no *argument* for their lists, while Plato sometimes just assumes a list, as in the *Protagoras*, and sometimes presents an unconvincing argument for a different list, as in the *Republic*. So none of them discovered a single correct list of virtues of character. Neither, then, can we.

Connecting Virtues: Advances in Ethics, Epistemology, and Political Philosophy.
Edited by Michel Croce and Maria Silvia Vaccarezza.
Chapters and book compilation © 2018 Metaphilosophy LLC and John Wiley & Sons Ltd.

Objection 4. Moreover, the virtues are those dispositions of character that people admire. But what people admire changes all the time and includes many contradictions and perplexities. No stable single list can be founded upon this mutability, contradictoriness, and perplexity. *Ergo*, etc.

Objection 5. Again the virtues are those dispositions of character that are always beneficial. But no dispositions of character are *always* beneficial; social structures and environmental conditions change constantly, and we change with them. Therefore there are no virtues of character, and hence no single correct list of such virtues, or indeed any list at all.

Objection 6. Again, the virtues are those dispositions of character that no one can make bad use of. But there is *no* disposition of character that no one can make bad use of: a soldier who fights knowingly in a bad cause can be courageous, a burglar who incidentally passes treasures on his way to the burglary he intends can temperately ignore them, justice can be unloving through harshness, love can be unjust through partiality, faith and hope can be sincere but misplaced. *Ergo* there are no virtues, and hence no list.

Objection 7. Again, the virtues are those dispositions of character that promote or instantiate human flourishing. But human flourishing is an evolutionarily determined notion, and what promotes it is not only different depending on the human animal's environmental conditions but also sets a standard that is not so much an ethical one as, in Bernard Williams's words, the "ethological standard of the bright eye and the gleaming coat" (*Ethics and the Limits of Philosophy*, p. 46). By this way, then, either the list of virtues of character includes such things as ruthlessness and cunning and dissimulation and promiscuity, *quod minime convenit* [which would be entirely unfitting], or there is no list of virtues of character.

Objection 8. And the true virtues are those dispositions that *necessarily* express and promote the good of and for any rational creature. But if we were a different kind of creature then different dispositions would be virtues for us (see Philippa Foot, *Natural Goodness*, on wolves and bees and plants). Therefore all of these dispositions only contingently express or promote our good; so none of them is truly a virtue. So there can be no list of virtues of character.

Objection 9. Moreover, the virtues are deep dispositions in us, as Bernard Williams says in several places. But as Williams also says, it is impossible for us to state consciously and explicitly the depth of these dispositions without detaching ourselves from their motivational power. Therefore, if there can be a single correct list of the virtues of character, it is one we cannot state. Therefore we must either speak knowingly falsely or say that we know of no single correct list of the virtues of character.

Objection 10. Moreover, a list of virtues implies a plurality of virtues. But "virtue" means "a quality of soul that resides in the will." And the soul and the will are unities. So therefore is virtue. So there is only one virtue, and unless a singleton "list" is a list, there can be no *list* of virtues.

Objection 11. And while a list of virtues implies a plurality of virtues, Augustine says in *De libero arbitrio*, book 1—following Socrates and the Stoics, and followed by Kant—that virtue means the capacity of the will that makes use of everything else, including all other capacities. So we have it on the authority of Socrates, the Stoics, Augustine, and Kant that virtue is a unitary capacity. So there is only one virtue. So no *list* of virtues.

Objection 12. And while a list of virtues implies a plurality of virtues, Aristotle says—following Socrates—that virtue of character is the knowledge of something specific: Socrates says knowledge of the good, Aristotle says knowledge of the mean. So there is only one virtue. So no list.

Objection 13. And while a list of virtues implies a plurality of virtues, John Lennon says—following the Epistles of St. John and, indeed, most of the rest of the New Testament—that love is all you need. So there is only one virtue. So no list.

Objection 14. Again, the object of those lists of virtues that have typically been offered, as by St. Paul or by spiritual directors, is not philosophical but devotional; St. Paul in such lists as he offers in his letters aims to exhort his readers to live better lives, spiritual directors aim to get their dirigees to consider with compunction in what ways they might have failed to live up to the Christian standard. Such lists are simply *ad gregem aedificandam* [for the edification of the flock] and have no bearing upon philosophical truth, and they do not imply that there can be a list of the virtues of character.

Objection 15. Again, the virtues are by definition the dispositions of character that we need to fulfil our highest destiny, that is, to get to heaven. But St. Paul and the Gospels say clearly that all we need to get to heaven is to be forgiven and redeemed. And to be forgiven and redeemed is not a disposition of character at all but a work of grace in us. So there are no dispositions of character that we need to get to heaven. Hence there are no virtues. And no list.

Objection 16. Moreover, the life of perfect goodness is what interests the ethicist. The life of perfect goodness is the life that we shall live in heaven; and supposedly, the life of perfect goodness is the life of the perfected virtues. But the virtues are, as St. Thomas says, *circa difficilia* [concerned with what is hard for us]. And nothing will be hard for us in heaven. So the life of perfect goodness will involve no virtues. So even if there is a single correct list of the virtues of character, it is of no interest to the ethicist.

But on the other hand, St. Thomas says, on the authority of the whole tradition, including scripture, Plato, Aristotle, Cicero, Augustine, and innumerably many others, that the cardinal virtues are fittingly enumerated as justice, self-control, courage, and wisdom (*Summa Theologiae* [ST] 1a2ae.61.2), and that the theological virtues are fittingly enumerated as faith, hope, and charity (ST 1a2ae.62.3). This, then, is our list of the seven virtues of character.

What needs to be said is that the virtues of character are those permanently admirable and reliably beneficial dispositions of the will that always express our attachment and orientation to the good.

"Permanently admirable" because every virtue of character always has something beautiful (*kalon, pulchrum*) and something great about it, and it is the nature of admiration to fix on what is beautiful or great or both. Admiration is often misdirected, sometimes even by entire societies: as it can be directed to honour killings of oneself or others, as it has been in Afghanistan and Japan; or to military violence, as it was by Homer's heroes and is by many eleven-year-old boys; or to racial purity or racial baiting, as it was in Nazi Germany and the Old (and alas not so old) South of the United States; or to the acquisition of fame and money and column inches in *Hello!* magazine, as it most inexplicably (*unintelligibilissime*) is in Britain and Italy today. Yet the admirable is not what *is* admired but what most intelligibly *can be*, what *should be*, admired.

"Reliably beneficial" because the virtues do not in every case or inevitably benefit either their possessor or those around her; as when a person herself suffers or dies exactly because of her virtue, as Edith Stein and Dietrich Bonhoeffer did, or as when some great common good can only be achieved by some evil act that a virtuous person rightly refuses to do for the sake of that great common good—as Caiaphas should have refused, John 11:50. Yet the virtues are those dispositions that do *in most cases* and *reliably* benefit both their possessor and those around her. And they are those dispositions that will benefit us in these ways, irrespective of the differences between societies and individuals and times.

"Dispositions of the will" because every virtue of character is a habit of choice. A habit of choice means two things: first, a way of putting the practical question what to do and, secondly, a way of answering it.

By "a way of putting the question what to do" I mean a particular kind of moral vision, a specific way of framing the alternatives between which we deliberate and choose, that is distinctive and definitive of the good person. So a good person who is confronted by a fat man stuck in a cave entrance will certainly think to look around for unguents, whereas it will not even occur to her to look around for explosives. And a good person who has been shipwrecked and is in a life raft with no food or water and three companions will certainly think to hope and wait and pray for a shore or a rescue ship, and to encourage and distract his companions, and to try his teeth on his leather belt and wallet, and to catch fish and seaweed and turtles and gulls and insects, and upturn his hat in order to pool rainwater, whereas it will not even occur to him to kill and eat the cabin boy.

From this way of putting the practical question, our answers to it in various contingencies will almost immediately follow; or will follow perhaps not immediately at all and with the greatest imaginable difficulty, yet still *conveniens virtuti* [in a way that befits virtue].

And the virtues of character "always express our attachment and orientation to the good," because to act out of virtue *per se* is always—however inchoately and unconsciously—to act out of allegiance to the good. It is expressive action with this force, that it states one's past and present commitment to the good and one's future intention always to continue to be guided by and towards the good. This force can rightly be called *love of* or *loyalty to* the good; it is the force that Iris Murdoch has in mind in *The Sovereignty of Good*. And this is the sense, or one sense, in which every act that is *per se* done out of virtue is always an act of love and an act of loyalty.

Now the virtues that always and in every case fit this description are at least these seven: faith, hope, love, justice, self-control, courage, and wisdom. Each of these is a single virtue, because it embodies a responsiveness to a specific kind of difficulty in life that is based in a specific group of the dispositions in us. Each of these virtues has subparts, but those parts are properly regarded as *sub*-virtues, not themselves as virtues, because of their ordering to the difficulties in life and the dispositions in us.

It is possible that there are not just sub-virtues but also wholly other virtues that should be listed. Possible in principle, at least.

It would be surprising for us to make a new discovery about this *now*, but we should always be open to future possibilities. If they seem remote to us now, this may simply be because they are *future* possibilities.

It is possible too that the division of the unity that is virtue overall into just these seven specific virtues could validly be framed a different way by a philosophical culture or tradition different from our own.

Notwithstanding these possibilities, these seven virtues will always be members of at least one possible correct list of the virtues of character. There can therefore be at least one single correct list of the virtues of character, though perhaps not one single *uniquely* correct list of the virtues of character; and we know at least seven of the items that it must contain.

So to *Objection 1*, this objection could not show that there cannot be a correct list of virtues of character; only that there could not be a *single* correct list, because there is no single correct principle of individuation for virtues. But the virtues are, as Thomas Aquinas says, *circa difficilia* [concerned with what is difficult for us]; so they can be individuated if the needs and difficulties that rational agents are necessarily bound to face can be individuated. And this can be done—though of course more than one need can occur at once, the need for courage is one thing, the need for temperance quite another. Hence it is possible at least to argue about how the virtues might be individuated; and this argument could have an outcome in a single list of virtues that reasonable interlocutors might accept as correct.

And on *Objection 2*, there may be no single list of the virtues that has in fact been accepted *semper ubique ab omnibus* [always and everywhere by everyone], or even by most people, or most wise people, in most times. But that is not to say that there cannot be a single correct list of the virtues of character. For it remains possible that there is a single list that *deserves* to be accepted *semper ubique ab omnibus*, and that we can say something interesting and substantive about what this list might contain: as I have argued above.

And this also answers *Objections 3 and 4*. Aristotle and Plato and St. Paul and many many others are labourers for the discovery of the truth, but we are co-labourers with them, and the task of discovery goes on, perhaps—indeed, probably—for ever, both *in via* and in heaven.

As to *Objection 5*, it is not true that the virtues are those dispositions of character that are *always* beneficial; they are rather dispositions of character that are *reliably* beneficial.

And on *Objection 6*, while acts that proceed from the virtues *per se* [in and of themselves] necessarily involve love of and loyalty and allegiance to the good, there are also acts that proceed from the virtues *per accidens* [incidentally]; these are actions that have the outward form and much of the dispositional structure of *per se* virtuous actions, yet with some disordering of the underlying inward prerequisites of love, loyalty, and allegiance to the good. In this sense there are indeed no dispositions of character that no one can make bad use of. Yet when courage, self-control, and so on take this *per accidens* form, it is also right, as Philippa Foot observes in "Virtues and Vices," to see a sense in which the corresponding acts are not truly actions *of those virtues* at all.

To *Objection 7*, it should be said that human flourishing is not an evolutionarily determined notion, and that it is the genetic fallacy to think so. Evolution sets up and historically precedes the conditions within which distinctively human life and flourishing arise. To think that evolution therefore determines the nature of human flourishing is like thinking that, since human feet phylogenetically correspond to flippers in one distant evolutionary ancestor of humans, therefore human feet are still really flippers. But the mistakenness of this thought is manifest.

On *Objection 8*, likewise, the apt comment is that at least the *principal* virtues will be the same for any rational creature, and that if there are characteristics of human life which we are inclined to call virtues, but which would not be shared by the life of some other conceivable rational creature, a Martian, say, then what we should doubt is that *these* characteristics are virtues at all, or at the very least that they are *principal* virtues. And closer attention to examples confirms this. Thus we can perhaps imagine a life of which the ability to put up with pain is not a necessary part, because there is no pain. But it is impossible to imagine a rational creature's life—if it is to be a *life*—where there could be no scope at all for courage. Now the ability to put up with pain is a subpart of the virtue of courage. Courage, then, is the same good for all rational creatures, even if the ability to put up with pain need not be. So this way we do not prove that there can be no list of virtues of character; we prove only that the true list of virtues of character must rise well above the contingencies of any particular mode of life. But *that* we knew anyway.

As for *Objection 9*, what is impossible for us is to state consciously and explicitly the *full* depth of these dispositions without detaching ourselves from their motivational power. It does not follow that we cannot say anything at all about the depth of our guiding dispositions; if that were true we could not even be having the present discussion without that detachment, and we can. Nor therefore does it follow that we cannot state a single correct list of the virtues of character.

To *Objection 10*, we should reply that the soul and the will and virtue are all of them unities; but all *complex* unities. And, moreover, *ideal* unities. The complete unity and integration of the soul and the will and of virtue is never actually achieved by any of us but is always the horizon towards which we aim. Yet even in its full achievement there will still be a place for at least some kinds of complexity in unity, just as, in the apt image of Protagoras (*quasi a veritate coactus* [as if he was magnetised to say it by the attraction of the truth]), the face is a unity by consisting of a mouth, nose, eyes, cheeks, chin, eyebrows, and forehead. So from the claim that the soul or the will is one, it does not follow that there is only one virtue; because that claim is false. Yet neither, from the fact that virtue is one, does it follow that there is only one virtue; for virtue, as said, is one by being a complex unity.

Objection 11. Likewise it is true that virtue means the capacity of the will that makes use of everything else, including all other capacities; which does indeed imply that virtue is a unitary capacity. But again, the fact that virtue is one does not imply that there is only one virtue.

The same can be replied to *Objection 12*.

And also to *Objection 13;* regarding which we may add that the love that is implicit in all other virtues is love of and loyalty to the good, as is clear from what was said in the body of the essay.

As for *Objection 14*, there is no reason any list of virtues should not have both a philosophical and a devotional point. The best philosophy and the best devotion go hand in hand. Indeed, in the Beatific Vision they become the very same thing.

Turning to *Objection 15*, it is quite true that all we need to get to heaven is to be forgiven and redeemed; but the objection evinces a misunderstanding of what redemption and, indeed, grace actually involve. To receive redemption and grace is to be transformed by the Holy Spirit's infusion into us of all the virtues; until this has happened—and it is only completed in heaven—the work of redemption and grace in us has hardly begun. So there are dispositions of character that we need to get to heaven, without which we are not fit for the life of heaven, and which God brings to being in us through the indwelling of His Spirit. And these are the infused virtues.

So finally, on *Objection 16*, it is for one thing quite untrue that the life of perfect goodness is the *only* thing that interests the ethicist; our struggles on the way to that life are of the greatest interest to her too. And for another, while we are still on the way we can know very little indeed of the life of heaven. But to say as the Objection does that "nothing will be hard for us in heaven" is to suggest that spending the rest of eternity going deeper and deeper into the ecstatic contemplation of the infinite, aweful, and ineffable mystery, majesty, and love of almighty God will be *easy* and so will not call at all significantly upon our reserves of virtue. As suggestions go, it is hard to see how any could be more rash or unpersuasive than this.

CHAPTER 2

GENEROSITY

A PRELIMINARY ACCOUNT OF A SURPRISINGLY NEGLECTED VIRTUE

CHRISTIAN B. MILLER

It is hard to explain why some virtues have received a great deal of attention from contemporary analytic philosophers in the West, whereas others have been almost completely neglected. Dozens of papers have been published on the virtue of modesty, for instance. Almost nothing has been written in the past fifty years on the virtue of honesty (for an exception, see Miller 2017).

What about generosity? I would have expected a lot of interest by analytic philosophers in this character trait. Not so. As far as I can tell, there have only been three articles in mainstream philosophy journals going back at least to the 1970s on generosity (Hunt 1975; Kupfer 1998; Stout 2015).

In this essay, I aim to draw attention to this neglected virtue. By building on what work has already been done, and trying to advance that discussion along several different dimensions, I hope that others will take a closer look at this important and surprisingly complex virtue.

My focus is on better understanding what it is to be a generous person. But much of the first half of the essay is about particular generous acts and the motives behind them. This will help to pave the way to developing an account of the virtuous character dispositions that are capable of giving rise to such acts.

I should be explicit from the start that I do not address two kinds of generosity in this essay: being generous-minded in how one thinks about things, and being generous-hearted in forgiving others. Each of these dispositions has complex features of its own that deserve a separate treatment

Connecting Virtues: Advances in Ethics, Epistemology, and Political Philosophy.
Edited by Michel Croce and Maria Silvia Vaccarezza.
Chapters and book compilation © 2018 Metaphilosophy LLC and John Wiley & Sons Ltd.

elsewhere (see Wallace 1978, 132, 136–39, and especially the excellent discussion in Kupfer 1998).[1]

One more qualification. We sometimes say things like "That was a generous helping of potatoes" and "They let out a generous amount of the waist on those jeans." Here "generous" is used to mean something like "larger than normal" or "plentiful." That is not my concern here either (see Wallace 1978, 132–33). I am interested in the moral virtue of generosity and the actions to which it gives rise.[2]

With these qualifications out of the way, we shall proceed as follows. First, I introduce two fictional cases of generous actions and use them to make some preliminary observations. Then in the next three sections of the essay I discuss three central elements of a generous action. Section 5 puts these pieces together in constructing a partial account of what a generous disposition looks like. Section 6 considers some other candidates for necessary conditions, while section 7 briefly tries to sort out the relationship between generosity and closely related traits like benevolence and compassion.

1. Preliminary Observations

Let's begin with two fictional cases.

1. Lillian is moved to make a donation to charity, and she spends some time researching organizations that work with the poor in India. Finally, she chooses one with an excellent track record of impactful work and makes an anonymous donation of $1,000. The website of the organization thanks her for her generous donation and vows to put it to good use in alleviating child poverty.
2. William is the CFO of a regional health care provider. His job keeps him very busy, but he still makes time to volunteer every Thursday night for an hour at the local community center to meet with anyone who needs help filing taxes, figuring out how to get a mortgage, navigating payroll for a small start-up company, or other financial challenges. He is often thanked profusely by the people he helps for being so generous with his time, not just for being generous with them personally but for being willing to volunteer in general in the first place.

These uses of "generous" are perfectly familiar and appropriate. They also serve to highlight certain features of generous actions. First, these acts are not limited to monetary donations, although that is the paradigm case of a generous act. William is generous with his time, not his money. We can be

[1] Although it would be an advantage of an account of generosity if it were able to explain these additional uses as well. Whether the account proposed here does such explanatory work, will have to be considered on another occasion.
[2] Hence if there is an epistemic virtue of generosity distinct from the moral virtue, I won't be taking it up here. For relevant discussion, see Roberts and Wood 2007, chap. 11.

generous with all kinds of things (opportunities, possessions, space, information, labor, and so forth), and while they may sometimes have a monetary value attached to them, this is not a necessary feature.

Second, generous actions can be onetime, momentary actions, like Lillian's online donation. Or they can be forms of commitment to a pattern of behavior over the course of months or even years, as with William's volunteering.

Third, it seems that both Lillian and William are focused on helping other people. Their attention appears to be directed outside themselves, rather than on benefiting themselves. But we don't know this for sure, and it could be that ultimately they are motivated by egoistic considerations of some kind, such as rewards in the afterlife or guilt avoidance. Their motivations cannot simply be read off from their behavior. We shall return to the motivational dimension of generous actions in section 3.

Finally, Lillian and William are commended for their behavior. But that does not entail that they are generous people. If their actions do not arise from some underlying virtuous disposition that is stable and cross-situationally consistent, and instead the actions are uncharacteristic and out of character, then they are not linked to the virtue of generosity.

This last observation highlights the importance of distinguishing between the following categories:

  (i) a generous action;
  (ii) acting from generosity; and
  (iii) being a generous person.

A generous action can be an action from generosity, due to the person's being generous. But a generous action can be a one-off action, done by someone who is not a generous person. Acting from generosity entails having the virtue of generosity. But performing a generous action does not. For all we are told about Lillian and William, it is natural to say that they performed generous actions. But that's it. Whether they acted from generosity, and whether they are thereby generous people, remains unknown given the thin descriptions of the cases (for helpful related discussion, see Hurka 2006).

I make use of these distinctions in the sections to come. For now, our focus will be on generous actions. This might seem surprising. For one common way to understand a virtuous action is as what a virtuous person would do in the relevant circumstances. So in the case of generous actions, even if Lillian herself does not have the virtue of generosity, her donation to charity can still be generous provided it is the same action that someone who was generous (perhaps even a different, virtuous version of herself) would have done too when researching poverty in India. Hence there doesn't seem to be much to say about generous actions, and the interesting work has to do with acting from generosity and being a generous person.

As we shall quickly see, I don't adopt this approach. On my view, there are conditions that must be met by Lillian herself that have nothing to do with how a virtuous person would behave in her circumstances.

2. The Cost of Generous Actions

With these preliminary observations in mind, let's try to go deeper and see if we can outline some central features of generous actions. Here is one about which there seems to be a fair amount of agreement in the literature on generosity.[3]

(C1) An action is generous only if what is bestowed by the action is of value to the giver.

A sum of $1,000 is of value to Lillian. That is a lot of money to her, as her annual salary is $40,000. Similarly, William leads a busy life as the CFO of the corporation. His free time is very limited, and there are many other ways he could be spending it. Yet he chooses to use his financial knowledge to help others.

Suppose we told one of these stories differently. Suppose, for instance, that Lillian is actually a frivolous billionaire. For her, $1,000 is completely insignificant; she would hardly blink an eye if it went missing. One day she makes an online donation of $1,000 to a charity working in India. Her action is still helpful, perhaps even compassionate. But it is less clear that it is generous.

Or imagine Sam. Sam used to care a lot about his model train set. But now he is bored with it and wants to get rid of it. Rather than just throw it away, he donates it to Goodwill. Helpful for Goodwill, perhaps, as it can resell the set and use the money for a good purpose. But hardly, it would seem, generous of Sam.

There is some intuitive plausibility to (C1), and it is widely accepted. But (C1) is ambiguous. Here are at least two different versions of the claim:

(C1$_{objective}$) An action is generous only if what is bestowed by the action is *objectively valuable* to the giver, such that she has normative reason to value it, even if as a matter of fact she does not.[4]

(C1$_{subjective}$) An action is generous only if what is bestowed by the action is *subjectively valued* by the giver, such that she does in fact value it, even if as a matter of fact it is not valuable.[5]

---

[3] See Wallace 1978, 133–34; Kupfer 1998, 358; Roberts and Wood 2007, 287; Curzer 2012, 95.

[4] Wallace seems to lean in this direction (1978, 135–36). Behind this condition are metaethical assumptions about the objectivity of value. But the condition is suitably vague, so that even expressivists and quasi-realists can accept it, since they can talk in terms of objective value too. Nihilist positions about value in metaethics, however, may have a harder time accepting this version of (C1).

[5] Kupfer (1998, 358) and Roberts and Wood (2007, 287) seem to favor this view. A third option is to combine these two requirements, such that an action is generous only if what is

We care about and value plenty of things that, in fact, are not good for us. And we don't value plenty of things that, in fact, it would be good for us to value.[6]

Instead of his model train set, Sam might care a lot about a bucket of mud. Yet he decides to donate the set anyway, because for some reason he thinks Goodwill can put it to good use and he cares about those less fortunate than himself. He certainly values the bucket of mud. But in fact it is not objectively valuable or good for him. Does that mean that Sam's action cannot be generous?

My own view is that it would be too restrictive to think that actions like this couldn't be generous. Even if Goodwill can't put the donation to any use, I am still inclined to say that Sam has done something generous, and to praise him for his "sacrifice."

Take the inverse case of something objectively valuable for a giver that she does not in fact value at all. Jessica, for instance, might give away several containers of sunscreen, thinking (mistakenly) that she doesn't burn and that there is no harm in being in the direct sun on the beach. She recognizes that other people might find the sunscreen helpful, but she couldn't care less about it.

What should we say about this case? Here, I am initially inclined to say that her action would not be generous, even though she is donating something that is objectively valuable to her. The fact that it has no subjective importance means that there is no cost—in her eyes—to donating the containers, and so nothing to admire about her action, at least as far as it's generosity is concerned (for a similar example see Wallace 1978, 133).[7]

So my view is that we should favor ($C1_{subjective}$) as the more plausible option for spelling out our first component of a generous action. Generous actions involve the giving of a gift (broadly construed), and that gift needs to be valuable in the eyes of the giver, at least to some extent.[8]

Here is a challenge to my view. Imagine someone who one day is struck by the needs of a family recovering from Hurricane Irma. She immediately donates five pairs of jeans and ten shirts from her closet to the family. This

bestowed by the action is subjectively valued by the giver *and* is objectively valuable too. Since I will be arguing against one of these requirements, my arguments will apply to this combined position as well.

[6] I am taking valuing, seeing something as having worth or being worthwhile, and caring about something to be equivalent for the purposes of this discussion.

[7] Suppose, however, that she has to go out of her way to make the donation, say, by driving all the way across town to a donation center. Then it might be harder to go with my position, even though it is still true that the containers don't have any value in her eyes. But I think there is a plausible way to account for the donations being generous. What is of value is not the containers per se but Jessica's time. She values *that*, yet is willing to give up her time to make this donation. And that is a generous thing to do, other things being equal. Thanks to several people at the University of Mississippi for helpful discussion of these issues.

[8] An interesting question, which I can't pursue here, is whether religions that demand relinquishing all attachments can still make conceptual room for generous action.

certainly could count as a generous action, I'd want to say, but it also seems that in donating the clothes she need not consciously consider their value to her.[9]

Fortunately, I can allow for cases like this to count as generous actions. I only require that what is bestowed by the giver be of value in her eyes, *other things being equal*. Yesterday, perhaps, she had been trying on the clothes and thinking to herself how well they fit and how much she looked forward to wearing them. But when she is struck by the needs of the family, naturally enough she doesn't give any conscious thought to how valuable they are to her. That is no longer on her conscious radar screen. And this is compatible with the proposal on offer in (C1).[10]

We can draw a deeper lesson from this example. The case serves as a helpful illustration of how (C1) can be true and someone still act wholeheartedly in generously giving to another. It might seem that if what is bestowed is costly in the eyes of the donor, then even if she does give it away, she might have to struggle and overcome internal opposition to do so. If this were the case, then her character could at best only rise to the level of continence, not virtue, at least on a standard Aristotelian picture.

But as we've just seen in the case of the clothing donation, (C1) need not have this implication. In the moment, the person may not give any thought to how valuable the items in question are to her. Her focus could rather be on those in need, and she can wholeheartedly come to their assistance.[11]

By way of concluding this section, recall that we are focusing on generous actions for now. This is important, since it doesn't automatically follow that (C1$_{subjective}$) is plausible as a requirement on *actions from generosity*. I suspect that when it comes to actions caused by the virtue of generosity, there will be more temptation to adopt an objective requirement like (C1$_{objective}$) on the value of the gift. We will return to this question in section 5 when we transition from generous actions to the virtue of generosity.

---

[9] Thanks to Alan Wilson for raising this challenge.

[10] Something similar can be said about the following case, which I owe to Dennis Earl. Suppose a professor has one dollar automatically deducted from his paycheck each month to go to his school. His monthly donations seem generous, but suppose that he rarely gives any thought to the dollar, and when he does, he isn't moved by losing the money. Two things can be said in response to this case. First, his *initial* act of signing up for the donation arrangement likely involved forgoing something the professor valued: namely, dozens of dollars over many years. And second, it is unlikely that he doesn't value one dollar, *other things being equal*. A penny could be a different story; most of us don't seem to care about single pennies anymore. And if the arrangement by the professor had been to donate a penny a month to his school, I'm not so sure that his monthly donations would then count as generous.

[11] Thanks to David Holiday for suggesting that I consider this issue. For relevant discussion in Aristotle, see 1120a–1121a.

3. The Motivation of a Generous Action

We don't know anything about the motives behind why Lillian donated the $1,000 and why William volunteered to help others with their finances. Could their motives make a difference to whether they were behaving generously or not? Or would we say that they were doing generous things no matter how reprehensible their motives might be?

Suppose it turned out that William was really volunteering so that he could look for psychologically vulnerable people to scam out of their money. Or perhaps he was trying to find ways to prey on them sexually. Perhaps Lillian donated the money only because she was required to do so as part of her conviction for tax evasion. Or she donated only to appease a guilty conscience.

These discoveries would matter to me a great deal. I initially would have said that both Lillian and William were doing generous things with their money and time, respectively. Now I wouldn't think that at all. They are just out to benefit themselves in some way (or so they think). I was wrong to believe that these were generous actions, especially since our focus in this essay is on *moral* generosity.

The few philosophers who have discussed this issue seem to agree. Motivation does matter for generous actions. What kind of motivation, though? My proposal is that there is an altruistic motivational requirement on generous actions.[12] Here is one way to formulate it:

> (C2) An action is generous only if in so acting the giver is ultimately motivated to give something in order to benefit the recipient for his or her own sake, regardless of whether the giver benefits in the process.[13]

Thus in the case of generous actions there must be an ultimate motive that is altruistic. Let me explain.[14]

---

[12] For related discussion see Hunt 1975, 239–40; 1987, 221–24; Wallace 1978, 132; Machan 1990, 62; Kupfer 1998, 357; Hurka 2006; Roberts and Wood 2007, 286; Curzer 2012, 95. Roberts and Wood do not technically accept (C2), as they allow for cases of generous actions in which the person acts from a sense of a duty to be generous (2007, 289).

[13] This formulation is restricted to generous actions aimed toward other persons. But if there can be generous actions toward nonhuman animals, and even toward communities or ecosystems or planets, then (C2) and the discussion that follows could be adjusted accordingly. Another complication is that in some cases the recipient of the gift and the object of the altruistic desires need not be the same person. As Alan Wilson helpfully pointed out to me, there are "cases where you help the child of a stressed friend out of an ultimate motivation to benefit the friend rather than the child. This wouldn't be a case where the ultimate motivation is to help the recipient, but it would be a case where the ultimate motivation is altruistic (as defined later on). Intuitively, I think that such a case could count as generous." I agree. One way to revise (C2) to address such cases would be to say, "An action is generous only if in so acting the giver is ultimately motivated to give something in order to benefit the recipient, *or someone suitably connected to the recipient*, for his or her own sake, regardless of whether the giver benefits in the process." To keep things simpler, I have omitted this complication from the main text.

[14] The next two paragraphs draw, with permission from Oxford University Press, from my earlier account in Miller 2013, chap. 2.

Ultimate desires are contrasted with derivative or instrumental ones.[15]
For instance, I might have this desire:

   (i) My desire that I help a student with his paper.

This would not be an ultimate desire if it was caused in me by prior mental
states like:

   (ii) My desire to get good course evaluations.
   (iii) My belief that helping this student with his paper will lead him to
       give me a better course evaluation.

The desire in (ii) itself could be instrumental with respect to

   (iv) My desire that I get a good raise from my university.

So (i), given its causal history back to (ii) and (iii), is clearly not an ultimate desire. Nor is it an altruistic one.[16] Altruistic desires are such that in
the process of being satisfied, someone else is benefited for his or her own
sake according to what counts as being benefited by the person who has
the desire. For example, the following could count as an altruistic desire:

   (v) I desire that you get better from your illness.

Here my focus, let us suppose, is on what is best for you, not on whether I
benefit in the process. In fact, such a desire might lead me to act against my
self-interest, but that's fine as far as I am concerned.[17]

---

[15] I have moved from talking about motives to talking about desires, but nothing hangs
on this in the essay. Other accounts of motivation can be substituted instead. For proposals
about how to formally distinguish ultimate and instrumental desires, see Sober and Wilson
1998, 217–19 and 218, n. 15; Stich, Doris, and Roedder 2010, 151–52.

[16] There may be desires that are both ultimate and instrumental, such as a desire for pleasure or the avoidance of pain (Stich, Doris, and Roedder 2010, 151–52). If so, I put them
under the heading of ultimate desires.

[17] Generalizing from cases like this one, we can say that:

The ultimate desire of a person is *altruistic* just in case:

   (i) It concerns what she thinks benefits (at least) one person who is not herself.
   (ii) The desire cannot be satisfied unless someone other than herself would be bene-
      fited in her eyes, and benefited in such a way that is independent of what would
      subsequently benefit her.

Here I have been helped by Sober and Wilson 1998, 217–19, 224–31; May 2011, 40–43. See
also Adams 2006, 65, 74; Batson 2011, 20–29. Note that (A) is formulated narrowly in terms of
what benefits another *person*. But as Sober and Wilson rightly observe (1998, 229), a broader
formulation would need to include ultimate desires concerning the environment, particular
animals, a group of people, and so forth. (A) can be easily adjusted to have such a broader
focus when need be. In addition, I understand "benefits" broadly so that they include, for
instance, protection of rights and intellectual and aesthetic pursuits.

With this background in mind, we can now restate the second component of a generous action as follows:

(C2*) An action is generous only if the action is motivated by an ultimate desire that is altruistic.[18]

Let me briefly make three observations. First, some might find the language of "altruism" distracting, or start to think in terms of evolutionary psychological accounts of "altruism" where the word can have a rather different meaning. If so, the term can be dropped and replaced with talk of benefits.

Second, this requirement is doing more work than just excluding egoistic ultimate motives. Egoistic and altruistic motives are not exhaustive; dutiful motives, for instance, exist too, and would be excluded by (C2*). This is intentional, but for those who want to allow for dutiful motivates to give rise to generous actions, (C2*) can be easily adjusted so that its job is only to exclude egoistic ultimate motives.

Finally, (C2*) should make us cautious about the accuracy of judgments of generous actions (ours or anyone else's). For it is hard to discern people's motives, and we can be mistaken about many of our own as well. We can easily think that an action is generous, and yet, unbeknownst to us, on motivational grounds it is not.

(C2) is a necessary condition on generous actions. It does not purport to tell a complete story about their underlying motivation. For good reason, too, since it is nowhere near sufficient. To see this, we can start with the familiar point that actions often have multiple motives. (C2) just requires *some* contribution from an altruistic desire. That is compatible with the *primary* source of motivation being crudely egoistic. Lillian might have some degree of altruistic concern that makes a modest causal contribution toward motivating the donation. Most of the action's motivation, let us suppose, instead comes from a desire to alleviate her feelings of guilt. That isn't the motivational profile of a generous action, I wouldn't think.

Rather, for generous actions there must be an ultimate motive that is altruistic *and* primary. Motives come in different strengths, and if multiple motives are causally relevant, the strongest one needs to be the generous one. The volunteering by William can still count as generous even if he is motivated in part to do this to pad his resume, so long as that motive is motivationally secondary to desires to help people in financial trouble for their own sake.

Even this, however, isn't enough. Suppose that, even though it is a secondary motive, William's desire to pad his resume is such that were he to

---

[18] As Hunt writes, "In the case of generous acts, there is no such 'because' or 'in order to' beyond the intention of benefitting someone: we do not do *that* in order to do something else" (1975, 239, emphasis his; see also 1987, 221, 224).

stop caring about his resume, he would stop volunteering too. The altruistic desires, in other words, are not strong enough by themselves to sustain him. Without some payoff for himself, he would bail out. And that doesn't seem like a particularly generous kind of behavior.

So the proposal we have arrived at for refining (C2) can be stated this way:

> (C2**) An action is generous only if the action is motivated by an ultimate desire that is altruistic, and in the case of mixed motives, this desire is primary and capable of leading to the behavior even in the absence of the other motives.

A natural question to ask at this point is whether we actually *have* any desires like this. If not, and if (C2**) is a genuine requirement on generous actions, then no one has performed any generous actions. That would lead to a deeply revisionary error theory about judgments of generosity.

The best place to look for such desires, at least at the present moment, is with research in psychology on empathy. For that is the only area of psychological research, so far as I am aware, that has found support of the existence of altruistic desires.

The leading figure here is C. Daniel Batson (for an excellent overview of his work, see Batson 2011). During the course of several decades of research at the University of Kansas, he found a robust causal relation between adopting an empathetic state of mind and increased helping behavior. When trying to explain this relationship, he tested many different egoistic hypotheses, such as the claim that people help more so as to relieve their distress after empathizing with the difficulties others face. Yet time and again he couldn't find any support for these egoistic explanations. Instead, the only hypothesis that repeatedly fit the data was what he called the empathy-altruism hypothesis, which he states as follows: "Empathy evokes motivation directed toward the ultimate goal of reducing the needy person's suffering; the more empathy felt for a person in need, the more altruistic motivation to have that need reduced."[19]

I suspect that other sources of altruistic motivation to help, besides empathy, will emerge in future research. But suppose not. Then if altruistic motivation is necessary for generous actions, and if empathy is the only source of altruistic motivation, we have the following:

---

[19] Batson 2002, 92. For different versions of the hypothesis, see Batson 2011, 29. Another area of psychological research that is relevant here is work in positive psychology using the VIA (values in action) classification of character traits. The classification has twenty-four character strengths, one of which is kindness, which encompasses generosity and altruistic love. Also relevant is Big Five research in personality psychology, since one of the facets of the Big Five trait of agreeableness is altruism. I have not discussed either of these research areas in the essay, both due to lack of space and because their measures are often based on self-report questionnaires. I am wary of how much such reports can tell us about the existence and sources of altruistic motivation.

The Empathy-Generosity Thesis. A person can perform a generous act toward another only if the person has empathized with the other person's situation in some relevant way.[20]

Again, I wouldn't be surprised if this thesis gets overturned someday on empirical grounds. But for now it is a defensible claim.

4. The Freedom of a Generous Action

We have looked at the costliness of generous actions and at the motives that underline them. In this section we turn to one more central component of generous actions, namely, that we are not required to perform them.

I have already invoked the language of "gifts" (see also Sanchez 2010, 443). Gifts by their nature are not things one is required to bestow on a recipient. They are freely chosen, praiseworthy if bestowed, but not blameworthy if omitted.

Lillian's donation is a kind of gift to the charity in India. Lillian wasn't required to make this donation, and ordinarily wouldn't be blamed if she had not. Similarly, William is making a gift of sorts with his time. His volunteering is praiseworthy but optional.

This leads to our third requirement on generous actions:

(C3) An action is generous for an agent to perform only if the action is not morally required but rather is morally optional.[21]

If Sam is morally required to give $50 to a starving person at his doorstep, that action might be compassionate and praiseworthy. But it would not be generous. If he is morally required to give $50 but instead chooses to give $100, then the action might be compassionate, praiseworthy, *and* generous.

Another way to put the point is in terms of supererogation. Sam's donation of $100 is supererogatory. So would have been Sam's donating $75 or $150. Hence we can restate (C3) as:

(C3*) An action is generous for an agent to perform only if the action is morally supererogatory.[22]

---

[20] A reviewer worried that this thesis might be tautological given condition (C2) and (C2*). But these conditions only require altruistic motivation. They don't say anything about the *source* of that motivation. The thesis here does—it claims that the source is empathy. Note that this could be false on empirical grounds, but that would have no bearing on the truth of (C2) and (C2*).

[21] See Hunt 1975, 236, 241, and 1987, 218–21, 225; Wallace 1978, 134–35, 140; Machan 1990, 61–63; Kupfer 1998, 359; Sanchez 2010, 443, 447, 450; Stout 2015, 142. For a challenge, see Stangl 2016, 359–60.

[22] A weaker view would say that an action has to either be supererogatory, or if it is morally required, it would be such that the person would still do it even if it were not morally required. But this would allow cases of acting from moral duty to count as generous actions, which I think is a mistake, and which (C3*) is designed to exclude. Thanks to Robert Westmoreland here.

Indeed, one dimension along which to measure how generous someone's action once was, is to see just how much it went above and beyond the call of duty.[23]

If this is right, it has interesting implications for certain debates in normative ethics. Some views, especially certain forms of consequentialism, deny that there are any supererogatory actions. We don't have to consider here their reasons for holding this claim. The only point to make is that, given (C3*), such views will also have to deny that there is any conceptual space by their own lights for generous actions. This would carry over to cases of acting from generosity, and to the virtue of generosity. Generosity as understood in this essay won't turn out to be a virtue.[24]

My goal is just to highlight these implications. Whether they are significant costs of the views in question would require looking closely at their details, which is a task for another essay.

Let me end here by noting that (C3) is ambiguous in a similar way as we saw happen with (C1). For it can be given both objective and subjective readings:

(C3$_{objective}$) An action is generous for an agent to perform only if, objectively, the action is morally optional, *even if* the agent takes it to be morally required.[25]

(C3$_{subjective}$) An action is generous for an agent to perform only if, subjectively, the agent takes the action to be morally optional, *even if* the action is objectively morally required.[26]

Back to Sam for a moment. Suppose he believed that giving \$100 to the person at his door was morally required, even though it wasn't. He only

---

[23] To clarify, (C3*) applies just to generous actions. It is compatible with the claim that becoming a generous person in the first place is morally required. It is also compatible with the claim that acting from generosity, at some point or other during one's life, is morally required. It is *even* compatible with the claim that, in a given instance, *generosity* requires one to help, so long as this does not entail that one is morally obligated to help. Finally, once one has performed a generous action, that in turn can *bring with it* certain moral obligations. For instance, once our CFO William has volunteered to help those with financial problems, he is subsequently obligated to, say, listen to their problems and not cut the meeting in half to go play golf. For discussion related to these various points, see Kupfer 1998, 363; Stout 2015, 150–52; Stangl 2016, 347–48.

[24] I owe this observation to Brandon Warmke. See Warmke unpublished. This is not the only virtue whose actions may necessarily be supererogatory. Acts of mercy may too. Perhaps charity as well.

[25] Wallace (1978, 135–36) seems to side with this view.

[26] Hunt (1975, 236, and 1987, 218) seems to adopt this view. Again, a third option is to combine these two requirements, and again since I will be arguing against one of these requirements, my arguments will apply to the combined position as well. (C3$_{subjective}$) could be construed as an intellectually demanding requirement—most people might not give any thought to whether their actions are morally optional versus morally required. If this is a genuine worry, then the condition can be restated negatively as follows: an action was generous for an agent to have performed only if, subjectively, the agent did not take the action to be morally required and did not take the action to be morally forbidden.

had to give \$50. According to the objective version of (C3), this can still count as a generous action.

But I am inclined to think that Sam *didn't* perform a generous action in this case. He just did what he thought he was supposed to do. Imagine this conversation with his wife when he returns to the living room:

Sam's wife: That was a very generous thing to do, Sam, giving him \$100.

Sam: Actually I really wasn't being generous. It just felt like the right thing to do, what I had to do.

Sam's wife: Well, I think you went way above and beyond what you had to do to help him. That's why I said it was such a generous thing to do.

This conversation seems perfectly intelligible to me.

Now consider a different version of what Sam did and the subsequent conversation with his wife:

Sam's wife: Where did you go?

Sam: There was someone at the door who needed help, so I gave him \$50. It was probably more than he needed, but I thought it wouldn't hurt to be a bit generous.

Sam's wife: Actually, you did exactly the right thing.

Reasons are given for why this was morally obligatory, followed by:

Sam: O.K., you convinced me. Now I see that I ended up doing what I was supposed to do all along. If I had realized that at the time, then I wouldn't have thought the \$50 was generous. Can we watch some TV now?

This conversation, too, seems perfectly intelligible to me. If another person in need comes to the door a minute later and now Sam gives him \$50 out of a sense of duty, then he and his wife can quickly agree this time that his action did not count as generous.

Hence I am inclined to accept ($C3_{subjective}$) and reject ($C3_{objective}$). I don't want to deny, though, that the subjective version might have some counterintuitive implications.[27] For instance, suppose someone starts out as a straightforward utilitarian and doesn't think that there are any supererogatory actions. Then on ($C3_{subjective}$) he wouldn't perform any generous actions. But suppose he has a crisis of confidence in utilitarianism and decides to convert to some form of folk morality. His donations to charity, which before were morally required in his eyes, now become supererogatory. He can suddenly perform generous actions all the time! That might seem odd. Or consider his twin, who remains a committed utilitarian. Even

[27] I am grateful to Alan Wilson for raising these concerns.

thought they might exhibit the same behaviors of writing a check in the same amount to the same charity, one of them might be acting generously and the other not. That too might seem odd.

These do not strike me as deeply counterintuitive implications, but they are worth highlighting rather than glossing over. Here is another challenge. It is well known that moral exemplars and heroes often downplay what they did in, say, saving a life or donating an organ. While to us their actions might seem supererogatory, they frequently report that in the moment they were just doing what they had to do or simply doing their duty. If their reports about their experiences are accurate, then my view would imply that in being motivated this way they couldn't have performed generous actions. And that seems like a tough pill to swallow.

I can't respond adequately here, and anything I do say will be hand waving. But a few possible moves are: (i) hold that in these cases exemplars are being modest, and so disbelieve the accuracy of their reports about what they thought was motivating them at the time; (ii) accept that there may have been a feeling of necessity to act in the way that they did in the moment but deny that the feeling was typically one of moral obligation or duty, and instead more along the lines of volitional necessity (Frankfurt 1999); or (iii) claim that if we were in the exemplar's shoes and performed the same actions, we would likely judge them to be generous but would not ourselves have taken them to be morally required.[28]

Overall the subjective version of (C3) still strikes me as more plausible than the objective one. That is, with respect to generous actions. As in the case of (C1), a different answer may be needed for actions that are caused by the virtue of generosity. At long last, it is time to turn to those actions and the virtue itself.

5. The Virtue of Generosity

We said that performing a generous action does not entail possessing the virtue of generosity and so does not entail that the action was done out of generosity. On widespread understandings of virtues as global character trait dispositions, to act out of a virtue like generosity is to act from a casual disposition with at least these two features (for more, see Miller 2014, chap. 9):

> *Cross-situational consistency.* A virtuous disposition, other things being equal, is likely to give rise to virtue-relevant thoughts and actions in a wide variety of different circumstances which are relevant to the virtue in question.

> *Stability.* A virtuous disposition, other things being equal, is likely to give rise to virtue-relevant thoughts and actions in the same relevant circumstances stably over time.

---

[28] Thanks to Danielle Wylie for raising this concern and to Michael Roche for very helpful discussion.

Thus if we knew not only that Lillian's donation of $1,000 was generous but also that it arose from her generous character, then we could expect that Lillian is likely to be generous again in similar ways in the future (assuming that she has the financial resources), and that she also will exhibit generosity in other ways in other kinds of situations. For instance, she may volunteer her limited time, say, to help struggling students as part of an after-school program.

Cross-situational consistency and stability are features of all moral virtues. But our goal is to better understand the virtue of generosity specifically. Fortunately the work of the past three sections can be put to good use in doing so. The virtue of generosity is, in large part, a disposition to perform generous actions with the motivational and normative features already outlined.[29] So we can say that:

(G) A person has the virtue of generosity only if she is disposed to perform actions, in a variety of different relevant situations and stably over time, which are such that:

   (i) What is bestowed by the actions is of value to the giver.
   (ii) The actions are motivated by an ultimate desire that is altruistic, and in the case of mixed motives this desire is primary and capable of leading to these actions even in the absence of the other motives.
   (iii) The actions are morally supererogatory and not morally required.

This should be a straightforward application of what has come before. In the remainder of this section, I want to return to the question of subjective versus objective interpretations.[30]

With respect to (i), would a generous person give only things that are objectively valuable to her, or is it enough that she merely thinks that they are valuable, even if they really are not? And with respect to (iii), would the virtue of generosity lead only to actions that really are morally optional, or is it enough that the generous person merely thinks that they are optional, even if they are required?

[29] See also Wallace 1978, 143. It is worth noting that there are other conceptions of generosity that are incompatible with the account offered here. Roberts and Wood, for instance, interpret both Aristotle and Nietzsche as denying the altruistic motivational requirement, since "the generous person's greatness as giver seems to be uppermost in his mind" (2007, 291). So I am not claiming to be putting forward an account that would be accepted by all leading philosophers of the past. Rather I am claiming to be offering an account that harmonizes well with our ordinary outlook about generosity and generous actions.

[30] One case that some have thought might be a challenge for my view is to explain how a professor giving extra credit on the final exam could be acting from generosity, as she certainly seems to her class to be doing. But I think (G) can handle this case. It is straightforward how the professor could be doing something supererogatory and also for altruistic reasons. (Of course, some cases of extra credit are motivated by egoistic considerations, like getting better course evaluations. But the motivation need not always be egoistic.) Finally, something is being given that is of value to the professor: namely, the opportunity to earn a higher grade in her class.

Note that the same kind of question arises with respect to condition (ii) as well. An altruistic motive aims to benefit or promote the good of someone else. But in the case of generous actions, does it actually have to benefit the recipient? Here again we get two alternatives:

($C2_{objective}$) An action is generous only if what the giver thinks would benefit the recipient really is objectively valuable to the recipient, such that she has normative reason to value it, even if as a matter of fact she does not (Stout 2015, 156; Stangl 2016, 341–42).

($C2_{subjective}$) An action is generous only if the giver thinks the recipient would be benefited, regardless of whether he really would be benefited.[31]

Sam really wants to help with a food drive. So he buys a carload of fruits and vegetables from a local farmer and drops them off at the food pantry. Unbeknownst to him, the food is infected with a microscopic parasite that causes all the people who eat it the next day to get terribly sick. Sam had the best of intentions, his action was costly to him, and it was supererogatory. But he ended up not benefiting these people at all but rather making their lives worse off. Would we still want to say that he did something that was generous? And when it comes to the virtue, would a generous person give only things that objectively benefit others, or is it enough that she merely thinks that they will benefit others (just as Sam thought), even if sometimes they do not?

For conditions (i) through (iii), the two natural options are to answer "objective" or to answer "subjective" for all three of them. Those are the options I shall focus on as well. But while I won't explore it further here, I think we shouldn't neglect the possibility of answering "objective" for at least one condition and "subjective" for at least one other condition.

I suspect the predominant approach, especially among contemporary Aristotelian philosophers, is to answer "objective" across the board. Aristotle would likely agree, as he famously claimed that "the generous person as well [as every other virtuous person] will aim at what is fine in his giving and will give correctly; for he will give to the right people, the right amounts, at the right time, and all the other things that are implied by correct giving" (Aristotle 1985, 1120a24–26; see also 1120b29–30; Sanchez 2010, 443–44). Philosophers tend to develop general accounts of what a virtue is, and their accounts tend to include objective versions of their conditions. So if generosity is to count as a virtue, then it would follow that it had better meet

---

[31] Hunt (1975, 240–41, and 1987, 226–27) seems to accept something like this view. Hence he writes, "There is no contradiction in saying 'He shouldn't have given her that money because she will certainly only use it to harm herself, but you can't fault him for his generosity'" (1975, 241). See also Roberts and Wood 2007, 287. As before, a third option is to combine these two requirements, such that an action is generous only if what is bestowed by the action is subjectively valued by the recipient and objectively valuable too. Again I will reject one of the requirements and so reject the combined view too.

those conditions as well. This is a top-down approach to deciding these questions.

My preferred approach is instead bottom-up. I have not worked with any background theory of virtue in this essay, other than assuming that the traditional virtues are cross-situationally consistent and stable. Instead I have started with generous actions rather than virtuous actions as such, and with occurrent actions as opposed to trait dispositions. I have relied upon my intuitive judgments about these occurrent generous actions to take me in the direction of a partial account of the virtue of generosity (here I have followed a similar approach to Hurka 2006.).

In doing so, I have arrived at conclusions that favor the subjective answers (Hunt [1975 and 1987] seems to draw similar conclusions). With respect to (i), I am moved by cases like this:

> Jones has more than a thousand dead ants in his insect collection. He has spent countless hours organizing all their bodies, labeling them and keeping them safely preserved. Objectively speaking, there is little to no value to the collection, monetarily or otherwise. But Jones clearly cares about it a great deal. He also, however, cares a great deal about those who are suffering, and so one day he donates the collection to a charity in the hope that the charity can sell it and use the proceeds to help alleviate child poverty in India.

This is a subjectively costly action for Jones, it is motivated altruistically, and it is morally optional. I am inclined to say that it is a generous action and that it could arise from the virtue of generosity.

With respect to (ii), I am moved by cases like that of Sam and the infected fruit that makes everyone sick. Even though his intention was to benefit people, they did not in fact benefit. But that, in my view, doesn't mean that he failed to act from the virtue of generosity in this case.

Finally, with respect to (iii), I am moved by cases like that of Sam helping the person at his front door. Sam might think that his giving $50 was morally optional, even though in fact it was morally required. I am not inclined to hold that against him doing something generous or acting from the virtue of generosity.[32]

A critic may object that even an objective approach can allow for cases like that of Jones and the dead ants, since it does not require perfect success at meeting the requisite conditions in order for someone to be generous. In other words, Jones can be a generous person if the case of the dead ants or other cases like it are suitably rare events in his life.

Likewise, according to the critic, my preferred subjective approach might be harder to maintain in the face of *systemic* errors on the giver's part.

---

[32] For those who are not moved to go quite as "subjective" as I am on the three conditions but are also worried about the objective versions, an intermediate option is to say that in cases like Sam and the infected fruit, he succeeded in *trying to perform* a generous action, even though he failed in *actually performing* a generous action. Thanks to Kyle Fritz for suggesting this possibility.

Suppose now, for instance, that *most* of what Sam donates to others is not objectively valuable to him. Suppose too that most of his charitable actions aim to benefit others but do not do so. And finally, suppose that routinely Sam is mistaken when it comes to determining his moral obligations. Do I still want to insist that he could be acting from the virtue of generosity?[33]

I do. Here are three reasons for my insistence.

Degrees

Virtues come in degrees, and generosity is no exception. Perfect generosity is an ideal that we likely cannot attain. But minimal or moderate possession of the virtue of generosity is attainable and is compatible with some mistakes and miscues.

Offloading the Mistakes

The mistakes and miscues at issue here, however, are not clearly failures of *generosity*. Being systemically mistaken about which actions are morally required, or about whether a gift will in fact benefit other people in the future, can be chalked up to failures of understanding, discernment, or the like. In other words, Sam could indeed have the relevant dispositions required for generosity; it is just that the information that is being inputted into and processed by these dispositions is faulty. If he is exhibiting failures of virtue in his behavior, they are failures with respect to other virtues, not generosity (for related discussion, see Hunt 1975, 241).

It is important to highlight that there are two aspects to this response. The first is to be able to identify some other defect in the person's psychology, such as a failure of a related intellectual or moral virtue. In some instances, it may even be a failure of baseline sanity or mental stability. The second aspect to the response is to hold on to the claim that the generosity dispositions themselves, abstracted away from the inputs they receive from the rest of the person's psychology, can still be virtuous. They are susceptible to "garbage-in, garbage-out" problems, but the garbage itself comes from elsewhere.

I find this way of handling the putative counterexamples plausible (and reminding people that the account is not purporting to offer sufficient conditions helps too). But in a longer discussion we would need to go example by example. And I also recognize that there are complications lurking in the neighborhood that I am not addressing here. One complication has to do with the doctrine of the unity of the virtues, since this response has more

---

[33] Relevant cases include individuals who perform morally horrendous actions but do so with the best of intentions, forgoing something they value and going above and beyond the call of duty for the sake of altruistically "benefiting" others, perhaps by torturing or killing them. For one such case that can be adapted to fit this description, see Kekes 1998, 219. Thanks to Alan Wilson for this reference.

plausibility if we deny the doctrine. Another complication has to do with whether practical wisdom is a part or component of generosity, and if so, what implications this might have for thinking about these cases. This is a huge topic that I cannot hope to tackle here.[34]

Implausibility of the Objective Requirements

Finally, it is simply implausible to expect of ordinary human beings that they meet the objective versions of conditions (i) through (iii) in order to qualify as generous. Sam had no reasonable way of knowing about the microscopic parasites in the food. To expect him to have detected the parasites beforehand is to expect him to behave like a supernatural being. It is not a reasonable expectation for a typical human being, given today's technology. Cases of blameless ignorance like this one are plentiful and should not render an action or, in systemic contexts, a person not generous.

To conclude, I am tentatively prepared to accept (G) with each of the three conditions being given a subjective reading. As Lester Hunt writes, "The fact remains that a fully generous act may be utterly misguided and miscarried" (1987, 226).

But I readily acknowledge that there is much more work that needs to be done on these issues. Furthermore, I am only making a claim about this one virtue. Objective interpretations might be more plausible for similar conditions that apply to other virtues. But I don't think we can decide how this is going to turn out merely by thinking about the nature of virtue as such. We need to go virtue by virtue.[35]

6. Some Candidates for Additional Necessary Conditions

It is highly unlikely that (i) through (iii) in (G), even if plausible, are exhaustive. Here I consider three additional candidates for necessary conditions. I do not, though, purport to have exhausted all possible candidates.

Reliable Success

Linda Zagzebski's influential account of virtue has as a necessary condition a success requirement. As Zagzebski writes, "A person does not have a virtue unless she is reliable at bringing about the end that is the aim of the motivational component of the virtue....A [generous] person aims at making the world a certain way, and reliable success in making it that way is a condition for having the virtue in question" (1996, 136).

Note that this reliability requirement is independent of the subjective versus objective disputes we have just considered in the previous section.

---

[34] For an excellent discussion of practical wisdom, with specific applications to generosity, see Russell 2009.

[35] For hints of a similar approach, see Hunt (1975, 240, 242, and 1987, 226–27). He notes that justice and prudence might require more objective conditions.

For instance, someone could have a radically distorted understanding of what would benefit other people in need, and yet there could still be a question about whether he is reliably successful in bringing those "benefits" about.

Issues about reliability and virtue are complex, and I do not have space to consider them properly here. Let me only register my view that, at least in the case of generosity, I do not find such a requirement to be plausible.

Suppose that Sam regularly makes donations to several charities to combat starvation. Can he reasonably be expected to discern ahead of time whether these organizations have a corrupt employee who pockets his donation? That does not seem reasonable. Or will Sam be able to tell when the work of these organizations will end up being fruitless due to a series of freak natural disasters? Again the answer is no. And this is not even to get into the philosopher's toolbox of skeptical scenarios like the evil demon or the Matrix hypothesis.

Of course, everything could go well for Sam. All of the charities he donates to could end up using his money appropriately, and many people in need could be benefited. But this looks like a happy accident. It is hard to see how he could have reliably discerned these things beforehand. To do so would have required a vast amount of information well beyond what can reasonably be expected of human beings. To have to be so reliable in discerning these matters puts generosity out of reach for most if not all of us.

This is the epistemic way of putting the worry for a reliability condition on generosity. The metaphysical way of putting the worry is that it is hard to accept that a failure to succeed in doing what you take to benefit others would entail a failure to act from the virtue of generosity.

The natural disaster case illustrates this point forcefully. Apart from a massive earthquake, Sam's donation would have benefited hundreds of people in a poor village. Instead, the earthquake destroys all the food that the donation purchased, and no one in need is benefited. It is hard to accept that Sam's action changes its status, based on this completely unforeseeable natural disaster, from acting from generosity to not acting from generosity.

Skeptical scenarios reinforce this point. If Sam lives in a Matrix environment, then even if there is no earthquake and the life-saving food is delivered to the village, his action does not get to count as arising from the virtue of generosity, since there are no real people who are benefited (only computer simulations). That strikes me as implausible.[36]

This is hardly the end of the story, however. Reliability conditions can be formulated in various ways, such as reliability in "normal conditions." So for all that is said here, the jury is still out on whether a reliability condition should be added to (G).[37]

---

[36] For similar cases, see Baehr 2007.

[37] For helpful discussion with respect to moral and intellectual virtues in general, see Baehr 2007.

The Manner of Acting

Up to this point nothing has been said about the manner in which someone goes about donating a valued possession for the sake of benefiting another person. That could seem to matter too. For example, if William the CFO volunteers to help others with their financial difficulties but then makes a big deal with each person who comes through the door about how important he is and how he is sacrificing so much of his valuable time to be there, we might question how generous he really is being. It seems he is just self-serving. On the basis of cases like this, perhaps we need to add a condition about the manner or way in which a person acting from the virtue of generosity goes about helping others.

But this is not immediately clear. For the second condition about altruistic motivation seems to block cases like this self-aggrandizing version of William. What makes him seem far from generous is that his focus is on himself and what a great guy he is to make this sacrifice, rather than focusing on the person in need. Recall that according to the second condition, the primary motive when acting from generosity needs to be altruistic and ultimate.

I think this is a plausible response with respect to cases like self-aggrandizing William. It won't work for other cases, however, like this one:

> Jones has brought to his local donation center a very heavy chest full of items to donate. For some reason, however, the center is overrun with people bringing in their items as well, although these folks just have one small item each. Unfortunately at the moment there is only one person working at the center, who looks frazzled and stressed trying to process these donations. Jones decides to wait in line with his chest, even though it will take the worker twenty minutes to catalog all his items and sort where they need to go. In the meantime, the line gets longer, and the people behind Jones get frustrated, as they could have all been finished long before Jones is done. And Jones knows this.

Here Jones was altruistically motivated in donating these valuable items, which he was not morally required to do. But there was still a failing on his part. The manner in which he carried out this donation was less than exemplary. He could have come back later in the day instead. Or he could have just stood to one side and let everyone else go first.

This failure, though, isn't clearly a failure of generosity. It is rather a failure with respect to some other virtue, such as conscientiousness, empathy, or thoughtfulness. Possession of these other virtues serves to naturally complement the functioning of generosity. But that is different from saying that a necessary condition needs to be added to the account of the virtue of generosity itself.

So for the moment I am not convinced that an additional condition is needed in this regard. But if it is, then it can easily be added to (G).

Presumptuousness

A different place where an additional condition might be needed is to address cases like the following:

> The grass has been getting long at Susan's house for several weeks now. One day Susan returns from work and discovers that her entire yard has been pristinely cut. It looks better than it has ever looked before. Susan asks her neighbor what happened, and the neighbor reports that a lawn company just came by and cut her lawn for free. The workers didn't leave a card or sign, as they wanted their gesture to be anonymous (for related examples, see Stout 2015, 143–45).

What should we make of this action by the lawn company? Susan's neighbor says that it was really generous—it was costly and morally optional for the company, which did it solely to help Susan out.

Susan, however, might have grounds for complaint. After all, these were complete strangers who entered her property without her permission, and they did something that she had not authorized. For all they knew, Susan might have *wanted* her lawn to look overgrown. Even though it turned out well, the lawn company's workers had bypassed her completely in the process and taken it upon themselves to decide what was best for her property. Far from being virtuous, what they did could be considered morally wrong.

Borrowing from a recent paper by Rowland Stout, I think we can say that the lawn company workers are guilty of being presumptuous.[38] It was presumptuous of them to think that they knew what was best for the property without consulting with Susan first.

Note that this does not seem to be blocked by the three conditions in (G). The actions of the lawn company appear to satisfy all three of them. Should we say that the company could have been acting from the virtue of generosity?

In my experience, people have different intuitions about cases like Susan's. Those who intuitively find the company to be generous and yet still at fault on moral grounds tend to make use of the strategy of appealing to another virtue that hasn't been exercised. This was a plausible strategy above, I suggested, when it came to Jones donating his pile of items at the donation center. Here we would be saying that the lawn company really was being generous and just failed with respect to, say, thoughtfulness or being respectful.

If that is the right thing to say about the case, then we are done here and (G) does not need any additional supplementation in this regard. Suppose, though, that Susan doesn't compliment the company's generosity. Instead she takes its presumptuousness to undercut what might otherwise have been an expression of generosity. Presumptuousness, on this way of

---

[38] See Stout 2015. Stout's paper provides a much richer and more complex treatment of presumptuousness and generosity than can be attempted here.

thinking, *undermines* generosity, and so something is missing from (G).[39] In the remainder of this section, let me provisionally accept this claim and see what could be added.

What is missing, one might say, is that the lawn company lacks suitable *authority* to cut Susan's lawn. It would be a completely different story if she had hired the company to work for her. Then she would be authorizing the workers to come onto her property and take care of it, even without contacting her ahead of time on the day when they show up.

The same applies to another case of presumptuousness:

> Drs. Jones and Bennett are colleagues chatting over lunch about the surgery Bennett needs to do tomorrow on one of her patients who is currently unconscious in intensive care. Early next morning, Jones goes ahead and does the procedure for Bennett without telling her in advance, in order to save his friend the trouble. The surgery is a complete success.

Again, Bennett can reasonably complain. This was not a patient under Jones's care, and Jones did not consult with Bennett beforehand. If he had, Bennett would have been fine with Jones doing the procedure. But in virtue of not consulting with him, Jones lacked the authority to perform the surgery on one of Bennett's patients.

If this approach sounds promising, then we can add the following fourth condition to (G):

> (G+) A person has the virtue of generosity only if she is disposed to perform actions, in a variety of different relevant situations and stably over time, which are such that:
>
> > (iv) The giver has the requisite authority to bestow the relevant kind of gifts to the relevant people in need, or to intermediaries who will use those gifts to benefit these people.[40]

Of course, a lot will depend on what "authority" amounts to in fleshing out condition (G+). But I hope to have suggested that there is some intuitive plausibility to this condition. The details will have to wait for another occasion.

Not surprisingly, this condition also lends itself to an "objective" and "subjective" reading. Suppose somehow that the lawn company thought it had the authority to cut Susan's lawn. Is that enough, or did it need to really be the case that the company had this authority?

---

[39] For more, see Stout 2015, 143–45. As Stout writes, "In behaving presumptuously you get wrong the very thing that you get right in behaving generously. Presumptuousness is a corruption of generosity" (145).

[40] Thanks to an anonymous reviewer for helping me refine this proposal. Stout's proposal is similar to mine, in that Stout thinks presumptuousness "involves adopting a role that you do not have and are not entitled to adopt" (2015, 145).

Here too it is not immediately clear which way to go, and I will not take a stand myself. In favor of the subjective version, we can imagine that the company had worked for the previous owner of Susan's property, and it is doing this act of kindness on what had been that owner's birthday (not realizing that Susan had recently moved into the house). The workers didn't have the requisite authority to do this work, but they reasonably thought they did. The fault wouldn't be with their generosity; it would be an epistemic fault. Or so the advocate of the subjective version could say.

On the other hand, there are cases in which you act presumptuously precisely in virtue of thinking that you have the requisite authority even when you don't. A familiar case would be grandparents who assume they have the requisite authority to make major decisions on behalf of their grandchildren without consulting the parents, and proceed to do so. A subjective reading of (G+) would allow such behavior to still count as generous; an objective reading would not. If presumptiveness is supposed to count against generosity, then that could favor the objective reading.[41]

Even if you do think (G+) is a plausible addition to (G), I don't want to claim that we now have sufficient conditions for acting from generosity or for possessing the virtue. I will return to this issue at the very end of the essay.

What I do claim, though, is that (G) gives us important and central necessary conditions.

7. Sorting Out Generosity and Some Related Virtues

In this brief final section I want to stand back from the details and use the account that has emerged to bring some clarity to the relationship between three related notions: benevolence, compassion, and generosity. Philosophers construe their relationship in a variety of different ways. The results of this essay suggest a natural organization.

Benevolence can be used as the broad notion, encompassing compassion and generosity and other notions as well such as kindness and charity (for a similar approach, see Wallace 1978, 128, and Kupfer 1998, 357). Compassion and generosity are types of benevolence. Are they the same thing? Is one a subset of the other?

My view is that generosity and compassion only partially overlap, as depicted in figure 1. One thing that compassion and generosity have in common is the altruistic motivational requirement. The virtue of compassion also gives rise to helping, which is primarily aimed at benefiting another person. But compassion and generosity do not share the supererogation requirement. Sam might come across a stranger who has been shot in the leg and drive him to the hospital. That is a compassionate thing for Sam to

[41] I have been helped here by Alan Wilson.

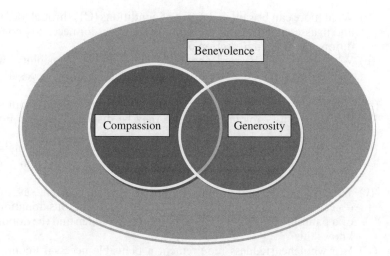

Figure 1   Benevolence, compassion, and generosity

do. But it may also have been morally required, and Sam could have even thought that it was what he had to do. If so, it can't qualify as a generous action, because of the supererogation requirement.[42]

On the flip side, there can be generous actions without their being compassionate (cf. Wallace 1978, 144). If compassion involves concern for the suffering or ill fortune of others, we can envision cases where someone does something generous toward a recipient who is not suffering. One such case is when a wealthy benefactor makes a large donation to a university, for instance. Let's suppose the benefactor values the money and is altruistically motivated to do this optional action for which she has the relevant authority. But the university is hardly suffering without her donation. It might have a twenty-billion-dollar endowment already.

Hence I conclude that generosity deserves its own unique place in the constellation of virtues of benevolence.

8. Conclusion: Looking Ahead

As this essay has illustrated, the virtue of generosity is surprisingly complex and multifaceted. I have, I hope, made some initial progress in understanding it better. But a book-length treatment is clearly the next step. Among the issues that should be discussed are the following:

---

[42] For related discussion, see Hunt 1987, 220. Also, it is not clear to me that a compassionate action need involve donating something to another person that is (subjectively or objectively) valuable to the donor.

   (i) What more can be said in defense of conditions (C1) through (C3), and in assessing the three additional candidates for necessary conditions considered in section 6?
  (ii) What more can be said about the comparative plausibility of subjective versus objective formulations of the various necessary conditions?
 (iii) Are there any requirements pertaining to *recipients* of acts of putative generosity—for instance, that they be disposed to welcome such acts?
  (iv) Can the account of generous people offered in this essay be plausibly extended to organizations, corporations, nations, and the like?
   (v) What should be said about gifts in which what is given, say, an object, is itself ill begotten? Can there still be a generous donation of a painting, for instance, if the painting was stolen and the donor knows this?[43]
  (vi) Is a wholeheartedness requirement a plausible necessary condition, such that when acting from generosity, a person must not have conflicting motives to both help and not help?[44]
 (vii) What does cross-cultural analysis reveal about the plausibility of the account, and in general about the universality of various claims about generosity?
(viii) What does empirical research reveal about the extent to which people actually possess the virtue of generosity? Is it, for instance, only rarely instantiated?
  (ix) How might generosity be cultivated and intentionally developed in ourselves and others?
   (x) Methodologically, what are the advantages and disadvantages of proceeding virtue by virtue, rather than developing a general account of a virtue as such?

And still other important issues could be mentioned as well.[45]

---

[43] Thanks to Chris Becker for raising these last two important questions. Kyle Fritz suggested to me that a plausible necessary condition to add here is that what is bestowed is the giver's to give in the first place. This is a promising proposal, I think, and worth considering in more detail, including whether an objective version (it really is the giver's to give) or a subjective version (the giver just has to think it is hers to give) is more plausible.

[44] As James Wallace writes, "A generous person, then, is not to be seen as reluctantly making burdensome sacrifices. He gives freely, wanting to give, with no practice in the background that requires such giving" (1978, 151). See also Hunt 1975, 244; Machan 1990, 61; Kupfer 1998, 364; Sanchez 2010, 450; Roberts and Wood 2007, 288–89. I find such a requirement plausible and hope to develop it more fully with respect to generosity in future work.

[45] Other interesting candidates for necessary conditions are the two forms of generosity excluded at the start of the essay: generosity of mind and of heart. For relevant discussion, see Kupfer 1998. Yet another candidate is Aristotle's condition that a person take pleasure (or at least lack pain) in acting from generosity (1120a28; see also Curzer 2012, 105).

Clearly the virtue of generosity deserves much more attention than it has already received from philosophers.

Acknowledgments

I am very grateful to Maria Silvia Vaccarezza and Michel Croce for having me be part of this collection. Thanks too for very helpful written comments from Alan Wilson and an anonymous reviewer, and to great feedback at Coastal Carolina University, the University of Mississippi, and Mississippi State University, especially written correspondence with Aaron Graham, Kyle Fritz, Michael Roche, and Chris Becker. Work on this essay was supported by a grant from the Templeton Religion Trust. The opinions expressed here are those of the author and do not necessarily reflect the views of the Templeton Religion Trust.

References

Adams, Robert. 2006. *A Theory of Virtue: Excellence in Being for the Good.* Oxford: Clarendon Press.
Aristotle. 1985. *Nicomachean Ethics.* Trans. T. Irwin. Indianapolis: Hackett.
Baehr, Jason. 2007. "On the Reliability of Moral and Intellectual Virtues." *Metaphilosophy* 38:456–70.
Batson, C. 2002. "Addressing the Altruism Question Experimentally." In *Altruism and Altruistic Love: Science, Philosophy, and Religion in Dialogue*, edited by Stephen Post, Lynn Underwood, Jeffrey Schloss, and William Hurlbut, 89–105. Oxford: Oxford University Press.
———. 2011. *Altruism in Humans.* New York: Oxford University Press.
Curzer, Howard. 2012. *Aristotle and the Virtues.* Oxford: Oxford University Press.
Frankfurt, Harry. 1999. *Necessity, Volition and Love.* Cambridge: Cambridge University Press.
Hunt, Lester. 1975. "Generosity." *American Philosophical Quarterly* 12:235–44.
———. 1987. "Generosity and the Diversity of the Virtues." In *The Virtues: Contemporary Essays on Moral Character*, edited by Robert Kruschwitz and Robert Roberts, 216–28. Belmont: Wadsworth.
Hurka, Tom. 2006. "Virtuous Act, Virtuous Disposition." *Analysis* 66: 69–76.
Kekes, John. 1998. "The Reflexivity of Evil." *Social Philosophy and Policy* 15:216–32.
Kupfer, Joseph. 1998. "Generosity of Spirit." *Journal of Value Inquiry* 32:357–68.
Machan, Tibor. 1990. "Politics and Generosity." *Journal of Applied Philosophy* 7:61–72.

May, Joshua. 2011. "Relational Desires and Empirical Evidence Against Psychological Egoism." *European Journal of Philosophy* 19:39–58.

Miller, Christian B. 2013. *Moral Character: An Empirical Theory*. Oxford: Oxford University Press.

——. 2014. *Character and Moral Psychology*. Oxford: Oxford University Press.

——. 2017. "Honesty." In *Moral Psychology, Volume V: Virtue and Character*, edited by Walter Sinnott-Armstrong and Christian B. Miller, 237–73. Cambridge, Mass.: MIT Press.

Roberts, Robert, and W. Jay Wood. 2007. *Intellectual Virtues: An Essay in Regulative Epistemology*. Oxford: Clarendon Press.

Russell, Daniel. 2009. *Practical Intelligence and the Virtues*. Oxford: Clarendon Press.

Sanchez, Carlos Alberto. 2010. "Generosity: Variations on a Theme from Aristotle to Levinas." *Heythrop Journal* 51:442–53.

Sober, Elliott, and David Sloan Wilson. 1998. *Unto Others: The Evolution and Psychology of Unselfish Behavior*. Cambridge, Mass.: Harvard University Press.

Stangl, Rebecca. 2016. "Neo-Aristotelian Supererogation." *Ethics* 126: 339–65.

Stich, Stephen, John Doris, and Erica Roedder. 2010. "The Science of Altruism." In *The Moral Psychology Handbook*, edited by John Doris and the Moral Psychology Research Group, 147–205. Oxford: Oxford University Press.

Stout, Rowland. 2015. "Adopting Roles: Generosity and Presumptuousness." *Royal Institute of Philosophy Supplement* 77:141–59.

Wallace, James. 1978. *Virtues and Vices*. Ithaca: Cornell University Press.

Warmke, Brandon. Unpublished. "Why Is Generosity a Virtue?"

Zagzebski, Linda. 1996. *Virtues of the Mind*. Cambridge: Cambridge University Press.

CHAPTER 3

AN EYE ON PARTICULARS WITH THE END IN SIGHT

AN ACCOUNT OF ARISTOTELIAN *PHRONESIS*

MARIA SILVIA VACCAREZZA

Introduction

This essay focuses on Aristotelian *phronesis* conceived as a rational excellence with an eye on particulars and general ends in sight. More specifically, I challenge the particularistic interpretation of phronesis and Aristotelian ethics in order to argue for a "qualified generalistic" interpretation. First, I lay out a Particularistic Reading (PR), which, according to a major proponent, John McDowell (1998), consists in interpreting phronesis and the other virtues merely as forms of practical perception. Second, I set out an interpretation that I call the Priority of Particulars Reading (PPR) and that I mainly extrapolate from the works of Sherman (1989), Nussbaum (1990), and Broadie (1991). Then I discuss some strategies to weaken PR that I take to be intrinsic to PPR, such as claiming Aristotle to be a "qualified particularist" (Sherman 1997) and appealing to the role of ethical theory to counteract the primacy of practical perception (Nussbaum 2000). Afterward, I offer further support to PPR by appealing to my own reading of Aristotle's phronesis, conceived as a virtue capable of grasping particulars while having general ends in sight thanks to its several subexcellences—which constitute a varied picture of subabilities to interpret and read the particular situation—and to its relation with the virtues and other forms of ethical knowledge. By doing so, I show that it is possible to defend PPR without ending in holding PR, and that Aristotle's own theory and work offer plenty of insights to ground a "moderate" reading such as mine. Finally, I draw some implications of my argument for real decision making by analyzing briefly the case of educational practice.

Connecting Virtues: Advances in Ethics, Epistemology, and Political Philosophy.
Edited by Michel Croce and Maria Silvia Vaccarezza.
Chapters and book compilation © 2018 Metaphilosophy LLC and John Wiley & Sons Ltd.

1. A Particularistic Reading of Aristotle's Ethics

Several neo-Aristotelian thinkers are committed to a Particularistic Reading (PR) of Aristotle's ethics that is clearly related to some of moral particularism's key assumptions. From a historical point of view, we can claim that the contemporary recovery of Aristotle has mainly taken this particularistic form, and that it has been among the main causes of an emphasis on the importance of particulars in ethics, as opposed to a relevance assigned to rules and general principles. Thus, indirectly, PR may even be listed as one of the main sources of moral particularism. No wonder, then, that many particularistic thinkers, such as Lawrence Blum, John McDowell, Jonathan Dancy, and Margaret Little, can all be identified as Aristotelian particularists, at least *lato sensu*.

This radical view (PR) equates the possession of virtue with perception and rules out any role of general knowledge and principles in ethics. This interpretation of PR is given by some of PR's exponents, such as, notably, McDowell, who is perhaps one of the most extreme of Aristotle's readers. In his essay "Virtue and Reason," McDowell identifies practical knowledge with a "reliable sensitivity," which in turn is "a sort of perceptual capacity" (1998, 51). He proposes a particularistic reading of Aristotle, claiming that the perceptual capacity has the following properties:

1 It is the only form of knowledge needed to possess virtue.
2 It consists in seeing an aspect of the situation "as a reason for acting in some way." This reason, in turn, "is apprehended not as outweighing or overriding any reasons for acting in other ways ... but as silencing them" (1998, 56).
3 It issues judgments that cannot be codified as general rules of conduct.
4 It is the complete explanation of the actions that manifest a virtue (1998, 52).
5 Thus it "turns out to be what the virtue is" (1998, 52).

Being virtuous, in this perspective, turns out to be nothing else than having a perceptual moral knowledge that consists in being reliably sensitive to the requirements of each situation. Being faithful to Aristotle means, therefore, for McDowell, dismissing the deeply rooted prejudice according to which virtue requires a set of rules and "formulable universal principles" (1998, 58). Such prejudice has to be removed not only as an homage to Aristotle but also in light of Wittgenstein's attack, in *Philosophical Investigations*, on the idea of following a rule. This argument, McDowell argues, is perfectly expressed by Cavell when he invites us to accept the "terrifying vision," "the vertigo, induced by the thought that there is nothing but shared forms of life to keep us, as it were, on the rails" (1998, 61). We should respect Aristotle's belief that "a view of how one should live is not codifiable" and that "the envisaged major premise, in a virtue syllogism, cannot be definitely written down" (1998, 67).

The particularistic reading of Aristotle, although influential and theoretically powerful, when taken as an interpretive stance of the Aristotelian ethical project does justice to only one side of it. Thus, in what follows I show how to complicate the picture by supporting a weaker particularistic position that I label the Priority of Particulars Reading (PPR).

2. Priority of Particulars Reading

Three influential works, published within a few years of each other, have been among the main works responsible for the PPR: *The Fabric of Character*, by Nancy Sherman (1989); *The Discernment of Perception: An Aristotelian Conception of Private and Public Rationality*, by Martha Nussbaum (1990); and *Ethics with Aristotle*, by Sarah Broadie (1991). Despite dealing with different topics, these three works share a key idea: restoring the intellectual virtue of phronesis as a form of knowledge of particulars so as to weaken the role of general knowledge and principles in ethics. Broadie, for instance, claims that only one who rules the polis needs a general knowledge of the good (or, in Broadie's words, of the "grand end"), whereas virtuous citizens simply need habituation and a good moral character. Nussbaum refers to the "priority of the particular" (1990, 66), aiming at stressing the chronological and normative priority of practical perception over general principles which function only to summarize wise choices and decisions and which might even be harmful if they came from above, as that would represent a failure of practical reason.

To oppose deontologism and consequentialism, PPR proposers emphasize two Aristotelian theses: (1) the *uncodifiability thesis* and (2) the *priority of practical perception* thesis. The uncodifiability thesis arises out of several methodological remarks Aristotle makes throughout his *Nicomachean Ethics* (NE), especially book I, where he explicitly states that the ethical field is, by its very nature, an imprecise one:

> But our account would be adequate, if we achieved a degree of precision appropriate to the underlying material; for precision must not be sought to the same degree in all accounts of things, any more than it is by craftsmen in the things they are producing. Fine things and just things, which are what political expertise inquires about, involve great variation and irregularity, so that they come to seem fine and just by convention alone, and not by nature. Something like this lack of regularity is found also in good things, because of the fact that they turn out to be a source of damage to many people: some in fact have perished because of wealth, others because of courage. We must be content, then, when talking about things of this sort and starting from them, to show what is true about them roughly and in outline, and when talking about things that are for the most part, and starting from these, to reach conclusions too of the same sort.

It is in this same way, then, that one must also receive each sort of account; for it is a mark of an educated person to look for precision in each kind of inquiry just to the extent that the nature of the subject allows it. (NE I.3, 1094b11–25)[1]

Such remarks have been read by PPR proposers as a powerful weapon against theories built upon rules and principles supposedly applicable in each and every situation. Similar theories appear incapable of making sense of the evidence that every moral situation is irreducibly complex— impossible to simplify without losing precision, detail, and an accurate grasp of the situation. Ethics deals with contingency, what admits of variation, and what cannot be fully captured by a general rule. Thus, ethics cannot be fully codified in advance. It does not need general norms, it needs a flexible method capable of approaching each situation with moral sensitivity. Every case is unique; thus, virtue consists in finding the right mean, by making use of the "Lesbian rule" (NE V.11, 1137b30–32): "For the rule of what is indefinite is itself indefinite, like the leaden rule used in building Lesbian-style: the rule adapts itself to the configuration of the stone, instead of staying the same shape, and the decree adapts itself to actual events."

As for the priority of practical perception thesis, let us deepen what it means to appeal to Aristotelian moral perception, which is the second key to understanding the contribution of Aristotle to the weak particularistic thesis and his relevance for contemporary moral theory. Aristotle, as is well known, holds we are accountable for how we perceive reality, since having a certain (virtuous or vicious) character is a matter not only of upbringing but also of voluntary choice, and character alters and conditions the quality of our moral perceptions. As he claims in *Nicomachean Ethics*, book III: "Suppose someone said that while every one of us aims at what appears to us good, we are not in control of the appearance, but rather the sort of person each of us is, whatever that may be, determines how the end, too, appears to him. Well, if each of us is himself somehow responsible for causing his disposition in himself, he will also be somehow responsible for the appearance in question" (NE III.5, 1114a30–1114b1).

It is typical of ethical virtue, as Aristotle conceives it, to allow an agent to see certain goods instead of others, to be sensitive to certain reasons, to grasp reality in its particular and contingent features with a certain moral outlook. The perfection of virtue, therefore, consists in a right perception of particulars, a quasi-visual capacity of concrete moral understanding (NE III.5, 1114b6). This capacity depends both on the intellectual virtue of phronesis and on the possession of properly ordered emotions—that is, emotions shaped by ethical virtues. Indeed, it is the emotional structure of one's character, shaped by the virtues, that gives one access to the

---

[1] All passages from *Nicomachean Ethics* are from Rowe's 2002 translation (Aristotle 2002). To facilitate reading, I omit accents when transliterating Greek terms.

goods that orient deliberation and choice—that is, to moral reasons and values.

By summing up these two elements, we can conclude that Aristotle cannot be a generalist *stricto sensu*, in that he assigns chronological and methodological priority to the perception of particulars and makes ethics an uncodifiable field. Also, Aristotle cannot be a generalist for a further reason, highlighted by Nussbaum: according to her reading, Aristotle's view lacks a "single standard" against which one can establish a hierarchy among the various goods (Nussbaum 1992). Thus, all authentic goods, and the related virtues, represent a genuine plurality, and no rules of maximization can be introduced to reduce such plurality to unity. The refusal to adopt a single standard means, for Nussbaum's Aristotle, rejecting the two Platonic principles that make Platonic ethics a science: (1) the *singleness principle*, according to which there is a single good making good all the others; and (2) the *metricity principle*, which establishes an external standard against which to measure the various goods. Thus, a good life is one that encompasses the various distinct activities that correspond to the virtues, and all the different goods are genuinely different and therefore incommensurable.

Despite assigning such strong priority to the perception of particulars, PPR does not attribute to Aristotle a form of particularism strictly speaking; rather, it attributes a "qualified particularism." To do so, PPR counterbalances the emphasis on practical perception by means of two strategies aimed at capturing other relevant features of the Aristotelian picture.

2.1 General Rules as Summaries of Particular Cases

The first of PPR's strategies has been proposed by Nancy Sherman. Contrary to the PPR thesis, Sherman maintains that Aristotle is committed to a qualified particularism, where general—yet nonuniversal—rules play a significant role. Such general rules, which summarize particular cases, can prove essential to deal with new cases, and they rule out the possibility of reading Aristotle as a particularistic intuitionist who would portray moral judgment as an intuition issued by a mysterious perceptive faculty that simply happens to "cotton on" (Sherman 1997, 254). As Sherman puts it, "If we understand intuitionism as implying a grasp of moral judgments that precludes more ordinary and reiterative processes of description, explanation, justification, or revision, then Aristotle is no intuitionist" (1997, 254). Even if Aristotelian moral judgment has much more to do with perception than do other kinds of judgments, it implies also the capacity of seeing particulars "under a description," and therefore involves a number of cognitive capacities, as we will see later. Thus, practical wisdom comprises, so to speak, a perceptive side and a cognitive one, which cannot be separated: there is no immediacy in approaching particulars. They can be reached only after a description and redescription, which allow an agent to recognize the case at hand in light of a certain interpretation. Practical perception is a case of recognition made possible by possessing adequate concepts, just as what happens in geometry, where one comes to recognize a triangle (NE VI.8, 1142a14–15) by recognizing that "this is a that" (cf. *Poetics*, 1148b15). Descriptions thus play a key role. What about rules and principles? In Sherman's view, there are no universal judgments to be taken as major premises of a practical syllogism. "Universal" is simply the name of what the moral expert is endowed with—that is, the competence enabling her to recognize particulars. On the one hand, therefore, one cannot entirely codify experience. On the other, Aristotle does not dispose entirely of rules, in that ethical competence involves some general principles that hold "for the most part" (NE I.3, 1094b13–22). This means, for instance, that even if there is no fixed hierarchy among virtues, a certain order holds for the most part, and, generally speaking, the contemplative life is superior to the active one.

2.2 The Role of Ethical Theory

The second strategy by means of which particularistic remarks have been counterbalanced in PPR is an appeal to the role of ethical theory. In two different papers, Nussbaum offers a sketch of how to account for the role of ethical theory as a counterbalance to particularism. In "Virtue Ethics" she claims that most ancient philosophers were strong universalists in that they believed in the existence of a very general concept of human flourishing, valid for all humans. What they proposed, therefore, was a theory universalism, rather than a rule universalism—that is, an "alliance between theory and a fine-tuned judgment of the particular circumstances of life," whereas "rules, standing in the middle, deliver neither the overall understanding nor the fine-tuned judgment" (Nussbaum 1999, 178). Generally valid rules, however, are "frequently valuable in the agent's deliberations. For often agents cannot assess the particular circumstances well enough, whether on account of time, or deficient information, or incomplete moral development, or special bias" (1999, 178).

Similar statements are made by Nussbaum in "Why Practice Needs Ethical Theory," where she develops the same argument further. While authors such as Baier, Williams, and Diamond reject the importance of theory in ethics, grounding their position on the idea that modern moral theories are too detached from the concreteness of real ethical life, Nussbaum restates the need for a retrieval of the (originally Stoic) distinction between theories, rules, and particular judgments. Such a distinction, according to Nussbaum, helps to establish a natural alliance between theory and judgments in that it is precisely ethical theory that allows one to see the limits of rules and to correct them. Criticizing systems of rules, therefore, does not imply ipso facto rejecting theories unless theories entirely correspond to rules. A theory is, for Nussbaum, "a set of reasons and interconnected arguments, explicitly and systematically articulated, with some degree of abstractness and generality, which gives directions for ethical practice" (2000, 233).

Thus, it does not coincide with a system or a list of rules (such as "don't kill," "don't steal," and so on); rather, it often "displaces" systems of rules typical of religion and custom by "giving *reasons for* the value of the rule in question" (2000, 237) in terms of a single end or of a plurality of ends. Thus, it corrects the obtuseness of a system of rules, and it provides the agent with reasons and motives to follow them or to make exceptions.

3. Aristotle as a "Qualified Generalist": Further Aristotelian Reasons

The two strategies outlined so far have already offered useful insights and shown that holding PPR does not ipso facto amount to supporting PR. What I want to propose now is an appeal to other Aristotelian reasons that should lead us to weaken PR. I will show that Aristotelian ethics consists of a two-way movement: from particularity to general ends, and vice versa. Paraphrasing Sherman, I define Aristotle as a "qualified generalist" whose account of ethical virtue and phronesis equally accounts for (1) the need to save the contingent, and (2) the orientation to general ends properly seen and desired as good. These two points represent, respectively, the minor and major premises of a practical syllogism. And, if I am right, they can both be written down, contrary to what McDowell claims. The reading I am about to propose, then, aims to show that, due to the two-way movement just mentioned, Aristotle is closer to generalism than particularists would accept, while at the same time being more particularist than generalists would admit.[2] My argument consists precisely in defending the Aristotelian priority of particulars while at the same time arguing that it is counterbalanced by powerful insights on the role of general principles and ethical theory. Therefore, Aristotle's position ultimately amounts to a form of qualified generalism that combines generalism and particularism's most valuable insights so as to account both for the movement from the perception of particulars to the appreciation of general principles and for the movement back from general principles and ethical theory to perception. Thus, my proposal of a qualified generalism is an alternative to both generalism and particularism, and consists in claiming that, despite the normative priority of the general pole, there is a mutual implication of the two movements, which makes it unrealistic and counterintuitive to analyze one of them while neglecting the other.

[2] A similar, though not identical, stand is taken by Terence Irwin. In "Ethics as an Inexact Science" he claims that refuting Aristotelian particularism implies rejecting the normative priority of particulars without at the same time assigning it to general principles, and that denying that Aristotle is a particularist does not require taking him as a kind of generalist. Thus, Irwin's refutation of particularism does not imply a defense of Aristotelian generalism—or universalism, in Irwin's words—given that "particularism and universalism ... are mutually exclusive, but not exhaustive. If we decide that Aristotle is not a particularist, we may then consider whether he is a universalist, or he rejects both particularism and universalism" (2000, 104).

3.1 Saving the Contingent: The Minor Premise of a Practical Syllogism

The first aspect, concerning practical perception and the salvation of contingent particulars, depends, as noted, on the possession of phronesis, which deals with a contingent matter that cannot be determined a priori by a scientific theory or a fixed set of universal rules to be applied. The excellence of phronesis consists in descending to the singular case in a nondeductive way and in identifying the particular action that represents the end here and now, in light of the circumstances. As Aristotle notes, the capacity of discerning and perceiving the situation in its singularity is not accidental to phronesis but rather represents its specific excellence.

But how does phronesis acquire its peculiar knowledge of the contingent, which enables it to understand and grasp the situation and the circumstances? The answer lies in the link in phronesis between practical reason and internal senses, a link that becomes visible when analyzing the habits Aristotle discusses right after phronesis. The habits represent, in my view, phronesis's subexcellences, or, as Thomas Aquinas would say a few centuries later, its "integral parts." In my view, these habits are the "eyes" of phronesis on the contingent, and its means of reaching into the sensible sphere.[3]

At NE VI.8, 1142a23–30, Aristotle lists several subexcellences of phronesis responsible for its cognitive quasi-sensible moral perception, such as *euboulia* (good deliberation), *sunesis* (comprehension), *gnome* (sense), and, above all, *nous*. Nous is understanding, or intelligence of particulars—that is, an immediate and intuitive capacity of acknowledging the moral relevance of a contingent situation.[4] Such habits, as Aristotle underlines at NE VI.11, 1143a24–34, have the same aim and belong to the same people, for all these dispositions concern particular cases (*ta kath'hekaston*). Nous, in particular, plays a key role in connecting phronesis with particulars. While this term normally indicates the faculty able to grasp by intuition the first indemonstrable principles of knowledge, here it is the name of a practical faculty concerning particular actions. When introducing nous, Aristotle states that it concerns what is last and contingent, which is "the starting point of that for the sake of which" (NE VI.11, 1143b4), because *Ek ton kath'hekasta gar to katholou:*

---

[3] That these three habits can be seen as "parts" of phronesis is far from uncontroversial. As Kenny notes, however, "they share the same subject matter as *phronesis* (EN VI.11, 1143a25–b6) and therefore inhere in the same part of the soul as it and seem not to be separable from it as a distinct virtue" (2017, 166).

[4] Aristotle uses the term "nous" in different ways. For example, in *Posterior Analytics* B 19, nous grasps the highest principles of science, which are universals. Here, however, it seems quite uncontroversial that nous is an immediate grasp of particulars. That it can be also an intellectual knowledge of general practical principles has been argued by, among others, Kenny. Of the vast literature on the topic, see at least Broadie 1998.

"Universals come from particulars" (NE VI.11, 1143 b5).[5] Regardless of how we interpret this passage, Aristotle is implying here that of particular cases "one must have perception ... and this is intelligence." Thus, grasping particulars is a sort of intelligence whose immediacy is comparable to that of a kind of sensation (*aisthesis*). Nous, therefore, is an intelligent sight, an ability to grasp particulars.[6] It provides phronesis with knowledge of the singular case by means of a sensorial and intellective intuition. It is a form of perception capable of grasping data as particular specifications of the universal end of action. As such, then, nous is one of the cognitive pre-conditions of phronesis, providing it with the knowledge of the singular it needs to give birth to good actions.

Establishing the second premise of a practical syllogism—the premise according to which "this is a that"—is a matter of seeing particulars in a morally correct way. This, in turn, implies being capable of perceiving the situation, deliberating, and judging. To deliberate well (euboulia), the agent needs a good disposition of her imaginative power, enabling her easily to see different data. Moreover, she needs an immediate intellectual grasp (nous) of experience. Experience is the first source from which she can obtain indications and data. It results from several empirical perceptions and memories and can therefore convey to the agent general guidelines enabling her to solve a practical problem without an excessive expenditure of cognitive energies. To judge well (sunesis, gnome), finally, she needs a developed common sense.

Phronesis, therefore, to obtain the knowledge of the contingent it needs to operate well, must lean on the external and internal senses, whose excellences are represented by the subvirtues mentioned so far.

3.2 The Orientation to General Ends: The First Premise of a Practical Syllogism

Nicomachean Ethics, besides outlining Aristotle's account of phronesis and its role in finding the minor premise of a practical syllogism, also offers plenty of insights on the role of general ends in deliberation and choice.

---

[5] What Aristotle is referring to in this central passage might be the process of habituation, *ethismos*, already explained in NE I.8, 1098b3–4: "Of starting points, some are grasped by induction, some by perception, some by a sort of habituation." This means that by accomplishing certain kinds of actions, one gets used to a certain kind of ends. Broadie, on the contrary, translates the passage as "Things that are universal consist of particulars" (Aristotle 2002, 186). Such a reading means that perceiving a concrete action transforms a vague tendency to aim at the end in a decision. That is, "generalities come into being only as particularized."

[6] It might even be translated as "attention" or "sensibility," since the peculiarity of nous seems to be a sort of attention, an opening to reality able to perceive its relevant aspects, similar to the attitude of those who are called "sensitive," who are able understand at a first glance that the person they are talking with is sad or that one aspect of a situation is more relevant than others.

I will recall four of them here in order to argue for the possibility of establishing the major premise of a practical syllogism, contrary to what McDowell claims.

First of all, in book II, Aristotle defends the idea that some acts do not admit of intermediacy, for they are bad in themselves and cannot be performed in a virtuous way: "But not every action admits of intermediacy, nor does every affection; for in some cases they have been named in such a way that they are combined with badness from the start, as e.g. with malice, shamelessness, grudging ill will, and in the case of actions, fornication, theft, murder; for all these, and others like them, owe their names to the fact that they themselves—not excessive versions of them, or deficient ones— are bad" (NE II.6, 1106b34–35). This remark might be taken as pointing in a generalist direction in that it takes some reasons as invariant in every case, no matter the context or the particular circumstances.

Second, in book VI, Aristotle mentions a *skopos* or *horos* to which the virtuous agent has to aim in order to hit the right mean: "Since we have said earlier that one must choose what is intermediate, not excess, and not deficiency, and that what is intermediate is 'as the correct prescription prescribes', let us delimit this. For with all the dispositions we have discussed, just as with everything else, there is a target, as it were, that the person with the prescription has in view as he tenses and relaxes, and a kind of mark that determines the intermediate states" (NE VI.1, 1138b15, 1138b24). Some interpreters who argue for a dominant view of *eudaimonia* and identify the final end with contemplative life take this passage as suggesting that in choosing and determining the mean, the agent should aim at promoting contemplation.[7] But even if we reject such a strong thesis and adopt an inclusive view of the final end, it is easy to see here something quite similar to what Nussbaum would call a "single standard": namely, a criterion against which to evaluate and establish a hierarchy among goods.

The third and central point concerns the way first practical principles enter into the practical syllogism: Are they objects or knowledge or desires? And, in case they are known, are they established by means of deliberation or known by phronesis? Quite clearly, the affective orientation to general ends is provided by moral virtues. But how do the moral virtues relate (if they do) to rational components in knowing or determining the ends of action? What is at stake here is the very nature of phronesis, of the deliberation it involves, and of its relation with the ends of action. Aristotle famously claims that deliberation is concerned only with "particulars" and that "we deliberate, not about ends, but about what forwards those ends" (NE III.3, 1112b11–12, 33–34; cf. *Eudemian Ethics* II.10, 1226b9–12, 1227a5ff.). As Russell notes, according to a "quasi-Humean" reading of such passage, our grasp of ends is nonrational, and phronesis only works out "means and constituents of ends that motivate from outside the

---

[7] Among others, Kenny 1992 and Kraut 1989.

intellect" (2009, 6).[8] On the other hand, a non-Humean view holds that while the end is not established by deliberation, it is nonetheless grasped by phronesis. Some interpreters, famously Kenny, point to the above passage on nous and read it as suggesting the existence of a peculiar kind of intelligence concerning the good and the universal practical principle.[9] Thus, they read the mentioned passage on nous as implying both an immediate grasp of particular data and a similar (intellectual) grasp of first practical principles. There would be a link, according to this reading, between the ability to see particulars and that of knowing first practical principles, two abilities that would make each other possible, since "things that are universal consist of particulars" (NE VI.12, 1143b5); that is, knowledge of universals is made possible either by intuition or, as others claim, by induction. Natali, for instance, reads the same passage as referring to *ethismos*, a kind of induction that derives general ends and rules of conduct from a summary of particular cases. In any case, nous, even when implying a perception of particulars, would be related to the possibility of summarizing particulars as general ends. Thus, no matter how we read this passage, the non-Humean view seems the more appropriate to account for the genuine Aristotelian picture of how phronesis works and for the link between nous, ethismos, and the grasp of general ends: "Although Aristotle holds that we acquire the virtues through habituation of emotion and desire, such habituation results in a rational recognition of the appropriateness of the actions and ends desired" (Russell 2009, 6; see also Sorabji 1980, 216). In support of such view is what Aristotle says at NE VI.8, 1141b15–17: "Nor is wisdom *only* concerned with universals: to be wise, one must *also* be familiar with the particular, since wisdom has to do with action, and the sphere of action is constituted by particulars" (my emphasis).

Finally, as pointed out, for example, by Irwin and Berti, it is possible to envisage throughout *Nicomachean Ethics*, especially at the beginning of book I, the idea of practical philosophy conceived as distinct from phronesis and, more specifically, as a form of science.[10] This would mean acknowledging a habit of theoretical reason, which aims at knowing the good and has a degree of rigor inferior to that of theoretical sciences. According to this reading, "practical philosophy would be the science of the supreme good for man, that is happiness—the full flourishing of all human capabilities—which is determined by means of a dialectical discussion with the thesis of the various philosophers" (Berti 2005, 1). The role of such science—which, as noted by Irwin, Aristotle calls "political science" at NE I.2, 1094a26–b11 and *Magna Moralia* 1181a243–b27, and which makes

---

[8] Among the most notable anti-intellectualist interpretations of Aristotelian virtue and orientation to the good, I should at least mention Jessica Moss's (2012).

[9] Among the many voices in this huge debate, we may recall here at least Irwin 1978; Kraut 1993, 361–74; Tuozzo 1991, 193–212; Reeve 1992.

[10] On the distinction between phronesis and practical philosophy, see also Berti 1989.

use of a dialectical method (Irwin 1990, 347)—would be that of elaborating general principles, even if with a certain degree of flexibility, and of guiding phronesis in its knowledge of particulars. As Irwin puts it, even if ethical generalizations have exceptions, they are still scientific principles. Furthermore, it is possible (and even easy) to draw a list of generalizations that do not admit of exceptions. For example, "happiness is everyone's ultimate good; everyone's happiness consists in activity of the soul in accordance with complete virtue in a complete life; it is always better to aim at the mean than to aim at either the excess or the deficiency; it is always better to be brave than to be cowardly; it is right to care more about fine action for its own sake than about honour," and so on (Irwin 2000, 111). Or, as Kraut argues by drawing on his dominant reading of *Nicomachean Ethics* books I and X, "One should be either a philosopher ... or a statesman since the best life is devoted to exercising the virtues of theoretical reason, and the second-best to the full exercise of the moral virtues" (1989, 5).[11]

This kind of general knowledge, whose limits Aristotle clearly acknowledges but whose status as science he seems to preserve, is often overlooked by particularistic readings.

4. Particularism and Generalism in Educational Practice

So far, my argument has been concerned with defending qualified generalism at an interpretive level. In this final section, I want to show briefly the advantages of holding a nonparticularistic account of phronesis at a theoretical level, and of applying it to a particular kind of practice—namely, educational practice.

A place where we can easily see the educational implications of a particularistic view of phronesis is what Kristjánsson calls the PPP: the phronesis-praxis perspective on education, proposed mainly by Joseph Dunne and Wilfrid Carr. Such a perspective is grounded in a particularistic account of phronesis, conceived as a form of vision whose discerning capacity is ultimately experiential. In this perspective, knowing what to do is a matter of looking at the situation until one comes to see the right course of action, and referring to the experienced person (the *phronimos*) in case one doubts one's own decision. From an educational standpoint, the perspective's main move is that of linking "educational reasoning and reflection to *phronesis*, and education itself to *praxis*" (Kristjánsson 2005, 456), and of denying that education represents a theoretical activity (Carr 1995, 33) rather than a practical one. What does all of this mean in terms of real educational practice? Surely, according to Carr, it implies that education does not consist in the application of a theory, nor is it a form of technical rationality guided by abstract theories. Rather, even if it is guided by some form

---

[11] Proposers of so-called inclusivism, however, might easily add other generalizations that would equally admit of no exception.

of theory, the latter is a "*theory* in a non-traditional sense, theory that is practice-confined and perspectivist," theory that is "internal to the [educational] practice and liable to all the exigencies of the latter" (Kristjánsson 2005, 458).

Thus, the PPP conceives teaching as praxis and teaching excellence as phronesis. It follows, as Kristjánsson points out, that the ends of both can be neither specified in advance nor fully codified (see Dunne 1993, 15), and that in such a view "expertise ... does not consist of designing a set of sequenced means or techniques which 'drive' learners towards expected learning outcomes. It consists of spontaneous and flexible direction and redirection of the learning enterprise, guided by a sensitive reading of the subtle changes and responses of other participants in the enterprise" (Carr and Kemmis 1986, 37).

As we have seen throughout the essay, we have no reason to embrace a particularistic view of phronesis from a theoretical viewpoint, in that phronesis, to put it once again in Kristjánsson's words, "while not unproblematically codifiable, ... is also not necessarily, but only contingently, uncodifiable" (2005, 467), because of the Aristotelian generalizing remarks seen above.

Thus, qualified generalism holds true also at an applied educational level. Contrary to Dunne and Carr's view, there is no "good Aristotelian reason" (Kristjánsson 2005, 471) to see teaching exclusively as a praxis and to oppose theory to the concreteness and perceptiveness of practical teaching activity. To sum up, there is no reason to keep good moral and educational theory outside the picture, depriving teaching practice of its guidance and insightfulness.

Conclusion

I have made an attempt to show that there are a number of good intrinsically Aristotelian reasons to preserve both phronesis's capacity of dealing with particulars—perceiving them in their contingent detail—and its openness to the knowledge of general ends, whether the ends are provided by nous, ethismos, or practical science. If this is true, Aristotle can be said to be a "qualified generalist," a generalist who takes the salvation of the contingent very seriously.[12] Also, I have shown that holding such a view of phronesis has an advantage over rival accounts as far as real decision making is concerned. For example, in educational practice, the excellent (phronimos) teacher can—and should—make use of general knowledge as a guide to the practice of teaching.

---

[12] Kristjánsson puts it quite nicely: "There are generalists like myself who believe *phronesis* involves reasoning, based on general first principles delineated in Aristotle's ethical works, about one's appropriate and rational combinations of desires and beliefs. Such generalists readily concede that although the verdicts of *phronesis* will be acutely context-sensitive and only problematically codifiable, they are not essentially uncodifiable" (2013, 159).

64 MARIA SILVIA VACCAREZZA

Acknowledgments

I am grateful to Kevin Flannery, participants at the Jubilee Centre 2017 annual conference, and two anonymous reviewers for helpful comments on earlier versions of this essay.

References

Aristotle. 2002. *Nicomachean Ethics.* Translation (with historical introduction) by C. Rowe. Philosophical introduction and commentary by S. Broadie. Oxford: Oxford University Press.
Berti, E. 1989. *Le ragioni di Aristotele.* Bari: Laterza.
———. "Saggezza o filosofia pratica?" *Etica e Politica* 2:1–14.
Broadie, S. 1991. *Ethics with Aristotle.* New York: Oxford University Press.
———. 1998. "Interpreting Aristotle's Directions." In *Method in Ancient Philosophy*, edited by J. Gentzler. Oxford: Clarendon.
Carr, W. 1995. *For Education: Towards Critical Educational Inquiry.* Buckingham: Open University Press.
Carr, W., and S. Kemmis. 1986. *Becoming Critical: Education, Knowledge and Action Research.* London: Falmer.
Dunne, J. 1993. *Back to the Rough Ground: "Phronesis" and "Techné" in Modern Philosophy and in Aristotle.* Notre Dame: University of Notre Dame Press.
Irwin, T. 1978. "First Principles in Aristotle's Ethics." *Midwest Studies in Philosophy* 3:252–72.
———. 1990. *Aristotle's First Principles.* Oxford: Clarendon Press.
Irwin, T. "Ethics as an Inexact Science: Aristotle's Ambitions for Moral Theory." In *Moral Particularism*, edited by B. Hooker and M. O. Little, 100–129. Oxford: Oxford University Press.
Kenny, A. 1992. *Aristotle on the Perfect Life.* Oxford: Clarendon Press.
———. 2017. *The Aristotelian Ethics: A Study of the Relationship Between the Eudemian and Nicomachean Ethics of Aristotle.* Second edition. Oxford: Oxford University Press.
———. 1989. *Aristotle on the Human Good.* Princeton: Princeton University Press.
———. 1993. "In Defense of the Grand End." *Ethics* 103:361–74.
Kraut, R. 1989. *Aristotle on the Human Good.* Princeton: Princeton University Press.
Kristjánsson, K. 2005. "Smoothing It: Some Aristotelian Misgivings About the Phronesis-Praxis Perspective on Education." *Educational Philosophy and Theory* 37, no. 4:455–73.
———. 2013. *Virtues and Vices in Positive Psychology: A Philosophical Critique.* New York: Cambridge University Press.
McDowell, J. 1998. "Virtue and Reason." In *Mind, Value and Reality*, 50–73. Cambridge, Mass.: Harvard University Press.

Moss, J. 2012. *Aristotle on the Apparent Good: Perception, Phantasia, Thought, and Desire*. Oxford: Oxford University Press.

Nussbaum, M. C. 1990. "The Discernment of Perception: An Aristotelian Conception of Private and Public Rationality." In *Love's Knowledge: Essays on Philosophy and Literature*, 54–105. Oxford: Oxford University Press.

———. 1999. "Virtue Ethics: A Misleading Category." *Journal of Ethics* 3:163–67.

———. 2000. "Why Practice Needs Ethical Theory: Particularism, Principle and Bad Behavior." In *Moral Particularism*, edited by B. Hooker and M. O. Little. New York: Oxford University Press.

Reeve, C. D. C. 1992. *Practices of Reason: Aristotle's Nicomachean Ethics*. Clarendon Press.

Russell, D. C. 2009. *Practical Intelligence and the Virtues*. Oxford: Oxford University Press.

Sherman, N. 1989. *The Fabric of Character: Aristotle's Theory of Virtues*. Oxford: Clarendon Press.

———. 1997. *Making a Necessity of Virtue: Aristotle and Kant on Virtue*. Cambridge: Cambridge University Press.

Sorabji, R. 1980. *Necessity, Cause, and Blame: Perspectives on Aristotle's Theory*. Ithaca, N.Y.: Cornell University Press.

Tuozzo, T. M. 1991. "Aristotelian Deliberation Is Not of Ends." In *Aristotle's Ethics: Essays in Ancient Greek Philosophy*, edited by J. P. Anton and A. Preus, 193–212. Albany: State University of New York Press.

CHAPTER 4

HONESTY AS A VIRTUE

ALAN T. WILSON

Introduction

Honesty is widely accepted as an important moral virtue. And yet, honesty has been surprisingly neglected in the recent drive by virtue theorists to account for specific virtuous traits. This neglect is surprising, not only because of honesty's endorsement by influential virtue theorists, but also because of the trait's obvious relevance to current debates within (for example) politics, journalism, and sports. Efforts to encourage increased levels of honesty in these areas would be enhanced by having a clearer account of the nature of the trait.

In this chapter, I aim to encourage an increased focus on the virtue of honesty. I do this by, first, proposing four success criteria that will need to be met by any successful account (in section 2). After surveying Christian Miller's recent discussion of honesty (in section 3), I set out and defend my own motivational account of honesty, and demonstrate how that account can satisfy the required criteria (in sections 4 and 5). This requires a discussion of why (and when) honesty should be accepted as a moral virtue. Finally, I highlight some implications that accepting a motivational account of honesty has for future work on the development of honesty, and on the relationship between different types of virtue (in section 6).

1. The Importance of Honesty

The claim that honesty is widely accepted as a moral virtue is likely to be met with little resistance. However, it is worth emphasising just how strong this acceptance has been. Influential virtue theorists have gone as far as to take for granted the virtue status of the trait. For example, in *Virtues of the Mind*, Linda Zagzebski tells us that "honesty is on all accounts a

Connecting Virtues: Advances in Ethics, Epistemology, and Political Philosophy.
Edited by Michel Croce and Maria Silvia Vaccarezza.
Chapters and book compilation © 2018 Metaphilosophy LLC and John Wiley & Sons Ltd.

moral virtue" and that "to think of virtue is almost immediately to think of examples of particular traits such as courage, generosity, compassion, justice, honesty, wisdom, temperance, and self-respect" (1996, 158, 86). The same assumption in favour of honesty's virtue status is made by Rosalind Hursthouse. For example, when testing her own naturalistic approach to identifying the virtues, Hursthouse (1999, chap. 9) includes honesty as one of the traits that ought to be accommodated.

Importantly, the endorsement of honesty is not limited to theorists working in the Aristotelian tradition. For example, Julia Driver (2003), a consequentialist virtue theorist, dismisses rival attempts to identify the moral virtues partly because of their supposed failure to accommodate honesty. And Michael Slote (2011) uses an assumption in favour of the virtue status of honesty when arguing for his controversial claim that some virtues necessarily conflict with one another. Given this widespread endorsement of honesty, there is good reason for virtue theorists to explore the nature of the trait.

Further reason for exploring the nature of honesty is provided by current debates within politics, journalism, and sports (to mention just three examples). The demand for honesty from our politicians (and the suspicion that honesty is not always forthcoming) may be nothing new. But the use of social media appears to have exacerbated concerns about whether politicians and the media can be trusted to engage truthfully with the electorate. Such concerns have been well documented in recent times, as have concerns about levels of dishonesty and manipulation in the sporting world. The credibility of many sporting contests has been damaged by a series of recent scandals involving dishonesty and cheating, be that through illicit use of performance-enhancing substances or through more mundane methods, such as match fixing (tennis); diving and playacting (football); using fake blood capsules to feign injury (rugby); or even insufficiently inflating footballs (American football). In all of these areas, there is a suspicion that participants are not being honest, and a concern that the very legitimacy of these enterprises may be damaged as a result of (the perception of) widespread dishonesty.

And yet, the candidate virtue of honesty has been almost entirely neglected by virtue theorists. This is true despite a recent move in virtue theory away from attempting to give an overarching account of virtue *in general* and towards providing accounts of *specific* virtuous traits.[1] If we believe that honesty is important, and if we want to correct for a lack of honesty (either in ourselves or more generally), then it will be vital to have an account of the nature of the trait. In the next section, I begin the task

---

[1] See, for example, Timpe and Boyd 2014, Battaly 2010, part 4, and Roberts and Wood 2007, part 2. The neglect of honesty is illustrated by the fact that not only does Timpe and Boyd's important collection on virtues and vices fail to have a chapter dedicated to honesty, honesty does not even appear once in the book's index.

of encouraging an increased focus on honesty by generating success criteria that can be used to assess any proposed account of the trait.

2. Generating Success Criteria

Success criteria for an account of honesty can be generated by considering why some initial attempts to explain the trait are unsuccessful. For example, a basic starting point when attempting to get clearer about honesty would be to say that an honest agent is one who does not tell lies. But this will not do, because we can imagine an agent who does not tell lies but who does not deserve to be considered honest either. For example, a Robinson Crusoe figure who never interacts with another human being, and so never tells a lie, would not thereby deserve to be considered honest.[2] This worry cannot be avoided simply by amending the initial basic claim and saying that an honest agent is one who does not tell lies *and* who regularly utters truths. We can imagine an agent who simply repeats everything that she overhears and who never happens to overhear a falsehood. Such an agent is not necessarily honest.

A slightly modified starting point would be to say that an honest agent is one who does *whatever is appropriate* with regard to either lying or telling the truth. One worry about the example of someone who merely repeats whatever she overhears might be that such a person is not properly responsive to whether it would be appropriate to tell the truth. But this modified approach is also problematic for (at least) two reasons. First, the approach faces a worry concerning occasions where the appropriate act is to tell a lie (or to conceal a truth). While we might want to say that lying on these occasions is *compatible* with being virtuously honest, it would nevertheless be strange to say that the lie thereby *expresses* the agent's honesty. And yet, if honesty just is a disposition to do whatever is appropriate with regard to the truth, then that is the conclusion that we would have to accept.[3]

A second, and more damaging, worry for any account that focuses solely on lying (or on telling the truth) is that such accounts are too narrow. They miss out on the full range of what is involved in being honest. As has been noted elsewhere, there is more to honesty than an appropriate disposition towards telling the truth. For example, when discussing what we would expect from honest agents, Hursthouse provides the following list: "They do not lie or cheat or plagiarize or casually pocket other people's possessions. You can rely on them to tell you the truth, to give sincere references, to own up to their mistakes, not to pretend to be more knowledgeable than

---

[2] A Robinson Crusoe example is used by Driver (2001, chap. 2) to reject a similarly basic account of modesty.

[3] This worry is raised by Gary Watson for what he calls the *due concern* view of virtue. Having set out the implication, Watson points out that "no one would think to say such a thing" (1984, 68).

they are; you can buy a used car from them or ask for their opinion with confidence" (1999, 10).

Hursthouse is not alone in recognising the different ways in which honesty is manifested.[4] In a recent contribution, Christian Miller (2017) helpfully groups together behaviours associated with honesty into five seemingly distinct categories. The categories identified by Miller (2017, 240) can be paraphrased as follows:

> *Truthfulness*: Being disposed to reliably tell the truth.
> *Being respectful of property*: Being disposed to reliably respect the prop-
> erty of others.
> *Proper compliance*: Being disposed to reliably follow the relevant rules.
> *Fidelity to promises*: Being disposed to reliably keep reasonable promises.
> *Forthrightness*: Being disposed to reliably give a complete presentation
> of the facts.

Miller (2017, 240–41) refers to these as "virtues" or "subvirtues" of honesty, and he is open to the possibly that additional subvirtues could be uncovered. To avoid complications, I will avoid the terminology of subvirtues and instead refer to these as five possible *aspects* of honesty. I will not consider whether each aspect ought to also be considered virtuous in its own right. The important point is that honesty is plausibly connected to (at least) these different forms of behaviour, and so an account of honesty that focuses solely on telling the truth and avoiding falsehoods is likely to be inadequate.

These considerations present us with our first success criterion for an account of honesty. Immediately after identifying these five aspects, Miller proposes what he calls the "unification challenge." This is the challenge of explaining why honesty is thought to be manifest in seemingly distinct ways. I suggest that an initial criterion for any successful account of honesty is that it be able to meet Miller's unification challenge. That is, a successful account of honesty will shed light on why honesty is closely associated with a range of seemingly distinct forms of behaviour, including the five aspects of honesty listed above.

Basic accounts on which honesty is simply a matter of avoiding lies or telling the truth fail to satisfy this initial criterion. They cannot explain why an honest agent is also expected to behave in other ways, such as keeping promises and avoiding any temptation to pocket the possessions of others. But these basic accounts have also been shown to fail in another way. They result in implausible verdicts when applied to such cases as the Robinson Crusoe example, or the example of someone who just happens to utter exclusively true statements. This reveals a second success criterion. In addition to explaining why the five aspects above are relevant to the single

---

[4] For another theorist who does so, see Kamtekar (2004, 468–69).

trait of honesty, a successful account will lead to plausible verdicts concerning who is or is not an honest agent.

The importance of these initial success criteria can be shown by surveying two of the few discussions of honesty as a virtue that can be found in the literature. David Carr argues that "the soul of honesty as a moral virtue" is a "disposition to seek and honor truth" (2014, 9). Does this account meet Miller's unification challenge, at the same time as providing plausible verdicts about who is or is not honest? It is possible that Carr's account meets the unification challenge. This will depend on what it means to appropriately honour truth. Rather than pursue that question here, we can instead see that Carr's account fails to satisfy the second criterion of generating plausible verdicts. The claim that honesty centrally involves a disposition to "seek and honor" truth is too broad. An agent who is not motivated to seek out new truths might nevertheless avoid being dishonest, as long as she is generally forthright with the information that she does possess. Carr (2014, 9) mentions that, on his account, honesty bears some similarity to curiosity and open-mindedness. I think this is right, but it gives us good reason to question whether we have uncovered the correct account of *honesty*. By implying that an agent who lacks curiosity must thereby be dishonest (or at least lacking in honesty), this proposal fails to satisfy the second of the two criteria that have been proposed so far.

Another rare extended discussion of honesty as a virtue is provided by Louis Guenin (2005), although Guenin's focus is narrower, in that he is primarily concerned with *intellectual* honesty. According to Guenin, intellectual honesty is but one component of honesty in general and is concerned with "truthfulness and veraciousness" (2005, 180). These are understood, respectively, as "the attribute of being truthful" and "the disposition to be truthful." Honesty more generally is explained as "an inclusive disposition embracing veraciousness as well as dispositions not to cheat and not to violate rules of fair play. As it is said, one who is honest does not lie, cheat, or steal" (2005, 222). It is apparent that this account does not meet the unification challenge. When discussing honesty in general, Guenin recounts the different behavioural dispositions that we would expect from an honest agent, but does not offer an explanation of why those different aspects tend to hang together. This should not be taken as a criticism of Guenin, whose aim is not to provide any such explanation. But it does demonstrate that we will need to look elsewhere for an account of honesty in general that satisfies the initial criteria.

Before moving on, I want to suggest two further success criteria. While the virtue of honesty has been relatively neglected in the virtue literature, this is not the case for all candidate moral virtues. For example, the trait of modesty has been subject to a high level of scrutiny and debate.[5] While I will not discuss that debate here, the literature on modesty can provide

---

[5] See, for example, Driver 2001, chap. 2; Ridge 2000; McMullin 2010; and Wilson 2016.

inspiration for additional success criteria when assessing accounts of specific virtuous traits.

The flourishing debate concerning modesty is due, in large part, to an account proposed by Julia Driver. When setting out her account, Driver (2001, chap. 2) argues that it is capable of doing two things that any account of modesty ought to achieve. First, she claims that her account is compatible with a plausible corresponding account of the vice of false modesty. Second, she argues that her account can explain the value or virtuousness of (genuine) modesty. Regardless of whether Driver's account is, in fact, successful in these ways, these do appear to be relevant aims when proposing an account of a specific virtuous trait. I therefore suggest the following additional success criteria for an account of honesty. First, the account ought to be compatible with a plausible corresponding account of dishonesty. Second, the account ought to go some way towards explaining why honesty is widely accepted as a moral virtue. Adding these two criteria to those considered above results in the following list of what we should expect from any plausible account of honesty:

> *The unification challenge*: An account of honesty ought to explain why the trait is thought to be manifest in a range of seemingly distinct behaviours, including the five aspects of honesty noted earlier.
> *Plausible verdicts*: An account of honesty ought to produce plausible verdicts concerning who should (or should not) be classed as an honest agent.
> *Corresponding account of dishonesty*: An account of honesty ought to be compatible with a plausible corresponding account of dishonesty.
> *Explanation of value*: An account of honesty ought to at least point in the direction of an explanation for why honesty is a moral virtue.

By setting out these four success criteria, I aim to provide a framework for further discussion of honesty as a virtue. The challenge, then, is to offer an account of the nature of honesty that can satisfy these criteria. In the remainder of this chapter, I take up this challenge by proposing and defending a motivational account of honesty, and by explaining what this account has to say about the virtue status of the trait.

3. Miller's Starting Point

In order to provide an account of honesty that can satisfy all four of the proposed success criteria, it is necessary to first meet Miller's unification challenge. This requires explaining what lies at the core of honesty, such that honesty would be expected to be manifest in the seemingly distinct ways highlighted by the five aspects of honesty that have been identified: *truthfulness, being respectful of property, proper compliance, fidelity to promises,* and *forthrightness*. Given the aim of meeting this challenge, it is worth considering Miller's own proposal.

The initial proposal from Miller is as follows: "The virtue of honesty is, centrally, a character trait concerned with reliably not intentionally distorting the facts" (2017, 244). Miller is clear that he views this mainly as "a promising starting point" aimed at encouraging future work (2017, 244). We can see both why the account is promising and why it will require revision by assessing it in terms of the success criteria generated in the previous section.

Does this proposal meet the unification challenge? Miller (2017, 241–44) first explains how the account can accommodate four of the five aspects of honesty mentioned above, before then discussing more problematic cases. It is plausible that *truthfulness* will involve not intentionally distorting the facts, as will *proper compliance* (such as by avoiding match fixing or feigning injury in sports) and *being respectful of property* (such as by avoiding passing off another's possessions as one's own). We can also see how not intentionally distorting the facts is connected to *forthrightness*. An agent who is less than forthright might typically be hoping to induce a false understanding of the facts, either through implication or by omission. In these ways, Miller's initial proposal can explain why honesty is associated with four of the five aspects of honesty that were highlighted above.

The first of the more problematic cases discussed by Miller (2017, 242) is *fidelity to promises*. In what way does the breaking of a promise involve an intentional distorting of the facts? First of all, we can see why making false promises is associated with (dis)honesty. By promising to repay the money despite having no intention of doing so, I distort facts about what I can be expected to do in future (and about my current intentions). But what about cases where an agent genuinely intends to keep a promise but later fails to do so? Is breaking a promise in this way a sign of dishonesty, and, if so, can it be understood as an intentional distorting of the facts? The correct response to this issue is to recognise that not all failures to keep a promise indicate a lack of honesty.

Fidelity to promises is properly associated with honesty, but only because a consistent failure to keep one's promises will justifiably raise suspicions about whether those promises are being made in good faith. If they are not, then one is being dishonest, and Miller's initial proposal is able to accommodate this. But the breaking of a promise does not always indicate a lack of honesty, such as when the promise is made in good faith but cannot ultimately be fulfilled due to unanticipated complications. In these cases, an agent might reveal a failure of character, but this is likely to be a failure of due care, or perhaps a failure of justice. Such cases do not necessarily reveal a lack of honesty.[6] Given this, we can explain why *fidelity to promises* is rightly associated with honesty, even if not all cases of breaking a promise should be thought of as dishonest.

---

[6] Miller (2017, 242) suggests that such cases instead indicate a lack of loyalty.

A second problematic case discussed by Miller (2017, 243) can be responded to in the same way. Even if the initial proposal does, in general, explain why honesty is associated with *being respectful of property*, there might be cases where stealing another's property involves no obvious distortion of the facts. Miller's example is of a "bald-faced theft" where the perpetrator is open about what he is doing and does not pretend that the stolen property belongs to him. Even if this is an example of lacking respect for property that does not involve any obvious distortion of facts, Miller is correct to suggest that this case is not necessarily one that involves dishonesty. As with the previous problematic example, we can say that an agent who engages in bald-faced theft reveals a failing of character. But this failure will be one of justice or of charity, not necessarily a failure of honesty. I believe that this is an intuitively plausible verdict in response to cases of bald-faced theft, and so Miller's initial proposal is also able to accommodate those instances of *being respectful of property* that are properly associated with honesty.

And so, having set up the unification challenge, Miller then provides an initial proposal that is capable of meeting that challenge. This demonstrates the promise of the proposal. That the proposal should only be thought of as a starting point is demonstrated by how it fares in relation to the second criterion generated earlier: the need to produce plausible verdicts concerning who should (or should not) be classed as an honest agent.

One worry for the proposal, as it stands, is that it provides only a negative requirement for being an honest agent. By this I mean that the proposal highlights a reliable *lack* of certain behaviours (intentional distortions of the facts) as the central feature of honesty. And yet, we can imagine an agent who has this central feature but is not necessarily honest. For example, an agent suffering from depression, or from a general apathy, might cease to care about the facts one way or another, and so be reliably disposed not to bother intentionally distorting any facts (at the same time as being reliably disposed not to bother checking any facts either). Such an agent appears to satisfy Miller's initial proposal, but it is not clear that this is enough to count as being a possessor of genuine honesty.

In addition to worries about the central feature of honesty being presented negatively (as a lack), there is a further worry that Miller (2017, 245) identifies. It is possible for an agent to be reliably disposed not to distort the facts, but where this reliability has a positive explanation that is somehow inappropriate. For example, someone might reliably not distort the facts only because of an active desire to avoid punishment.[7] If we think that this underlying explanation casts doubt on an agent's possession of

[7] Miller's own examples are of seeking to make a good impression and seeking rewards in the afterlife.

honesty (or of morally virtuous honesty), then this will be problematic for Miller's initial proposal.[8]

Miller is aware that his initial proposal may need to be amended. For this reason, he mentions four possible revisions to his proposal, while being clear that his goal "is not to argue either for or against these revisions" in his paper (2017, 244–46). The possible revisions he mentions are:

(1) The virtue of honesty is, centrally, a character trait concerned with reliably not intentionally distorting the facts *unless it is morally appropriate to do so*.

(2) The virtue of honesty is, centrally, a character trait concerned, *for good or virtuous motivating reasons*, with reliably not intentionally distorting the facts.

(3) The virtue of honesty is, centrally, a character trait concerned with reliably not intentionally distorting the facts *as the agent sees them*.

(4) The virtue of honesty is, centrally, a character trait concerned with reliably not intentionally distorting the facts *in one's own life and also with actively preventing such distortions in others (in morally appropriate ways)* (emphasis added).

It will not be possible to evaluate the four potential revisions to his initial proposal that Miller mentions. However, given the problem cases just discussed, I believe that the second potential revision is the most promising. The reliability of an agent suffering from depression, or of an agent seeking to avoid punishment, is plausibly not explained by any "good or virtuous motivating reasons," and so those agents will no longer satisfy Miller's account once it is revised in this way. One way of attempting to advance the debate on honesty, therefore, would be to develop this second potential revision by providing arguments in favour of it (perhaps by arguing that it can meet the four success criteria set out above) and by providing an account of how the "good and virtuous" motivating reasons are to be understood.

And yet, that will not quite be my approach here. I believe that Miller's discussion provides a vital starting point for the debate, particularly when demonstrating how an account might meet his unification challenge. I am also generally sympathetic towards accounts of virtue that emphasize an important role for an agent's motivations, as is suggested by Miller's second potential revision. As we will see, however, I believe that an agent's motivation needs to play two distinct roles (or a role at two distinct levels) when one provides an account of the nature of honesty as a moral virtue.

---

[8] Similar worries may arise for Tara Smith's account on which honesty is "a person's refusal to pretend that facts are other than they are" (2003, 518).

First, I believe that an honesty-specific motivation ought to be identified as the central feature of honesty in general (rather than a tendency to reliably act, or to avoid acting, in certain ways). Only then should a further appeal be made to the idea of virtuous motivations in order to explain when and why honesty is rightly considered morally virtuous. In what follows, I want to propose and defend an account that has these features. This will involve proposing both what the honesty-specific motivation could be and how we might think of the additional virtuous motivations that are present when honesty is a moral virtue. I will argue in favour of this account by demonstrating that it can satisfy the success criteria outlined above.

4. A Motivational Account of Honesty

The account of honesty in general that I want to propose can be set out as follows:

> *The motivational account of honesty*: The trait of honesty centrally involves a deep motivation to avoid deception.

This account can be categorized as a *motivational* account of honesty for the simple reason that it identifies a motivation as the central feature of honesty, as opposed to a reliable behavioural disposition, or a tendency to produce certain outcomes. On this account, honesty requires a deep motivation to avoid deception. What is meant by a "deep" motivation in this context? We should not accept that just any motivation to avoid deception is sufficient for honesty. Instead, an agent's motivation must have certain features (discussed also in Wilson 2017). Firstly, the motivation must be sufficiently *persistent*, in the sense that it is neither fleeting nor sporadic. Secondly, the motivation must be sufficiently *strong*, in the sense that it is capable of actually influencing the agent's behaviour. And thirdly, the motivation must be sufficiently *robust*, in the sense that it is not easily defeated by competing considerations. We would not consider an agent to be honest if her persistent and strong motivation to avoid deception was consistently overridden by her competing desire to be well liked. Only when her motivation has these three features can we say that an agent possesses a *deep* motivation to avoid deception, and only then can she be considered truly honest.

This account of honesty can respond to the unification challenge. An agent who is deeply motivated to avoid deception can be expected to avoid telling lies and to avoid making false promises, and this explains why honesty is associated with *truthfulness* and *fidelity to promises*. Similarly, an agent who is deeply motivated to avoid deception will avoid presenting only a partial and misleading picture of the truth, and so honesty can also be expected to result in *forthrightness*. In this way, the motivational account explains the connection between the trait of honesty and three of the five aspects of honesty mentioned above.

The remaining two aspects of honesty can be accommodated in a similar way. Efforts to cheat or to violate the rules of fair play typically involve deception. This is true, for example, when a footballer pretends to have been unfairly challenged by an opponent, or when a tennis player pretends to be trying to win her match despite having secretly agreed to lose in exchange for a cash payment. An agent who is deeply motivated to avoid deception would not be expected to act in these ways, and this explains why honesty is associated with *proper compliance*. And it is also true that most cases of theft also involve deception. This is the case, for example, when an agent poses as a security guard in order to rob a bank or, more commonly, when one claims stolen possessions as one's own after the fact. Again, an agent who was motivated to avoid deception would not be expected to act in these ways, and this explains why honesty is associated with *being respectful of property*. By accommodating all five of the aspects of honesty that have been identified, the motivational account provides a satisfying response to Miller's unification challenge.

There may be cases where an agent fails to demonstrate either *fidelity to promises* or *being respectful of property* without engaging in any deception. These cases will include the problematic examples discussed by Miller and considered above. An agent who makes a promise in good faith might later fail to fulfil that promise due to unforeseen complications while not engaging in deception of any kind. An agent who is guilty of bald-faced theft when stealing from others might fail to be respectful of property while not engaging in deception of any kind. If this is possible, then these actions will be compatible with a deep motivation to avoid deception, and so will be judged as compatible with honesty on the proposed account. And yet, this is not a problem for the account. We saw above that the failings involved in these problematic cases are better viewed as failures of justice or of charity, rather than as failures of honesty. That verdict is compatible with the motivational account of honesty. Therefore, we can maintain our initial verdict in response to these problematic cases and say that the motivational account is able to explain why the five aspects of honesty are all properly associated with the single trait of honesty.

The motivational account is also able to produce plausible verdicts in response to examples that proved problematic for rival accounts. Neither Robinson Crusoe nor someone who merely repeats whatever she overhears will be considered honest on this account. This is because their behaviour (of avoiding falsehoods and uttering truths) is not explained by a deep motivation to avoid deception. And unlike Carr's account, the motivational account does not demand the seeking out of new information in order for someone to be considered honest. If an agent is not motivated to uncover exciting new truths, then this might tell against her possession of an important virtue (such as inquisitiveness or intellectual curiosity). But it will not tell against her possession of honesty, so long as she does have a deep motivation to avoid deception. In these ways, the motivational account is better

able to meet the second criterion of generating plausible verdicts than were
proposals considered above.

The motivational account can also satisfy the third criterion of being
compatible with a plausible corresponding account of dishonesty. According to the motivational account, dishonesty consists in a problematic failure to be deeply motivated to avoid deception.[9] The most extreme way of
failing in this regard is to have a positive motivation to deceive. Any agent
motivated in this way clearly deserves to be considered dishonest. And yet,
we might expect that such agents will be rare. More common will be those
who lack honesty as a result of having a motivation to avoid deception
that falls below the necessary levels of persistence, strength, or robustness.
Someone who deceives others because her motivation to avoid deception
is always overridden by her competing desire to be well liked ought to be
considered dishonest. Someone who deceives others because her motivation to avoid deception is problematically weak or sporadic ought to be
considered dishonest. The understanding of dishonesty that follows from
the motivational account of honesty gains plausibility by securing these
results.

In these ways, the proposed motivational account of honesty satisfies
three of the four success criteria. It can explain why honesty is thought
to be manifest in seemingly distinct behaviours; it generates plausible verdicts concerning who is and who is not honest; and it is compatible with a
corresponding account of dishonesty that is intuitively appealing. Can the
proposed account also explain the moral virtuousness of honesty, thereby
satisfying the final criterion? I do not believe that the account is sufficient,
as it stands, to achieve this result. In the next section, I explain why this
is the case, before detailing an amendment to the account that allows it to
satisfy all four of the proposed success criteria.

5. Honesty as a Moral Virtue

Approaches to identifying which traits are morally virtuous can be separated into two broad categories. On an *outcomes-based* approach, the moral
virtues are those aspects of an agent that reliably lead to positive outcomes.
On a *motivations-based* approach, the moral virtues are those aspects of
an agent that involve intrinsically valuable motivations.[10] Different theorists then disagree about which are the relevant positive outcomes, and
about which motivations are intrinsically valuable. The challenge for any
account of honesty, then, is to demonstrate that honesty (on the proposed
understanding) will be accepted as a moral virtue by one, or both, of

---

[9] Some will fail to possess a sufficiently deep motivation in ways that are not problematic.
Very young children, for example, might lack a sufficiently deep motivation to avoid deception
and yet not be properly thought of as dishonest.

[10] For more on these two approaches, see Battaly 2015.

these two approaches. I will focus here on whether honesty would be accepted as a virtue by a motivations-based approach to identifying moral virtues.[11]

I have argued that honesty centrally involves a deep motivation to avoid deception. If this motivation is accepted as having intrinsic moral value, then honesty will be accepted as a moral virtue by a motivations-based approach to identifying moral virtues. In that case, the proposed account will already satisfy all four of the required success criteria. It is not clear to me, however, that the characteristic motivation of honesty does deserve to be included as being of fundamental or intrinsic moral value. It seems possible to possess a deep motivation of this sort in a way that is not morally virtuous.

When discussing Miller's proposal, I used the example of someone who reliably does not intentionally distort the facts, but only because of a fear of being punished. Such an agent is not obviously morally virtuous. However, we can also imagine an agent who is deeply motivated to avoid deception only because of a further, more fundamental, motivation to avoid punishment. Even if such an agent should be accepted as being honest, this is not an obvious case of moral virtue. For this reason, the proposed motivational account of honesty requires additional support so as to properly explain when honesty should be accepted as morally virtuous. The necessary amendment can be explained by first taking inspiration from an influential account of the intellectual virtues.

In *Virtues of the Mind*, Zagzebski (1996, part II) sets out an understanding of the intellectual virtues that appeals to a distinction between proximal motivations and underlying motivations. A proximal motivation is one that is grounded in a more fundamental, underlying motivation. For example, I might have a proximal motivation to save a percentage of my income every month, where this proximal motivation stems from an underlying motivation to live well in retirement. Crucially, Zagzebski argues that intellectual virtues involve both a proximal motivation and an underlying motivation. First of all, each intellectual virtue has its own characteristic proximal motivation. For example, the virtue of intellectual rigour might involve the characteristic proximal motivation to thoroughly examine evidence, while the virtue of intellectual courage involves the characteristic proximal motivation to respond fearlessly to intellectual challenges (see Zagzebski 1996, 269, for more examples). But in the case of intellectual virtues, these proximal motivations are grounded in a shared underlying motivation—the motivation to achieve "cognitive contact with reality."[12]

---

[11] This may actually be the more difficult task, given the general acceptance that honesty is beneficial in producing positive outcomes such as well-functioning social groups and intimate relationships. See, for example, Hursthouse 1999, 209–10, and LaFollette and Graham 1986.

[12] For explanation of this term, see Zagzebski 1996, 131–32. I also provide a slightly more detailed summary of Zagzebski's account in Wilson 2017.

And it is this shared underlying motivation that explains why they are intellectually virtuous. I believe that Zagzebski's idea of proximal and underlying motivations can be used to amend the proposed account of honesty so as to explain the status of honesty as a moral virtue.

In addition to an account of the nature of honesty, it is important to explain why (and when) honesty is morally virtuous. The account that I have in mind is as follows:

> *The motivational account of honesty as a moral virtue*: Honesty is morally virtuous only when the characteristic motivation to avoid deception is grounded in an underlying motivation that is of intrinsic moral value.

Different theorists can accept this account, even if they then disagree about which motivations have intrinsic moral value. It will not be possible here for me to argue in favour of any particular position on this issue. I have argued elsewhere, however, that fundamentally valuable moral motivations include the motivation to protect and promote well-being, and the motivation to ensure fairness (see Wilson 2017). Just as intellectual rigour is an intellectual virtue when its characteristic motivation to examine the evidence is grounded in an underlying motivation for "cognitive contact with reality," so too will honesty be a moral virtue when its characteristic motivation to avoid deception is grounded in, for example, an underlying motivation to ensure fairness.

Using the motivation to ensure fairness as an example of a morally valuable motivation, we can see how the proposed account can lead to plausible verdicts concerning when honesty is morally virtuous. We should not say that an agent who is deeply motivated to avoid deception only because of a fear of being punished is morally virtuous. Even if this agent is properly considered honest (if the motivation is sufficiently deep), she should not be considered *virtuously* honest. A deep motivation to avoid deception is only morally virtuous when it is grounded in an intrinsically valuable underlying motivation, such as the motivation to ensure fairness. An agent who is deeply motivated to avoid deception because she thinks that it would be unfair to deceive others can be both honest and morally virtuous. An agent who is deeply motivated to avoid deception only because she is afraid that she will be punished may well be honest, but she will not thereby be morally virtuous.

Combining the initial motivational account of honesty with this further account of when honesty is a moral virtue renders the overall account better able to explain why (and when) honesty can be included as a moral virtue. As a result, the motivational account becomes able to satisfy all four of the success criteria that were generated in section 2. By explaining how these criteria can be satisfied, I hope to have demonstrated the promise and plausibility of the proposed account.

6. Further Implications

Before concluding, I want to briefly discuss two implications of my proposal. The aim of this section is to highlight possible areas of future research for those interested in honesty as a virtue.

6.1 Encouraging the Development of Virtuous Honesty

The claim that honesty centrally involves a characteristic motivation, as opposed to a characteristic behavioural disposition, has important implications concerning how to encourage the development of honesty. If our aim is only to encourage certain behaviours, then it might be thought effective to provide rewards for the desired behaviour and to enforce punishments for any undesired behaviour. This is a strategy that could be suggested in an educational context. For example, a school might include a selection of "virtue awards" at the annual prizegiving ceremony in order to reward virtuous behaviour, or even choose to amend grades on the basis of students' perceived virtues (or vices). In these ways, parents and educators might choose to use rewards and/or punishments when viewing the aim of virtue education as being to encourage virtuous behaviour.

This will not, however, be an effective strategy for encouraging the development of honesty as a virtue, once we accept that honesty centrally involves a deep motivation. This is because there is evidence that offering external rewards (and threatening external punishments) may actually have a negative impact on motivational development. As Heather Battaly explains: "There is mounting evidence that extrinsic motivation for tangible rewards (e.g., money, awards) does not facilitate, and even undermines, intrinsic motivation. According to Edward Deci, Richard Koestner, and Richard Ryan, a host of psychological studies have shown that offering students tangible rewards for tasks like reading and writing actually *decreases* their intrinsic motivation to perform such tasks" (2015, 155).[13] If this is correct, and if honesty centrally involves a deep motivation to avoid deception, then it may be important to *avoid* offering rewards or punishments in response to behaviour that is associated with honesty (such as the behaviours identified by the five aspects of honesty). Such incentives to act honestly have the potential to decrease an agent's characteristically honest motivation, and so make it more difficult for virtuous honesty to develop.

The evidence discussed by Battaly suggests that existing strategies used by parents and educators when attempting to inculcate honesty may be self-defeating if our aim is to encourage virtuous honesty. This has implications for work that will need to be carried out by those interested in encouraging the development of honesty. First, it will be important for virtue theorists

---

[13] The study mentioned by Battaly is Deci, Koestner, and Ryan 2001.

to engage with psychological studies, with the aim of either confirming or refuting the negative impact of rewards and punishments on motivational development. Secondly, it will also be important for more work to be done on uncovering and assessing alternative methods for encouraging the development of virtuous honesty. This will include focusing on strategies that do not involve obvious external incentives. It is possible that such strategies will include role-modelling, the use of art and literature, and perhaps educating children directly about virtue concepts.[14]

6.2 Other Forms of Virtuous Honesty

A second implication of the motivational account concerns the possibility of forms of honesty that are virtuous but not morally virtuous. A key feature of the motivational account is that it separates the explanation of the central feature of honesty (the deep motivation to avoid deception) and the explanation of why and when honesty is morally virtuous (the grounding of the honest motivation in a morally valuable underlying motivation). This has implications for the virtue status of honesty.

As discussed above, the motivational account makes it possible for someone to be properly considered honest (by having the required deep motivation) while at the same time not possessing honesty as a virtue (if the required motivation is grounded in an underlying motivation that is somehow inappropriate). The account also leaves open, however, the possibility that someone could possess honesty as a non-moral virtue. For example, the idea that honesty might be better understood as an intellectual virtue has been discussed elsewhere.[15] The motivational account makes it possible to understand how this could occur.

Honesty is a moral virtue when the motivation to avoid deception is grounded in a morally valuable underlying motivation, such as the motivation to protect and promote well-being or the motivation to ensure fairness. But it may also be possible for the motivation to avoid deception to be grounded in an underlying motivation that is intellectually valuable, or perhaps aesthetically valuable. Honesty might be possessed as an intellectual virtue, such as when the motivation to avoid deception is grounded in a love of truth. Or honesty might be possessed as an aesthetic virtue, such as when the motivation to avoid deception is grounded in a desire for artistic authenticity or in a belief that the truth is somehow beautiful. The opening up of these possibilities ought to encourage virtue theorists to explore the idea that familiar candidate virtues are not necessarily restricted to one particular category of virtue. Instead, future work on honesty might allow for a more open-minded discussion about the exact relationship between

---

[14] A list of seven methods for encouraging intellectual virtues in the context of education is provided by Jason Baehr (2013, 256–59).

[15] See Driver 2003, 381, and Carr 2014, 4. Intellectual honesty is the focus of Guenin 2005.

a range of different types of virtue, including moral, intellectual, and aesthetic virtues.[16]

In these ways, the motivational account of honesty points towards important future work at both a practical and a conceptual level for those interested in honesty as a virtue. It is hoped that this chapter will encourage such work, and that it will result in an increased engagement by virtue theorists with the neglected virtue of honesty.

Conclusion

In this chapter, I have attempted to address the current neglect of honesty by virtue theorists. I have provided a framework for future discussions by generating four success criteria that can be used to assess proposed accounts of honesty. And I have proposed a motivational account of honesty, arguing that this account satisfies the required criteria. It is hoped that this will encourage others to join in the task of accounting for the nature of honesty, and that it will prompt future research on how best to encourage the widespread development of honesty as a virtue.

Acknowledgments

For helpful comments and discussion, I am grateful to Christian Miller, participants at the Aretai Conference in Genoa, and the anonymous reviewers. I am also grateful to Michel Croce and Maria Silvia Vaccarezza for including my work in this collection. It was supported by a grant from the Templeton Religion Trust. The opinions expressed here are those of the author and do not necessarily reflect the views of the Templeton Religion Trust.

References

Baehr, Jason. 2013. "Educating for Intellectual Virtues: From Theory to Practice." *Journal of Philosophy of Education* 47, no. 2:248–62.

Battaly, Heather. 2015. *Virtue*. Malden, Mass.: Polity Press.

———, ed. 2010. *Virtue and Vice, Moral and Epistemic*. Oxford: Wiley-Blackwell.

Carr, David. 2014. "The Human and Epistemic Significance of Honesty as an Epistemic and Moral Virtue." *Educational Theory* 64, no. 1:1–14.

Deci, Edward L., Richard Koestner, and Richard M. Ryan. 2001. "Extrinsic Rewards and Intrinsic Motivation in Education: Reconsidered Once Again." *Review of Educational Research* 71, no. 1:1–27.

Driver, Julia. 2001. *Uneasy Virtue*. Cambridge: Cambridge University Press.

---

[16] I take steps in this direction in Wilson 2017.

———. 2003. "The Conflation of Moral and Epistemic Virtue." *Metaphilosophy* 13, no. 3:367–83.

Guenin, Louis M. 2005. "Intellectual Honesty." *Synthese* 145, no. 2:177–232.

Hursthouse, Rosalind. 1999. *On Virtue Ethics*. Oxford: Oxford University Press.

Kamtekar, Rachana. 2004. "Situationism and Virtue Ethics on the Content of Our Character." *Ethics* 114, no. 3:458–91.

LaFollette, Hugh, and George Graham. 1986. "Honesty and Intimacy." *Journal of Social and Personal Relationships* 3, no. 1:3–18.

McMullin, Irene. 2010. "A Modest Proposal: Accounting for the Virtuousness of Modesty." *Philosophical Quarterly* 60, no. 241:787–807.

Miller, Christian B. 2017. "Honesty." In *Moral Psychology, Volume 5: Virtue and Character*, edited by Walter Sinnott-Armstrong and Christian B. Miller, 237–73. Cambridge, Mass.: MIT Press.

Ridge, Michael. 2000. "Modesty as a Virtue." *American Philosophical Quarterly* 37, no. 3:269–383.

Roberts, Robert C., and W. Jay Wood. 2007. *Intellectual Virtues*. Oxford: Oxford University Press.

Slote, Michael. 2011. *The Impossibility of Perfection*. Oxford: Oxford University Press.

Smith, Tara. 2003. "The Metaphysical Case for Honesty." *Journal of Value Inquiry* 37, no. 4:517–31.

Timpe, Kevin, and Craig A. Boyd, eds. 2014. *Virtues and Their Vices*. Oxford: Oxford University Press.

Watson, Gary. 1984. "Virtues in Excess." *Philosophical Studies* 46, no. 1:57–74.

Wilson, Alan T. 2016. "Modesty as Kindness." *Ratio* 29, no. 1:73–88.

———. 2017. "Avoiding the Conflation of Moral and Intellectual Virtues." *Ethical Theory and Moral Practice* 20, no. 5:1037–50.

Zagzebski, Linda Trinkaus. 1996. *Virtues of the Mind*. Cambridge: Cambridge University Press.

PART 2

EPISTEMOLOGY

CHAPTER 5

VIRTUE EPISTEMOLOGY, ENHANCEMENT, AND CONTROL

J. ADAM CARTER

1

According to Ernest Sosa's virtue epistemology (e.g., Sosa 2009, 2010b, 2010a, 2015), the normative structure of epistemic performances can be fruitfully modelled within a wider framework for assessing performances more generally. The basic features of the wider framework are as follows:

A. Any performance with an aim can be evaluated along three dimensions: (i) whether it is *accurate*, (ii) whether it is *adroit*, and (iii) thirdly, whether it is accurate *because* adroit.
B. A performance in some domain of endeavour *D* is accurate because adroit when its success issues from a (complete) *D competence*; such performances are *apt*.
C. A competence, in a given domain of endeavour, is a disposition to perform well in that domain of endeavour.
D. Competences have a "triple-S" constitution—*seat, shape*, and *situation*—with reference to which three kinds of dispositions can be distinguished: the innermost competence (*seat*), the inner competence (*seat + shape*), and the complete competence (*seat + shape + situation*).

The theoretical core of (A–D) are Sosa's two "triples": (i) the "AAA" structure of the normativity of performances (accurate/adroit/apt); and the (ii) "SSS" structure of the constitution of competences (seat/shape/situation).

To appreciate how the "triple S" (that is, SSS) structure of the constitution of a competence works, just consider the illustrative example Sosa

Connecting Virtues: Advances in Ethics, Epistemology, and Political Philosophy.
Edited by Michel Croce and Maria Silvia Vaccarezza.
Chapters and book compilation © 2018 Metaphilosophy LLC and John Wiley & Sons Ltd.

offers concerning one's competence to drive a car: "With regard to one's competence in driving, for example, we can distinguish between (a) the innermost driving competence that is seated in one's brain, nervous system, and body, which one retains even while asleep or drunk; (b) a fuller inner competence, which requires also that one be in proper shape, that is, awake, sober, alert, and so on; and (c) complete competence or ability to drive well and safely (on a given road or in a certain area), which requires also that one be well situated, with appropriate road conditions pertaining to the surface, the lighting, etc. The complete competence is thus an SSS (or an SeShSi) competence" (2017, 191–92). We test for an innermost competence to drive a car by asking: Would the driver drive reliably enough *if in proper shape and properly situated?*[1] (We don't test for a driving competence by asking: Would the driver perform reliably enough if deprived of oxygen and placed on a slick road?) Likewise, the possession of a visual-perceptual competence requires just that one's perceptually formed beliefs are reliably enough correct when one is in proper shape (that is, awake, alert) and properly situated (not in the dark, in thick fog, and so on).

Crucially, for Sosa, a performance may be apt *even if* it issues (nondeviantly) from a complete competence (hereafter, competence) in circumstances under which the obtaining of certain elements of the competence is *unsafe*—namely, when you are in the proper shape and properly situated but very easily might not have been. (Imagine, for example, your hitting a bull's-eye manifests your competence to shoot reliably enough under conditions where you might easily have been in improper shape because you might easily have been struck by a bolt of lightning but luckily were not.) That said, a performance is not apt *unless* its success manifests such a competence.

This all matters for epistemology because beliefs are themselves a kind of epistemic performance, one that aims at truth. Apt belief, on Sosa's view— namely, belief whose correctness manifests an epistemic competence— is *knowledge*. More specifically, apt belief is *animal* knowledge. Animal knowledge (like any other kind of apt performance) must manifest a complete competence but doesn't require that all of the individual components of the complete competence *safely* hold. Thus, one might attain animal knowledge even in circumstances where (for instance) the shape or situational components of the first-order competence could easily, and unbeknownst to the thinker, have *not* been in place.[2] What Sosa calls *reflective knowledge* demands more, that one's apt belief is aptly noted—namely, that the belief's aptness *itself* manifests a second-order competence of the

---

[1] What counts as "reliable enough" for Sosa is determined by the norms governing particular performance domains. See Sosa 2010 for discussion.

[2] For instance, one might have animal knowledge when one uses one's visual-perceptual conditions to identify a red wall when there is no funny business with the lighting conditions, but even if there *easily could have been* funny business with the lighting—such as a jokester waiting in in the wings, who just so happened not to tinker with the lights, bringing about a lighting condition under which you'd believe the wall was red when it was not.

thinker, one that requires taking a reliable perspective on one's first-order competence and environmental conditions such that not too easily would one have formed one's first-order belief inaptly.

2

We may, for present purposes, set aside the complexities of reflective knowledge.[3] The focus will be more basic—on apt belief (animal knowledge) and, even more fundamentally, the SSS components of a complete competence.

Here is a question rarely asked: Does it matter how one comes to acquire the relevant seat/shape? In the default case, where one forms a visual-perceptual belief by looking at an object while sober/awake and in normal lighting conditions, the *acquisition conditions* of the seat/shape don't seem particularly interesting. (Consider, after all, that on Sosa's view one can believe aptly *even when* one very easily could not have been in proper shape but is, and could likewise easily have been, improperly situated but was not. One might be inclined to reason thus: (i) Sosa says explicitly that it doesn't matter, vis-à-vis an apt performance, whether any of the SSS elements of a competence might easily have not obtained, so long as they do obtain. (ii) Therefore, by parity of reasoning, it shouldn't matter, vis-à-vis an apt performance, whether the seat and shape elements of a subject's competence have been acquired by the subject through abnormal means, so long as they *have* been acquired.

But on this point, Sosa has—very recently (2017)—taken a different tack. Here are some interesting remarks from his latest book: "For simplicity, I leave aside restrictions on how you acquire the relevant elements of competence, such as the seat and the shape, restrictions that have come to the fore with the cyclist Lance Armstrong (regarding drug-induced shape) and with the baseball player Alex Rodriguez (regarding drug-derived seat). Each of these athletes enhanced his performances by enhancing his complete SSS dispositions to succeed, but these dispositions did not remain competences once drug-enhanced" (Sosa 2017, 195, n. 2). These remarks indicate a kind of *acquisition restriction principle* in Sosa's thinking: if an SeShSi condition of a complete competence is *drug enhanced*, then the associated SSS disposition to succeed is not a *competence*. And given that successes that do not derive from genuine competences are not apt, it follows from such an acquisition restriction principle that no successes (epistemic or otherwise) that issue from drug-enhanced SSS dispositions to succeed are *apt*.

Of course, "drug-enhanced" does not simply mean "affected by a drug." Caffeine and vitamin supplements might temporarily sharpen one's

---

[3] For some criticism of this distinction, see Kornblith (2004, 2009, 2012). Compare, however, Carter and McKenna (2018) for a defence of this distinction in light of Kornblith's criticisms.

senses before a performance; moreover, some drugs (for example, anti-depressants) might help one to perform better by simply aiding in restoring one to normal healthy levels of functioning. In his examples Sosa is refer-ring to individuals who are using medicine to enhance themselves *beyond* normal healthy levels of functioning in order to gain an advantage. He is accordingly using "enhanced" in a way that comports with the distinction in the bioethics literature between mere *therapeutic improvements*, which restore one to normal healthy levels of functioning, and *enhancements*, which aim to take healthy individuals beyond such normal levels, gener-ally by availing them of the latest science and medicine.[4]

3

Why does Sosa take such a line? He doesn't explicitly say. But others have (in various ways) defended similar ideas, albeit to different ends. In *The Case Against Perfection*, the political philosopher Michael Sandel writes: "As the role of the enhancement increases, our admiration for the achievement fades. Or rather, our admiration for the achievement shifts from the player to his pharmacist.... . This suggests that our moral response to enhancement is a response to the diminished agency of the person whose achievement is enhanced. The more the athlete relies on drugs or genetic fixes, the less his performance represents his achievement" (2012, 25–26). In a similar vein, the bioethicist John Harris has suggested that performance enhancements take away a valuable kind of freedom we have, a freedom to *fail*, by almost guaranteeing our success in a way that renders our own agency in the course of our endeavours otiose. Drawing inspiration from Milton's *Paradise Lost*, Harris writes: "Milton's insight is the crucial role of personal liberty and autonomy: that sufficiency to stand is worthless, literally morally bankrupt, without freedom to fall," and he remarks elsewhere that "our freedom to fall is precious" (2011, 110). One point in common between Sandel's and Harris's assessments is that both see enhancements as undermining respon-sibility for the performance in a manner that has a deleterious effect on performance's value, even if it may successfully attain its end.[5]

4

What Sosa says about athletic performance enhancement applies, mutatis mutandis, for cognitive performance enhancement. Consider, for example,

---

[4] Enhancement comes by degree. Plausibly, Sosa has in mind something like "signifi-cantly" (drug-enhanced) relative to non-enhanced levels of performance, where significance will partly be fixed by domain of performance. For further discussion on the distinction, see, for example, Bostrom and Savulescu 2009, Bostrom 2009, and Bostrom and Roache 2007.

[5] A critical discussion of Sandel and Harris on these issues is in Carter and Pritchard forthcoming. See also Bradford 2013 for related remarks on the value of achievements in connection with the overcoming of obstacles.

Modafinil, a nootropic "smart drug" prescribed to patients suffering from narcolepsy, which is often used off-label as a kind of eugeroic cognition-enhancement agent. Modafinil is an effective way to boost cognitive performance. Comprehensive metastudies show that Modafinil consistently boosts (in non-sleep-deprived healthy individuals) attention, executive functions, and learning, especially in complex cognitive tasks (Battleday and Brem 2015).

Here is a dilemma: if we embrace Sosa's acquisition restriction principle, then—absent some compelling disanalogy between athletic and cognitive performance enhancement that would justify a difference in how we normatively assess the two from within Sosa's framework—Modafinil-enhanced cognitive successes are not *knowledge*, animal or otherwise. (After all, knowledge minimally requires *apt* belief, true belief that manifests a competence; but it follows from Sosa's acquisition restriction principle that Modafinil-driven cognitive successes don't derive from competence and so *a fortiori* fall short of knowledge.) This is an uncomfortable result.

But—and here is the dilemma—we can't very well avoid the above result simply by jettisoning wholesale Sosa's acquisition restriction principle. Suppose, for *reductio*, that we did, while attempting to retain the broader performance normativity framework in claims A–D. It would follow that one's performance may qualify as apt even in circumstances in which the enhancement seems to be doing *all* the work.[6]

My inclination is to think there should be a principled way to split the horns of this dilemma, one that is in principle compatible with Sosa's performance normativity framework. I'll turn now to developing how I think such a rationale might proceed.

5

Take as a starting point a simple idea connecting apt belief and epistemic responsibility. Your believing correctly manifests *your* competence (rather than, say, someone else's) only if *your* epistemic agency (for example, cognitive traits, capacities that are in some way owned by you) is in some significant way responsible for your cognitive success.[7] Note that this kind of epistemic responsibility doesn't presuppose that you have direct control over your beliefs. (You don't.) (See, e.g., Williams 1970; cf. McCormick 2014.) The idea, rather, is that the kind of responsibility an apt believer has for the correctness of her belief at least requires that the mechanisms giving

---

[6] Consider, for example, the plight of Jeremy Renner's character Aaron Cross in the 2012 film *The Bourne Legacy*. In the film, Cross uses pills called "chems" that enhance him both physically and mentally, permitting him to function at a superhuman capacity as a black ops agent. *Without* the pills, Cross is—and this is crucial to the plot—of below-average intelligence and capable of none of the things that make him otherwise highly effective in field operations.

[7] This is, in effect, what Duncan Pritchard has termed the "ability intuition" on propositional knowledge. See, for example, Pritchard 2012.

rise to the belief are suitably her own mechanisms, whatever these may involve.

Suppose now that a benevolent demon *causes* you to believe *p* (making it impossible for you to believe otherwise), and *p* is true. In such a case, that you believe correctly seems to have nothing to do with your own epistemic agency; your own cognitive traits play no role in accounting for why you believe truly rather than falsely. We can vary facts about your own epistemic agency anyway we like, but the outcome remains the same—you believe (correctly) that *p*.

Such a case is suggestive of something like the following initial idea: a subject is epistemically responsible for some cognitive success, *X*, only if it's not the case that no matter how we alter facts about the subject's epistemic agency, the result *X* remains the same. Put another way: the agent isn't responsible for the cognitive success if the subject *couldn't have avoided that success*. This idea comports with a more general idea: that responsibility of any kind requires alternative possibilities.

Frankfurt-style cases, however, famously cast doubt on this general claim (see Frankfurt 1969). And likewise, *epistemic* Frankfurt cases— namely, where a benevolent demon waits in the wings and will intervene only if the subject doesn't come to form the target belief correctly, but since the agent forms the target belief correctly, the demon accordingly doesn't intervene—cast doubt on the supposition that alternative possibilities are necessary for epistemic responsibility.[8] There is, however, plausibly a freedom-relevant necessary condition on epistemic responsibility that doesn't trade on alternative possibilities, one that has to do with what Fischer and Ravizza (2000) call *guidance control*.

In what follows, (i) I briefly explain guidance control as a freedom-relevant feature of moral responsibility and show how (a tweaked version of) a guidance control condition is a plausible necessary condition on epistemic responsibility of the sort that apt belief plausibly demands; and (ii) I then attempt to show why *some* kinds of pharmacological cognitive enhancements may fail such a condition while others satisfy it. The upshot, or so I suggest, is that there is room to manoeuvre in a principled way between the two horns of the dilemma: the virtue epistemologist who embraces a Sosa-style performance normativity model of epistemic assessment can allow that some beliefs formed via the aid of cognitive enhancing drugs are apt (and so knowledge) while others are not.

6

Fischer and Ravizza (2000) define *guidance control* as the freedom-relevant aspect of moral responsibility. The pithy statement of the view is as follows: an agent has guidance control over an action if and only if that action is

---

[8] For a recent discussion of epistemic Frankfurt-style cases, see Kelp 2016.

caused by a reasons-responsive mechanism M, and S owns M.[9] As Fischer and Ravizza note, and as is suggested by the preceding definition, there are two key dimensions of guidance control: *reasons-responsiveness* and *mechanism ownership*. On the Fischer-Ravizza view, a mechanism (in short: a way of doing something) is reasons-responsive provided that, *holding fixed that mechanism*, "the agent would presumably choose and act differently in a range of scenarios in which he is presented with good reasons to do so" (Fischer 2012, 187). The mechanism that is normal practical reasoning functioning in normal conditions is reasons-responsive; even if this mechanism issues act A in the actual world in light of the presence of the actual reasons on which A is based, if we hold fixed this mechanism and vary the presence of reasons so that there are, say, overwhelming reasons for B rather than A, normal practical reasoning will go for B on the basis of these other reasons. The mechanism of *coerced* practical reasoning is not likewise reasons-responsive (after all, even if we adjust the reasons, that mechanism will continue, holding fixed the coercion as a feature of the mechanism, to issue the same action).

Given that one could be manipulated or brainwashed to acquire a reasons-responsive mechanism (in the sense just specified) but would not intuitively be responsible in such a circumstance for the deliverances of such a mechanism, Fischer and Ravizza specify further that the mechanism that issues in the relevant behaviour must (in an appropriate sense) *be the agent's own mechanism*. They articulate this mechanism ownership condition as follows: S owns a process/mechanism of type M iff S reasonably takes himself to be the agential source of the outcomes of M and S takes himself to be a fair target of reactive attitudes regarding the outcomes of M.[10]

We may initially define *epistemic guidance control* as an analogous condition on *epistemic* responsibility, one that likewise admits of dimensions that will be epistemic variants on reasons-responsiveness and mechanism ownership.[11] For our purposes, an epistemic variant on reasons responsiveness (which Fischer and Ravizza are of course thinking about in the context of moral, rather than epistemic, responsibility) will involve—on a first pass—the following core idea: a *belief-forming mechanism* is (epistemically) reasons-responsive provided that, *holding fixed that mechanism*, "the agent would presumably form beliefs differently in a range of scenarios in

---

[9] See Kruse 2017 for a helpful and concise presentation of Fischer and Ravizza's key definitions. Compare Mele 2000 and 2006 and Todd and Tognazzini 2008 for some critiques of guidance control.

[10] See Fischer 2012, 190, and Fischer and Ravizza 2000, 210–13. I am taking this formalisation from Kruse 2017, 2814.

[11] McHugh (2013) is the first I'm aware of to use the term "epistemic guidance control," though McHugh is using the term to capture, in the main, the reasons-responsiveness element of (doxastic) guidance control. As will become clear, the interest here will primarily be to do with the mechanism-ownership component. We thus are using the term in different ways.

which he is presented with good reasons to do so." On such a view, the mechanism of normal induction is epistemically reasons-responsive—the process responds differentially in nearby worlds where we vary the inputs—while the mechanism of hypnotized believing is not. These are both intuitive results.[12]

7

I submit that belief-forming processes boosted by pharmacological cognitive enhancements are not going to have any obvious problems satisfying *epistemic reasons-responsiveness*—at least, not in ordinary circumstances. The idea, in sum, is this: Let M be a cognitive mechanism and let $E(M)$ be M operating at an enhanced capacity. If M is suitably reasons-responsive, then $E(M)$ will be too, provided $E(M)$ is really an *enhancement* of M, as opposed to a diminution of M. Suppose that M *ex hypothesi* involves attention and executive functions of the sort enhanced via Modafinil in complex cognitive tasks. If M is a suitably reasons-responsive, then when we hold fixed the mechanism (that is, involving attention and executive functions, and so forth) and vary the inputs, M responds differentially in light of the varied inputs. But then $E(M)$, an enhanced variation of this very mechanism, will if anything respond differentially *even better* in light of the varied inputs. And indeed, that's what the empirical evidence would suggest (see Battleday and Brem 2015).

The situation then seems to be as follows: if cognitively enhancing our ways of forming beliefs has as a consequence that the epistemic responsibility we have for our cognitive successes reached through such enhanced processes is undermined, then this isn't going to be for the reason that such enhancements undermine the guidance control condition on epistemic responsibility by way of the reasons-responsiveness dimension to guidance control. It must be, if anything, that such enhancements stand in tension with *mechanism ownership*.

---

[12] It might be thought that the above-sketched way of modelling the "epistemic reasons-responsiveness" component of what would be epistemic guidance control allies with a distinctively *epistemic internalist* gloss of epistemic responsibility but not so obviously with an externalist gloss of this notion. And Sosa's epistemology is externalist, a form of virtue reliabilism. Thus, as the line of thought would go, reasons-responsiveness as a component on guidance control is orthogonal to the kind of guidance control that would be germane to epistemic responsibility on an externalist programme like Sosa's. This is not, however, a deep worry. For one thing, as Sylvan and Sosa (2014) have pointed out, reasons possession itself may be explicable with reference to the more fundamental notion of competence possession. For another—and more important—thing, we may easily retain the core idea of reasons-responsiveness (as a component of responsibility-relevant guidance control) by simply maintaining this: a mechanism (that is, a belief-forming process) is reasons-responsive in the way that matters for guidance control provided the process type is suitably modally robust—viz., that the process responds differentially in nearby worlds where we vary the inputs.

8

According to Fischer and Ravizza, one *owns* a mechanism just in case someone reasonably takes herself to be the agential source of the outcomes, Ω, of that mechanism, and reasonably takes herself to be a fair target of the reactive attitudes (for example, approval, praise, disapprobation, blame, and so on) regarding Ω. We can—following Andrea Kruse (2017, 2814)—define *epistemic mechanism ownership* as the following restricted idea: S owns an epistemic process/mechanism of type M iff S reasonably takes herself to be the agential source of the outcomes of M and S takes herself to be a fair target of reactive attitudes regarding the doxastic outcomes of M (that is, the beliefs that M issues). Let's set aside what "reasonably" involves for the moment—though we'll return to this.

While beliefs formed via smart drugs will satisfy the reasons-responsiveness condition on epistemic guidance control, there's a worry that they'll *never* satisfy the epistemic mechanism-ownership condition, and that this may be so no matter how we unpack "reasonably."

To appreciate why, consider the following case in the moral-responsibility literature, due to Neal Judisch, which he intends as an objection to the Fischer-Ravizza account of moral guidance control. What's interesting in particular about the case is the kind of move Fischer thinks must be made in order to deal with it, and what this suggests for epistemic mechanism ownership and enhancement.

BYPASS. Suppose that one night, while Chum is soundly asleep, he spontaneously develops a debilitating brain lesion. The lesion is situated in his neural network in such a way that his capacity for practical reasoning is severely impaired—the relevant mechanism no longer even approximates the standards of moderate reasons-responsiveness. Imagine now that a benevolent neuroscientist, Dr. White, is somehow made aware of Chum's plight. Unfortunately, there is no way he can remove the lesion without causing irreparable damage to Chum's brain, but White has a few handy electronic devices that enable him (literally) to get around that problem. The first, placed just "upstream" of the lesion, takes as inputs the messages sent through the neural pathways headed right for the spot where the lesion is located, and it transmits the incoming data via radio signals to the other device located just "downstream" of the lesion, which device, in turn, relays the appropriate impulses to the neural pathways just downstream of it. The result is that the lesion is both successfully isolated and bypassed, its potentially deleterious effects completely cut off from the rest of Chum's brain; indeed, Chum's post-surgery cognitive architecture is functionally equivalent to his pre-surgery brain .... When Chum awakens, he is of course completely unaware of the evening's events; as far as he is concerned, it is business as usual. (Judisch 2005, 115–30).[13]

---

[13] Cited also in Fischer 2012, 201.

Judisch's diagnosis is as follows: (i) Chum is morally responsible for his subsequent behaviour; (ii) but contra the Fischer-Ravizza view according to which moral responsibility requires guidance control (as they specify it), Chum cannot qualify as morally responsible. Judisch's rationale for (ii) is that you can't *take responsibility* in the sense required for mechanism ownership of a mechanism that is manipulated in a clandestine fashion (after all, it seems that you are utterly mistaken in such a circumstance about what the mechanism actually is).

I suggested that Fischer's reply is interesting and bears relevance to how to think about enhancement cases vis-à-vis mechanism ownership. Fischer's reply, in short, involves an appeal to commonsense functionalism. Fischer writes: "If neuroscientists secretly installed a physically different part of my brain that functioned equivalently to the biological part, this would surely not create a different kind of mechanism. As far as I'm concerned, this would be like replacing one's carburettor with a functionally identical carburettor but made of slightly more durable material; it would still be the same kind of engine (for most conceivable purposes). Merely changing the physical realization of the processing that goes on (without changing the inputs or the processing of those inputs) does not, it seems to change the mechanism-kind" (2012, 202). A corollary of Fischer's diagnosis is that if the neuroscientists installed something that was *more than the functional analogue of a sturdier carburettor*—namely, one that didn't "function equivalently" but functioned *better*, then the situation would be different. And Fischer says as much explicitly in commenting on a twist on Judisch's case: "If the way Chum tends to process inputs is fundamentally altered, this changes Chum's mechanism. For example, if Chum is (say) highly risk-averse prior to the manipulation and very adventuresome after, or if he is egoistic before and altruistic after, the intervention has changed Chum's mechanism—his signature way of weighing reasons" (2012, 202).

The foregoing reasoning by Fischer suggests the following. Call the mechanism that is [*reasoning* + Modafinil] "*M(R)*." If Modafinil alters a thinker's mechanism in a manner broadly analogous to the moral case described above—such that $M(R)$ stands to normal reasoning, R, as the alteration to Chum's mechanism in the passage above stands to Chum's normal mechanism—then the use of Modafinil has fundamentally altered the mechanism. But then if the mechanism is fundamentally altered, there's a problem: it's not clear how the subject can *reasonably* take responsibility in the way required for mechanism ownership. After all, what would such evidence *be* in virtue of which such a taking of responsibility is reasonable? It's at best unclear.[14]

---

[14] Consider that such evidence would at least have to include evidence that one is the agential source of the outcomes of the enhanced mechanism, *as well as* additional evidence that S takes herself to be a fair target of reactive attitudes regarding the doxastic outcomes of M. If

9

At this point, though, we may anticipate an optimistic rejoinder: in the typical kinds of cases of cognitive enhancement under consideration, you are freely *choosing* to take Modafinil! This feature makes such cases very different from the BYPASS case, where you were manipulated against your will. Consideration of this difference may lead one to reason as follows: your responsibility for your choice to take Modafinil "carries over" to the known consequence of this choice (that is, your cognitive behaviour while on the drug) in such a way that you could be responsible for the cognitive success while on the drug *even if* you fail the mechanism-ownership condition on epistemic guidance control at the time at which you are forming Modafinil-fuelled cognitive outputs.

Such an appeal is, in effect, an appeal to what Fischer and Ravizza call a *tracing condition*. Indeed, Fischer and Ravizza help themselves to just such a condition in order to handle cases where it seems one is responsible at a time despite not having a reasons-responsive mechanism at that time—as in drunk driving. According to Fischer and Ravizza, "When one acts from a reasons-responsive mechanism at time T1, and one can reasonably be expected to know that so acting will (or may) lead to acting from an unresponsive mechanism at some later time T2, one can be held responsible for so acting at T2" (2000, 50).

Question: Can we say, then, that a cognitively enhanced individual may satisfy a plausible guidance-control requirement on epistemic responsibility simply because—even though the agent seems to fail the mechanism ownership condition on guidance control at a time T2—the agent nonetheless acted from an owned reasons-responsive mechanism at T1 (that is, through an owned mechanism used to take the pill in the first place)?

It's not clear that we can. I want to suggest now that a tracing condition, though it seems plausible in the case of *moral responsibility* as Fischer and Ravizza are adverting to it, looks quite a bit less plausible when we shift from moral to *epistemic* responsibility. Furthermore, a tracing condition—if plausible at all vis-à-vis epistemic responsibility—seems comparably more plausible in cases of epistemic blame as opposed to epistemic praise (for example, of the sort befitting an epistemic achievement).

To see this point, compare the plausibility of the tracing condition in a drunk-driving case (a case with a negative moral outcome—where the free choice at a previous time to knowingly put one in a position whereby one drove dangerously seems intuitively to warrant moral blame) with the following case of epistemic responsibility for a positive epistemic outcome.

Imagine an extreme case. Suppose there is a futuristic pill, Euler-Pro, that does the following: first, the pill incepts in one's memory detailed

one knows the Modafinil has been efficacious, it's not clear initially how either of these would be satisfied in normal cases of Modafinil use. I return to this point in section 10.

information about topology, graph theory, and analytic number theory; the pill further dramatically enhances one's raw mathematical skill. Aaron, an ordinary maths student with average grades, takes the Euler-Pro pill and, within five minutes, works out the connection between the Riemann zeta function and the prime numbers. He proceeds to write up a proof for what is effectively the Euler product formula for the Riemann zeta function (and his teacher gives him an A).

If an "epistemic tracing condition" were a plausible supplement to epistemic guidance control as a condition on epistemic responsibility, we should expect Aaron to be responsible, epistemically speaking, for his proof (regardless of what is going on while he is proving the Euler product formula for the Riemann zeta function), given that he had suitable guidance control over his previous action of taking a pill the taking of which put him in the state whereby this formula became provable for him.

But this doesn't seem right at all. To see why, consider a tracing-relevant variation on the famous case of Norman the Clairvoyant (BonJour 1980, 62) in the classic reliabilist literature.

NORMAN-PILL: Norman wants to know where the President is at all times, but the Secret Service frequently hide the President's whereabouts for security reasons, constantly frustrating Norman's desire to know where the President is. Fortunately for Norman, an angel decides to help him out. The angel gives him a pill with the following explanation. Taking the pill will cause two things: first, it will cause Norman to form a true belief about where the President is any time Norman thinks about this. Secondly, the pill will cause Norman to forget his encounter with the angel, and thus, will cause him to lack any appreciation for why he is believing what he does. Norman freely chooses to take the pill. The next day, Norman forms the (true) belief "The President is in Boston" and has no idea why he thinks this.

In NORMAN-PILL, Norman's belief is correct: the president really is in Boston. But upon recognising that he has no idea why he believes this, Norman acquires a defeater for his belief—what is called in the defeasibility literature a "no-reason defeater."[15] He's no longer justified in continuing to believe the president is in Boston, *even though* this belief issues from an infallible process. Continuing to believe the president is in Boston despite the presence of such a defeater is epistemically irresponsible.

Such epistemic irresponsibility isn't "cancelled" by pointing out the further fact that a tracing condition is met in NORMAN-PILL. After all, Norman *did* have full command of his faculties and made a free and informed decision to take the pill at an earlier time, a pill that he knew would bring it about both that he would know where the president was any time he

---

[15] A no-reason defeater is a type of psychological or mental state defeater (see Pollock 1986) that is a reason for thinking it's no longer reasonable to believe a proposition, given that one lacks any reason for believing it, and yet, it's the sort of belief that would be reasonable to hold only if one did have some reason for it (Bergmann 1997, 102–3). See also Sudduth 2013.

thought about it *and* that he would forget at the later time the explanation for why he believed this.

And what goes for Norman in NORMAN-PILL goes for Aaron who takes the Euler-Pro pill. What these cases indicate is an interesting way in which moral and epistemic responsibility come apart: regardless of whether we can supplement an account of guidance control with a tracing condition to handle problem cases with respect to moral responsibility (such as drunk-driving cases), the same doesn't seem to be the case with epistemic responsibility. In particular, looking to past free, fully informed decisions isn't always going to be helpful in assessing epistemic responsibility at a later time. And what *this* means is that attempting to explain how we may be suitably epistemically responsible for the correctness of beliefs which are formed via enhancement, but which seem to fail a mechanism ownership condition, simply by pointing to how such non-owned mechanisms are known consequences of owned reasons-responsive mechanisms exercised at a previous time is not going to be compelling. Accounting for how we are suitably responsible for the correctness of such beliefs in the face of the mechanism ownership problem requires, thus, looking elsewhere.

10

Let's take stock. We were initially faced with a dilemma: if we embrace Sosa's acquisition restriction principle, then it looks as though Modafinil-enhanced cognitive successes will inevitably fall short of *knowledge*, animal or otherwise—a result that seemed problematic (for surely we can know at least *some* of the things we come to believe through cognition-enhancing drugs). But if we tried to avoid this result by jettisoning wholesale Sosa's acquisition-restriction principle, it would follow that one's performance may qualify as apt, and accordingly that one's belief may qualify as animal knowledge, even in circumstances in which the enhancement seems to be doing *all* the work. The objective, then, was to seek a way to navigate through the horns of this dilemma.

Doing so, it was suggested, would seem to require some principled rationale for a difference in treatment in extreme enhancement cases as opposed to moderate ones—where Modafinil use would seem prima facie to fall in the latter category. A natural starting point was to consider how such a difference might be a difference in the level of epistemic responsibility the agent may have for the successful outcome. Here, a promising place to look was to the moral-responsibility literature, which is replete with rich discussion of how disconnections between agency and action can be responsibility undermining. In particular, one popular way of thinking of such a connection is as follows: (i) moral responsibility requires guidance control; and (ii) guidance control requires the satisfaction of two conditions: a reasons-responsiveness condition and a mechanism-ownership condition. Taking this line of thinking as a guide, we've seen that an analogous requirement on epistemic responsibility—namely, that epistemic responsibility for a cognitive output (for example, such that the success of the cognitive output is suitably a product of the agent's *own* cognitive agency) requires exhibiting *epistemic guidance control*, will—in the kind of cognition-enhancement cases of interest to us—ultimately turn on the mechanism-ownership condition on epistemic guidance control.

The problem, which as we saw in the previous section can't be fixed by adding a tracing condition of the sort that Fischer and Ravizza endorse in the case of moral responsibility, is that it's not clear how *any* cognitive enhancements, moderate or otherwise, are going to satisfy such a mechanism-ownership condition. The requirement, recall, is as follows: *S* owns an epistemic process/mechanism of type *M* iff *S* reasonably takes herself to be the agential source of the outcomes of *M* and *S* takes herself to be a fair target of reactive attitudes regarding the doxastic outcomes of *M*.[16]

At this point, it will be fruitful to consider more carefully what "reasonably" should be understood to involve in the mechanism-ownership condition. Plausibly, Fischer and Ravizza intended such a condition in what is on the whole a subjective account of mechanism ownership, to rule out cases where someone's taking herself to be the source of the outcomes of the mechanism and a fair target of the reactive attitudes regarding the doxastic outcomes of that mechanism are unfounded, delusional, or otherwise disconnected from reality.

But on what kinds of consideration might one base one's assessments of one's self, mechanism, and outputs in order for them to qualify as reasonable? Even more specifically, what kinds of evidence would actually serve to *favour* a given self-assessment, on the part of a subject, *S*, that *S* is the source of the outcomes of a given mechanism, as opposed to a competing self-assessment according to which *S* is *not* the source of the outcome of such a mechanism?

Fortunately, there is a burgeoning field at the intersection of epistemology and the philosophy of mind and cognitive science that has attempted to answer such questions with reference to considerations to do with *cognitive integration*.[17] For example, according to S. Orestis Palermos (2014a, 2014b, 2015) the relevant kind of evidence would consist in the presence of *feedback loops*. The idea, which is grounded in a dynamical systems theory (DST) approach to theorising about cognitive processes, maintains that when an external element (for example, a drug, a piece of technology, and so forth) is *non-linearly* related to the agent's biological cognitive system, it can count as a constitutive part of an overall cognitive system that extends

---

[16] This formulation is due to Kruse (2017, 2814).

[17] For some representative discussions, see Menary 2006; Pritchard 2010, 2018, and Carter et al. 2014, 2018.

to include all the contributing parts.[18] A key motivation for this is that, as DST maintains, such non-linear relations arising out of continuously and reciprocally interacting parts on the basis of feedback loops from one part to the other give rise to an overall non-decomposable system that consists of all of them. In short, when there are ongoing feedback loops or "continuous reciprocal causation" (CRC) between internal and external parts (see Palermos 2014b), the result is an *extended cognitive system* that consists of all of them.

Notice that, in (extreme) enhancement cases such as NORMAN-PILL, no such feedback loops are present. After all, the pill seems to be disintegrated from the rest of Norman's cognitive psychology, such that the pill is having distinctive cognitive effects on Norman (causing him to believe certain things), even though the mechanisms of the pill are in no way *affected* by anything Norman does or thinks.[19] The pill is certainly a causal antecedent of a process that is Norman's own, but if DST is any guide to what should be included in a cognitive process, the pill is not a *part* of Norman's process. Norman thus lacks at least one kind of evidence available to him (the would-be presence of feedback loops) for thinking that he would be the source of the outcomes of that mechanism (that is, the pill-induced beliefs about the president).

The same does not obviously hold in the case of Modafinil. Whereas nothing about one's own epistemic agency is going to have much of an effect with Norman in NORMAN-PILL, one can potentially monitor one's use of Modafinil. This might happen in various ways. For one thing, there are known side effects of Modafinil, including (in a minority of cases) dizziness, hallucinations, and unusual thoughts and behaviour, which may themselves affect the reliability of Modafinil use.[20] One may monitor for such symptoms and refrain from trusting the deliverances of one's enhanced mechanism if one detects such symptoms. In this respect, the causal relations between Modafinil and the user are not so obviously linear one-way relations as they are the case of NORMAN-PILL. Thus, one might have with respect to DST some defeasible evidence for reasonably taking it that one is the source of the outcomes of that mechanism, and likewise, a fair target of the reactive attitudes.

It may be, however, that additional evidence, beyond merely evidence for the presence of feedback loops (evidence that may be somewhat elusive) is needed in order for one to reasonably take oneself to be the source of the outcomes of a cognitively enhanced mechanism.

---

[18] For DST see, for example, Chemero 2009, Froese, Gershenson, and Rosenblueth 2013, and Palermos 2016.

[19] Indeed, we may suppose even that if Norman were to try to believe otherwise than that the president is where the pill causes him to believe the president is, then he would be unable to do so.

[20] https://www.emedicinehealth.com/drug-modafinil/article_em.htm

At this point it will be helpful to consider Duncan Pritchard's recent thinking about cognitive integration. Pritchard (2010) sets out to reconcile virtue epistemology and extended cognition, where—according to the latter—cognitive processes such as memory can supervene partly on instruments and technology which are located outside the agent herself, and which are not biologically endowed features of the agent. As one might be initially inclined to read the situation, the deliverances of "extended cognitive processes" (that is, those partly involving work done by gadgets located outside our heads) are not going to be due to *ability* or virtue to a sufficient extent in order to qualify as knowledge by virtue epistemology's lights. Of course, the proponent of extended cognition (Clark and Chalmers 1998) wants to insist that the matter of whether something is located outside one's head is irrelevant to whether that thing is part of a genuine cognitive process; what matters is just the functional role that the thing is playing.

Pritchard's novel move to reconcile these two programs takes as a starting point the following "cognitive integration" condition on knowledge:

(COGA$_{WEAK}$) If S knows that p, then S's true belief that p is the product of a reliable belief-forming process which is appropriately integrated within S's cognitive character such that her cognitive success is to a significant degree creditable to her cognitive agency. (2010, 136–37)

Pritchard's formulation is importantly neutral with respect to whether or not the process that gives rise to the belief must be entirely composed of one's biologically endowed faculties, or whether it may in some cases incorporate features that have been "added on" to the original process. What matters is that the overall (reliable) process responsible for the true belief is suitably integrated.

A brief consideration of this view suggests how it may fruitfully be applied to the vexed case of smart drugs, and to the present conundrum. To this end, let's run a quick case comparison. One well-known case in the reliabilist literature is Alvin Plantinga's (1993) case of someone (call him Al) who develops a brain lesion that (unbeknownst to Al) causes him to produce reliable beliefs on a given subject (say, for instance, mathematics). What is the epistemic status of the ensuing reliable beliefs?

The prevailing assessment is that they are not known, despite being reliably produced, and Pritchard's explanation is that such beliefs fail COGA$_{WEAK}$. But, crucially, such beliefs don't fail COGA$_{WEAK}$ *in principle*, simply because the tumour (an addition to the original cognitive process) was what was responsible. It's because the tumour in the initial case isn't suitably integrated. A corollary of this thinking is that if the tumour *were* suitably integrated, there would be no barrier to gaining knowledge through a process that relies on it. And this, Pritchard supposes, might be something that could happen over time. The following remarks Pritchard offers are illuminating on this score:

> For now suppose that Alvin becomes aware that there exists brain lesions of this sort, and gains additional good grounds for supposing that he possesses just such a brain lesion, such that he now knows that he has one of these brain lesions. Perhaps, for example, he comes across an article about these brain lesions in a reliable newspaper and researches the matter in reliable medical journals and on this basis comes to know that he is the victim of the brain lesion in question. Intuitively Alvin's beliefs in the target mathematical propositions now qualify as knowledge. But notice that it is also true that Alvin has in this way integrated this belief-forming process within his cognitive character to a sufficient degree that his cognitive success is now primarily creditable to his cognitive agency, rather than being creditable to something external to his cognitive agency (albeit a factor which was under his skin, and hence in this sense internal). (2010, 138)

We might then say something similar for beliefs produced through the assistance of smart drugs. Suppose that, rather than developing a brain lesion that aids him in his mathematical beliefs, "Al-Drug" begins using Modafinil or some other cognitive performance-enhancing drug, but with *no conception* whatsoever of what the drug does or how it effects his formation of mathematical beliefs. With no such conception (and no appreciation of how the drug may go wrong, when it does—namely, in the case of side effects), Al-Drug is in a relevant respect in a similar position to that Al is in in Plantinga's original case *prior* to any appreciation of the brain lesion or how it is affecting him.

Things seem very different, however, if we suppose that Al-Drug (like Al from Pritchard's variation on the case) comes over time, and through calibration and feedback, to appreciate the source of the reliability of his beliefs, along with a sensitivity to when things go wrong (such as tell-tale signs of any epistemically problematic side effects), an appreciation that may be developed and refined over time and through further feedback. In such a circumstance, there is, on Pritchard's rationale, no principled reason to treat Al-Drug any differently from "Al-Lesion"; both *may* potentially come to gain knowledge through the deliverances of their cognitive processes, respectively.

A pleasing result of the foregoing is that the very kinds of evidence one would plausibly require in order to cognitively integrate a drug into one's belief-forming process in such a way as to satisfy Pritchard's COGA$_{WEAK}$ condition would at the same time be evidence with respect to which one may (by taking a view of oneself on the basis of such evidence) plausibly satisfy the epistemic mechanism ownership condition for the guidance-control requirement on epistemic responsibility—namely, evidence on the basis of which one might *reasonably* take oneself to be the agential source of the outcomes of the relevant belief forming mechanism, and a fair target of the reactive attitudes.

This is good news in so far as we want to split the horns of Sosa's dilemma. Sosa's restriction principle indicated that no cognitively enhanced performances aspire to aptness, a consequence of which is that no beliefs formed via cognitive enhancement aspire to knowledge. I hope to have shown that there is scope to resist this strong conclusion *without* tolerating cognitive enhancement wholesale in our epistemic assessments. Apt beliefs (that is, knowledge) must be beliefs we are suitably responsible for, and this requires (among other things) that we *own* the relevant mechanism giving rise to our beliefs. We can't own our beliefs without being in a position to reasonably take ourselves to be the agential source of the outcomes of the mechanisms. Fortunately, the kind of evidence plausibly needed for such self-assessments to be reasonable can be found by looking to recent work at the intersection of epistemology and the philosophy of mind and cognitive science—namely, evidence of suitable cognitive integration.

Acknowledgments

Thanks to Emma C. Gordon, Michel Croce, an anonymous referee, and an audience at the University of Cologne for helpful feedback.

References

Battleday, Ruairidh M., and Anna K. Brem. 2015. "Modafinil for Cognitive Neuroenhancement in Healthy Non-Sleep-Deprived Subjects: A Systematic Review." *European Neuropsychopharmacology* 25, no. 11: 1865–81.

Bergmann, Michael. 1997. "Internalism, Externalism, and Epistemic Defeat." Ph.D. dissertation, University of Notre Dame.

BonJour, Laurence. 1980. "Externalist Theories of Empirical Knowledge." *Midwest Studies in Philosophy* 5:53–73.

Bostrom, Nick. 2009. "Cognitive Enhancement: Methods, Ethics, Regulatory Challenges." *Science and Engineering Ethics* 15, no. 3:311–41.

Bostrom, Nick, and Rebecca Roache. 2007. "Human Enhancement: Ethical Issues in Human Enhancement." In *New Waves in Applied Ethics*, edited by Jesper Ryberg, Thomas S. Petersen, and Clark Wolf, 120–52 Basingstoke: Palgrave Macmillan.

Bostrom, Nick, and Julian Savulescu. 2009. "Human Enhancement Ethics: The State of the Debate." In *Human Enhancement*, edited by Nick Bostrom and Julian Savulescu, 1–22. Oxford: Oxford University Press.

Bradford, Gwen. 2013. "The Value of Achievements." *Pacific Philosophical Quarterly* 94, no. 2:204–24.

Carter, J. Adam. 2017. "Intellectual Autonomy, Epistemic Dependence and Cognitive Enhancement." *Synthese* 1–25. https://doi.org/10.1007/s11229-017-1549-y

Carter, J. Adam, Jesper Kallestrup, Orestis Palermos, and Duncan Pritchard, eds. 2014. *Extended Knowledge*, special issue of *Philosophical Issues* 24, no. 1:1–482

Carter, J. Adam, and Robin McKenna. 2018. "Sosa Versus Kornblith on Grades of Knowledge." *Synthese* doi: 10.1007/s11229-018-1689-8

Carter, J. Adam, and Duncan Pritchard. Forthcoming. "The Epistemology of Cognitive Enhancement." *Journal of Medicine and Philosophy* 1–25.

Carter, J. Adam, Andy Clark, Jesper Kallestrup, Orestis Palermos, and Duncan Pritchard, eds. 2018. *Extended Epistemology*. Oxford: Oxford University Press.

Chemero, Anthony. 2009. *Radical Embodied Cognitive Science*. Cambridge, Mass.: MIT Press.

Clark, Andy, and David Chalmers. 1998. "The Extended Mind." *Analysis* 58, no. 1:7–19.

Fischer, John Martin. 2012. *Deep Control: Essays on Free Will and Value*. New York: Oxford University Press.

Fischer, John Martin, and Mark Ravizza. 2000. *Responsibility and Control: A Theory of Moral Responsibility*. Cambridge: Cambridge University Press.

Frankfurt, Harry G. 1969. "Alternate Possibilities and Moral Responsibility." *Journal of Philosophy* 66, no. 23:829–39.

Froese, Tom, Carlos Gershenson, and David Rosenblueth. 2013. "The Dynamically Extended Mind." http://arxiv.org/abs/1305.1958

Harris, John. 2011. "Moral Enhancement and Freedom." *Bioethics* 25, no. 2:102–11.

Judisch, Neal. 2005. "Responsibility, Manipulation and Ownership: Reflections on the Fischer/Ravizza Program." *Philosophical Explorations* 8, no. 2:115–30.

Kelp, Christoph. 2016. "Epistemic Frankfurt Cases Revisited." *American Philosophical Quarterly* 53, no. 1:27–37.

Kornblith, Hilary. 2004. "Sosa on Human and Animal Knowledge." In *Ernest Sosa and His Critics*, edited by John Greco, 126–34. Oxford: Blackwell.

——. 2009. "Sosa in Perspective." *Philosophical Studies* 144, no. 1:127–36.

——. 2012. *On Reflection*. Oxford: Oxford University Press.

Kruse, Andrea. 2017. "Why Doxastic Responsibility Is Not Based on Direct Doxastic Control." *Synthese* 194, no. 8:2811–42.

McCormick, Miriam Schleifer. 2014. *Believing Against the Evidence: Agency and the Ethics of Belief*. London: Routledge.

McHugh, Conor. 2013. "Epistemic Responsibility and Doxastic Agency." *Philosophical Issues* 23, no. 1:132–57.

Mele, Alfred R. 2000. "Review: Reactive Attitudes, Reactivity, and Omissions." *Philosophy and Phenomenological Research* 61, no. 2:447–52.

——. 2006. "Fischer and Ravizza on Moral Responsibility." *Journal of Ethics* 10, no. 3:283–94.

Menary, Richard. 2006. *Cognitive Integration: Mind and Cognition Unbound*. Basingstoke: Palgrave McMillan.

Palermos, S. Orestis. 2014a. "Knowledge and Cognitive Integration." *Synthese* 191, no. 8:1931–51.

———. 2014b. "Loops, Constitution, and Cognitive Extension." *Cognitive Systems Research* 27:25–41.

———. 2015. "Active Externalism, Virtue Reliabilism and Scientific Knowledge." *Synthese* 192, no. 9:2955–86.

———. 2016. "The Dynamics of Group Cognition." *Minds and Machines* 26, no. 4:409–40.

Plantinga, Alvin. 1993. *Warrant and Proper Function*. Oxford: Oxford University Press.

Pollock, John. 1986. *Contemporary Theories of Knowledge*. Savage, Md.: Rowman and Littlefield.

Pritchard, Duncan. 2010. "Cognitive Ability and the Extended Cognition Thesis." *Synthese* 175:133–51.

———. 2012. "Anti-Luck Virtue Epistemology." *Journal of Philosophy* 109:247–79.

———. 2018. "Extended Knowledge." In *Extended Epistemology*, edited by J. Adam Carter, Andy Clark, Jesper Kallestrup, S. Orestis Palermos, and Duncan Pritchard. Oxford: Oxford University Press.

Sandel, Michael J. 2012. "The Case Against Perfection: What's Wrong with Designer Children, Bionic Athletes, and Genetic Engineering." In *Arguing About Bioethics*, edited by Stephen Holland, 93–104. London: Routledge.

Sosa, Ernest. 2009. *A Virtue Epistemology: Apt Belief and Reflective Knowledge*, volume I. Oxford: Oxford University Press.

———. 2010a. *Knowing Full Well*. Princeton: Princeton University Press.

———. 2010b. "How Competence Matters in Epistemology." *Philosophical Perspectives* 24, no. 1:465–75. https://doi.org/10.1111/j.1520-8583.2010.00200.x.

———. 2015. *Judgment and Agency*. Oxford: Oxford University Press.

———. 2017. *Epistemology*. Princeton: Princeton University Press.

Sylvan, Kurt, and Ernest Sosa. 2014. "The Place of Reasons in Epistemology." In *The Oxford Handbook of Reasons and Normativity*, edited by Daniel Star, 155–80. Oxford University Press. https://eprints.soton.ac.uk/362902/.

Sudduth, Matthew. 2013. "Defeaters in Epistemology." In *Internet Encyclopedia of Philosophy*, edited by James Fieser and Bradley Dowden. http://www.iep.utm.edu/ep-defea/

Todd, Patrick, and Neal A. Tognazzini. 2008. "A Problem for Guidance Control." *Philosophical Quarterly* 58, no. 233:685–92.

Williams, Bernard. 1970. "Deciding to Believe." In *Language, Belief, and Metaphysics*, edited by Howard E. Kiefer and Milton K. Munitz, 95–111. Albany: SUNY Press.

CHAPTER 6

EPISTEMIC PATERNALISM AND THE SERVICE
CONCEPTION OF EPISTEMIC AUTHORITY

MICHEL CROCE

1. Introduction

Suppose a mother enrols her son in university and pays for the tuition fees while he is working to save money and is unsure whether to keep studying. Almost everyone would agree that she is acting paternalistically towards him. Some would argue that her interference is permissible; others would disagree. In this essay, I am interested in the specific phenomenon epistemologists call *epistemic paternalism*, according to which in some circumstances we are justified in interfering with the inquiry of others for their own epistemic good without consulting them on the issue (Ahlstrom-Vij 2013, 4). For now, let us consider the example above as a case of an epistemically paternalistic interference. Other examples may include a judge withholding information from the jurors about the track record of crimes committed by the defendant in order to preclude them from developing a bias against him; and a health department mandating the introduction of prediction models for medical diagnosis and prognosis in order to prevent clinicians from overestimating their expertise and clinical abilities.

Epistemic paternalism (EP) is commonly regarded as a harmful epistemic practice that could undermine our freedom, epistemic autonomy, or both. Over the past three decades, however, a few epistemologists have endorsed the view that there are both genuinely defensible forms of EP and epistemic goods that paternalistic interferences could allow the subjects interfered with to gain (see my section 2 below; Ahlstrom-Vij 2013; Bullock 2016; Goldman 1991; and Pritchard 2013). Surprisingly enough, not much work has been done on the question of who is rationally entitled to undertake paternalistic practices, and in virtue of which features one has this entitlement.

Connecting Virtues: Advances in Ethics, Epistemology, and Political Philosophy.
Edited by Michel Croce and Maria Silvia Vaccarezza.
Chapters and book compilation © 2018 Metaphilosophy LLC and John Wiley & Sons Ltd.

I aim to provide a compelling answer to this question. In particular, I shall challenge Goldman's view, according to which one's paternalistic interference is justified in so far as the interfering subject is an *expert*. I shall argue that the epistemic conditions for being a paternalist interferer substantially differ from the requirements of cognitive expertise (section 3). Specifically, they differ in a way that makes Goldman's own definition of an expert inadequate to justify epistemically paternalistic interferences, as paternalist interferers have a different task to accomplish from experts and therefore are required to display a different set of intellectual virtues. I shall also argue that *epistemic authorities*—which I take to differ from experts in a relevant sense (section 4)—cannot fulfil the function of paternalist interferers. Yet I shall show that epistemic authorities and paternalist interferers have some relevant features in common. In section 5, I offer what I consider a compelling account of virtuous paternalist interferers, while in section 6 I defend the idea that my account can apply to cases in which paternalist interferers are collectives, such as groups or institutions.

My argumentative strategy is grounded in a virtue-based framework, which—as I have argued elsewhere (see Croce 2017)—provides an extremely effective tool for distinguishing various ways in which a subject can be epistemically superior to another. For this reason, this essay purports to show how virtue theory contributes to the current epistemological research by providing insights into an underexplored topic in social epistemology. Some might feel disappointed about the scope of the project in that it does not purport to provide a conclusive straightforward answer to whether EP, in general, is an epistemically justified practice. That remains a fair question, one still open for debate. Research on epistemic paternalism could nonetheless benefit from the results of this project. Were my argument to be compelling, it would provide an effective corrective to a potentially wrong research line according to which only experts should be granted the entitlement to paternalistically interfere with someone's inquiry. It would also allow us to identify another type of authoritative subject in the epistemic realm, one that should not be confused with cognitive experts and epistemic authorities.

2. Epistemic Paternalism in a Nutshell

In Alvin Goldman's early formulation (1991, 118–19), EP has two fundamental features. First, it is a form of *protection* that a subject (or a group) A, who is more reliable than a subject (or a group) B, adopts towards B to improve the effectiveness of her epistemic agency, either by putting B in the conditions to acquire an epistemic good or by preventing B from developing various forms of epistemic deficiencies (such as cognitive biases, unjustified beliefs, or inappropriate heuristic reasoning). Second, EP involves A's *interposition* with B's agency to the extent that B lacks the opportunity to exercise her own judgment in the way she thinks most appropriate.

Both components of Goldman's view of EP are featured in Ahlstrom-Vij's more recent account (2013), according to which A undertakes an epistemically paternalistic practice towards B by doing (or omitting to do) X if and only if the following conditions are met:

(a) Doing X interferes with the epistemic autonomy or freedom of B to conduct inquiry in whatever way she sees fit (*interference condition*);

(b) A does so without consulting B on whether B should be interfered with in the relevant manner (*non-consultation condition*); and

(c) A does so for the purpose of making B epistemically better off (*improvement condition*).

Let us consider in detail these three necessary and jointly sufficient conditions for an interference to be epistemically paternalistic. The interference condition captures Goldman's point on A's interposition with B's agency. Assuming an involuntaristic framework, according to which we cannot believe things on command, interfering with one's epistemic agency—particularly with one's inquiry—amounts to compromising one's freedom to choose the most appropriate methods and strategies to perform some epistemic task and thus to attain an epistemic good.[1] The case mentioned above of a judge withholding information from jurors about past crimes committed by a defendant amounts to an example of an external constraint on information access in which the freedom of the jurors to evaluate the case is compromised by the fact that the judge withholds relevant information in order to prevent them from becoming biased against the defendant. The prediction-model case features a constraint on information collection because it forces clinicians to collect some, and not other, information about patients and to ground their diagnosis on the results provided by the model. The case of the mother who enrols her son in university is an example of a slightly different sort of interference, in that her intervention affects her son's freedom to decide how to deal with his academic and professional interests by making things easier for him to opt for studying.[2]

According to the non-consultation condition, for an interference to be (epistemically) paternalistic, A does not ask B whether B is happy with A's interference. On Ahlstrom-Vij's account, for the interference to be paternalistic it is not necessary that B would object to A's interference, had A been consulted, nor that B would not welcome the interference itself. What matters instead is that A act irrespective of what B might think about the

---

[1] On Ahlstrom-Vij's view, inquiry cannot be reduced to belief formation; rather, it is something done by the subject, whose purposes, methods, and activities "are selected specifically on account of their epistemic merits, that is, because of how they (as far as we can tell) tend to lead us towards true belief and away from false beliefs" (2013, 40).

[2] For further considerations on different kinds of constraints, see Bullock (2016, 2–3).

interference—that is, that A does not ask for B's opinion, or, in case A knows it, disregards what B wants.[3]

The improvement condition captures Goldman's point on protection, yet it goes beyond that concept, for it explains that the scope of A's interference is not merely that of protecting B from a potential epistemic harm. Rather, it aims at ensuring that B's epistemic agency benefits from the interference. One plausible way to account for how a paternalistic interference can make one epistemically better off is to refer to the notion of epistemic value as conceived by Pritchard (2009, 2013), amongst others. His take on epistemic paternalism sheds light on a relevant weakness of Goldman's and Ahlstrom-Vij's perspectives, which measure the epistemic benefits and harms of a paternalistic interference in a purely veritistic way—that is, by considering the number of true beliefs that A allows B to acquire, or the number of false beliefs that A prevents B from acquiring (see Ahlstrom-Vij 2013, 4). On a broader perspective, it sounds reasonable to concede that A's interference can make B epistemically better off in at least two more ways. First, B might improve her understanding of some subject matter x or avoid worsening her understanding of x as a result of A's interference. Second, B might acquire intellectual virtues or avoid forming epistemic vices because of A's interference. Notice that the improvement condition constrains A's purpose, rather than the outcome of A's interference. Thus, as Ahlstrom-Vij points out, for an interference to count as epistemically paternalistic it is not necessary that A promote B's well-being: A's failure in improving B's epistemic well-being might make the interference unjustified, but it does not affect its status as an epistemically paternalistic practice (2013, 49).

If we take a quick look at the debate on general paternalism, it is easy to notice that all three requirements for epistemic paternalism might be questioned. Ryan would presumably reject the non-interference condition, as he contends that "an action may be paternalistic without interfering in the liberty or autonomy of the object of the paternalist action" (2016, 126). Feinberg might reject the non-consultation condition since he believes that a coercive rule legislated for someone's sake and approved by the subjects interfered with is not paternalistic (1986, 20). And Dworkin (2017) would replace the improvement condition with a success-based condition, according to which A's interference will improve B's welfare or promote B's interest, values, or good. In what follows, I assume that Ahlstrom-Vij's conditions can nonetheless be defended; I shall leave a more detailed discussion of these requirements for another time.

---

[3] Ryan (2016) makes a similar point about general paternalism when he suggests that Dworkin's condition (2017)—according to which A's interference is paternalistic in so far as A acts without the consent of B—be replaced with the requirement that A acts irrespective of the consent of B.

All I have said so far concerns the requirements for one's interference with another's agency to count as epistemically paternalistic. For an epistemically paternalistic interference to be justified, however, some story has to be told about how the interference comes to have the relevant beneficial effects it is meant to generate. That is a very complicated matter because it has to be shown not only that (i) an epistemically paternalistic interference is likely to promote the epistemic good of the interfered-with subjects but also that (ii) it does not damage their overall welfare. The former requirement amounts to demonstrating that A must have a justified belief that his interference is likely to be beneficial for B. To account for this requirement, Ahlstrom-Vij introduces the *burden-of-proof condition*, which demands that "the would-be interferers are able to make a case that available evidence suggests that it is *highly likely* that everyone does or will benefit from the relevant form of interference, compared to relevant alternatives" (2013, 122). The latter requirement amounts to showing that the epistemic reasons for interfering do not clash with other relevant epistemic or non-epistemic reasons against intervention.

For the sake of argument, let us grant that (i) is fairly unproblematic, and focus on (ii). The first problem with this requirement is that any interference seems to violate at least the interfered-with subject's own autonomy or personal sovereignty. Some would presumably argue that such a violation might constitute a sufficient reason not to undertake any form of epistemically paternalistic interference. Yet there are ways to resist this objection. According to Bullock, the proponent of EP might respond that personal sovereignty is only pro tanto valuable, as there might well be circumstances in which our reasons for interfering outweigh the concern for one's autonomy (2016, 10). According to Pritchard (2013), EP need not clash with this legitimate concern, because a small violation of someone's autonomy today might be justified by the fact that it leads to improving the person's freedom and autonomy in the longer term.

The second problem with (ii) pertains to finding a compelling way to cash out this requirement. Ahlstrom-Vij's strategy amounts to introducing the *alignment condition*, according to which in order for an epistemically paternalistic interference to be justified, A's epistemic reasons for the interference need to be aligned with A's non-epistemic reasons for the interference either by constituting additional reasons for interfering or by being silent on the issue—that is, by not constituting reasons against interfering (2013, 117). This condition does not require—as rival options do[4]—that A knows the weight of the reasons to be balanced, but only their valence (their direction for or against a given interference). It presents a relevant weakness, however: as Ahlstrom-Vij admits, it does not constitute a stable necessary condition for justified epistemic paternalism, because there may

[4] See, for example, Bullock's balancing-goods condition (2016, 8).

be cases in which a weak non-epistemic reason against interfering fails to outweigh robust epistemic reasons for intervention (see also Bullock 2016, 9–10).

Despite these problems, Ahlstrom-Vij holds that the burden-of-proof condition and the alignment condition are jointly sufficient to justify epistemically paternalistic practices (2013, 114). It is important to notice that his justification of EP targets large-scale situations in which someone's interference is going to have an impact on a considerable number of subjects. This explains why in Ahlstrom-Vij's view the notion of evidence on the likelihood of an interference's beneficial effects is to be conceived in terms of statistical probability. Nonetheless, it seems possible to justify paternalistic interferences even in the absence of such statistical evidence, or so I shall contend. In several ordinary circumstances, some interferences can help particular subjects (or groups) in virtue of their specific epistemic situation. Think, for example, of parents hiding a joke history book—that is, a book including unreliable information and jokes about historical events—from their kids (Pritchard 2013, 15); of a doctor breaking the right of her patient not to know about his illness (Bullock 2016, 3), as she justifiedly believes he will benefit from knowing that he is out of danger; or of a teacher refraining from providing a student with the tools to solve a geometry problem in order to let her develop analytical skills. What matters in circumstances like these is that the interferer be an epistemically competent subject who has the ability to form justified beliefs about the benefits of the relevant form of interference as well as about why that course of action is meant to be more beneficial than relevant alternatives.

In this picture, Ahlstrom-Vij's burden-of-proof condition becomes a special instance of a more general requirement—call it the *epistemic-reasons condition*—according to which A must have robust epistemic reasons for believing that B will benefit from the intervention and that undertaking such intervention will be more beneficial for B than adopting other attitudes or courses of action. Those who fulfil the burden-of-proof condition are by definition satisfying the epistemic-reasons condition too, yet in several cases someone can fulfil the latter without being in a position to satisfy the former. In such circumstances, an interference is justified in so far as it fulfils the epistemic-reasons condition and the alignment condition. I shall argue that for paternalist interferers to be justified in intervening in someone else's inquiry as required by these conditions, they need to be *virtuous* interferers (see section 5).

3. Justifying Epistemic Paternalism: Against the Expertise Strategy

In several passages of his work on EP, Goldman suggests that expertise is a fundamental component for defending epistemic paternalism and argues that "to justify any particular instance of such paternalism ... we must have grounds for taking the agent to be an expert" (1991, 128). This claim seems to suggest that in his view expertise should be considered a necessary condition for one to be entitled to undertake epistemically paternalistic interferences towards another. If, however, someone thinks that, by definition, experts fulfil the justification conditions of paternalistic interferences, cognitive expertise would become a sufficient requirement for justified EP. After introducing the account Goldman provides of a cognitive expert, I shall argue that his notion of expertise is neither necessary nor sufficient for justifying epistemically paternalistic interferences.[5]

Goldman has recently remarked that any definition of an expert should reflect the person's function within an epistemic community. Specifically, he contends that such definition should explain "what expertise *is* by reference to what experts can *do* for laypersons by means of their special knowledge or skill" (2016, 1). Thus, any account of expertise should not only provide a definition of an expert (definition requirement) but also explain how this definition fits the function of expertise assumed by its proponent (function requirement). The definition of an expert on Goldman's 1991 account can be summarized as follows:

EXPERT.   A subject S is an expert in a domain D iff
[T-LC]   S has true answers to core questions in D; or
[AC]   S has the capacity to acquire true answers to core questions arising in D.

The former requirement is a *truth-linked condition* highlighting the veritistic flavour of Goldman's definition, in that it measures expertise based on the number of true beliefs an expert possesses about the main issues in D. The latter is an *ability condition* that allows us to also regard as experts those who have the ability to solve new problems arising within D, no matter whether they actually have done so. Thus, in this account, experts are supposed to perform what I call a *research-oriented function*, according to which S is an expert in domain D iff

[R-OF]   S has the capacity to contribute to the epistemic progress of D. S can provide such help by offering true answers to the questions under dispute in D.

Now, let us go back to the conditions for justified EP in light of this account of an expert. Someone, if not Goldman himself, might want to hold the view that experts satisfy the burden-of-proof condition. It could be argued that a subject A, in virtue of his expertise, is the best candidate to

---

[5] Henceforth I shall refer to cognitive experts simply as "experts." What Goldman means by the notion of *cognitive* or *intellectual expertise* is the expertise pertaining to an agent's propositional knowledge and understanding, whereas *practical* or *performative expertise* identifies the expertise pertaining to an agent's "competence at performing a task" (Watson 2016, 2), such as playing the piano, doing magic tricks, or driving a truck, and involves an agent's skills and know-how.

evaluate available evidence in D and make a case that his interference with B is highly likely to make B epistemically better off. In fact, it is plausible to contend that experts know much better than laypeople how to assess pros and cons of a given course of action in their domain of expertise in light of relevant alternative practices. Similarly, one might hold that experts are also better placed to evaluate potential non-epistemic reasons against intervention, thereby being in a position to satisfy the alignment condition.

On careful analysis, though, it is far from clear that Goldman's account of an expert can accommodate the requirements for justified EP. Let us focus on whether one's expertise is *sufficient* for one to be justified in undertaking epistemically paternalistic interferences. Consider the following example:

> PROF. EVERYT SOLVED. Suppose Joseph is a young mathematician based at MIT who is working at Hilbert's third problem. Joseph knows that this specific problem has already been solved, and he knows its solution. His supervisor, Prof. Everyt Solved, is not only one of the most important mathematicians who worked on Hilbert's problems but is also well known for her distraction and insensitivity to others' epistemic needs. During a meeting with Joseph, Everyt suggests that Joseph try to work at problem 3 from the beginning, as if it were still unsolved, in order to understand fully its structure and solution. A week later, she stops by Joseph's desk and, once she notices he is working on the problem, she tells him straight away the solution to the problem without allowing him to say a word.

I argue that this case satisfies the three conditions for an interference to count as epistemically paternalistic. Everyt's intervention fulfils the interference condition in that she limits the autonomy of Joseph to conduct inquiry into Hilbert's third problem in whatever way he sees fit. It also fulfils the non-consultation condition because she neither takes into consideration his opinion regarding her intervention nor consults him on the issue. Finally, it fulfils the improvement condition: due to her distraction and insensitivity to his needs, Everyt forgot the advice she gave to Joseph and now genuinely interferes to help him by offering the solution to the problem. I also maintain that Everyt satisfies Goldman's expertise requirement: she not only has lots of true answers to the core questions in mathematics but also possesses the ability to contribute to the epistemic progress of the discipline, as her outstanding list of recent and forthcoming publications shows.

Nonetheless, Everyt's intervention does not constitute a justified case of epistemically paternalistic interference. Her complete insensitivity to the student's epistemic needs prevents her from being in a position to satisfy the epistemic-reasons condition. As a matter of fact, she might possess epistemic reasons for believing that Joseph will benefit from her intervention and that any further non-epistemic reasons for intervening align with the epistemic ones. Nonetheless, the problem lies with the relevant-alternatives component, as she does not bother to evaluate which attitude is going to help him get the most out of his intellectual inquiry. A more careful evaluation would have easily allowed her to acknowledge that the strategy of letting Joseph work at Hilbert's problem on his own would have made him improve his understanding of the solution in a way that her intervention obviously cannot. Yet, assessing what course of action is going to be more beneficial for the subject interfered with is by no means a condition for one to be an expert. Thus, the example shows that someone's expertise does not ensure that the person's epistemically paternalistic interferences are justified.

Now, let us analyse whether being an expert is nonetheless a *necessary* condition for justified EP. The fundamental problem with the above definition of an expert is that neither of its conditions can ensure that an expert A has good reasons to think his interference will make B epistemically better off, for these conditions pertain to someone's having extensive knowledge in a given domain. Instead, what is required for an epistemically paternalistic interference to be justified is that the interferer have a clear view on what is epistemically better to do on behalf of B. Consider the following example:

> VIRTUOUS COLLEAGUE. Suppose Emma and Frank are in charge of the recruiting process for a big company that is hiring twenty new employees. Having recently noticed that Frank has developed a bias against female applicants, this time Emma wants to help him. So she asks for his help with the first step in the selection process: evaluating the CVs of two hundred applicants and selecting the best forty profiles. But she provides Frank with blind CVs in order to prevent his bias from affecting his judgment, and she reveals the identity of the applicants only after he completes his task.

Again, this case satisfies the three conditions of EP: it fulfils the interference condition because Emma prevents Frank from conducting inquiry in whatever way he sees fit; it fulfils the non-consultation condition since Emma does not consult Frank on the issue of whether he would be happy if she blinded the applicants' CVs for him; and it fulfils the improvement condition, as Emma intervenes with the aim of improving his epistemic agency, namely, of enhancing the chances that he get to know which are the most suitable profiles for the job positions that he needs to fill.[6] Furthermore, one might want to argue that her interference is justified, for the available evidence suggests it is highly likely Frank will benefit from the interference compared to relevant alternatives—such as letting him select candidates on the basis of his gender bias—and there are no relevant reasons against intervening that Emma should take into consideration. Nonetheless, it seems

---

[6] Clearly, Emma's interference would presumably have clear practical benefits, in that it could lead Frank to select better candidates. That is not in contrast with the epistemic benefit that the intervention by Emma provides, nor does it undermine the epistemic purpose of her actions.

clear that the justification of her interference does not depend on any specific kind of expertise she might have. Rather, what puts her in the best position to fulfil her function as a paternalist interferer is the fact that she is sensitive to her colleague's biased attitude and acquires good evidence of what is his best epistemic interest.

To further stress this point, let us consider which intellectual abilities allow one to fulfil one's function in the epistemic community. I contend that the intellectual virtues required for one to fulfil Goldman's account of the expert are largely different from those that allow one to satisfy the justification conditions of an epistemically paternalistic interference. Experts need to possess what elsewhere I have called *research-oriented abilities*: virtues that allow one to exploit their fund of knowledge to find and face new problems arising in their field of expertise, such as intellectual curiosity, intellectual creativity, open-mindedness, intellectual courage, firmness, and autonomy. On the other hand, paternalist interferers are virtuous in so far as they possess *novice-oriented abilities*: virtues that allow them to properly address B's epistemic dependency on them, thereby putting them in a suitable position for knowing what is epistemically best to do in the service of B. This set of abilities includes such traits as sensitivity to B's epistemic needs, intellectual generosity, intellectual empathy, sensitivity to B's epistemic resources, practical wisdom, and maieutic ability.[7]

This distinction bolsters the thesis that cognitive expertise is neither a sufficient requirement for one to be justified in undertaking epistemically paternalistic interferences nor a necessary one. Being an expert is not sufficient for justifying EP, because someone's expertise does not ensure that the person satisfies the epistemic-reasons condition, as he may well lack the ability to evaluate what among several options is the most epistemically beneficial way to interfere with another's inquiry. Furthermore, being an expert is not even a necessary condition for justified EP, for as the case of the virtuous colleague shows, someone can fulfil the requirements for justified EP without being an expert.

4. Justifying Epistemic Paternalism: The Epistemic-Authority Strategy

A plausible alternative to the idea that experts constitute the ideal profile of paternalist interferers is offered by a recent discussion on the topic of *epistemic authority* and, in particular, by the service conception of authority that Joseph Raz has proposed as a model of authority in the practical realm and Linda Zagzebski has recently adopted as a model of authority in the epistemic domain. According to them, the main function of authorities is to serve the governed (or novices)—that is, to do something in their service (see Raz 1986, 56). On my pluralistic reading of this view, epistemic

---

[7] For further clarifications on this distinction between sets of intellectual virtues, see Croce 2017, 19–20.

authorities can fulfil their function in various ways, ranging from imparting true beliefs to a layperson B (Zagzebski 2012) and helping B weigh available evidence (Jäger 2016; Lackey 2018), to imparting understanding to B and leading B to improve her understanding of some subject matter on her own (Croce 2017; Jäger 2016). I suggest we gather these specific services under a broader formula for the function of epistemic authorities, which I call *novice-oriented function*. According to the function requirement of epistemic authorities, a subject A is an epistemic authority for a subject B in domain D iff

[N-OF] A has the capacity to help B achieve epistemic goals in D that B might not be able to achieve on her own.[8]

The corresponding definition requirement can be introduced as follows:

EPISTEMIC AUTHORITY. A subject A is an epistemic authority for a subject B in domain D iff

[EPC] A is better epistemically positioned than B is in D; and
[AC*] A possesses at least sensitivity to B's epistemic needs.

A quick comparison between this notion and that of an expert should clarify why in principle epistemic authorities look like a more convincing exemplar of paternalist interferers than experts do.

The first distinction concerns the function requirements and illustrates that these categories of epistemic subjects have different roles in the epistemic community. The function of epistemic authorities is to help the interlocutor(s) achieve epistemic goals, as required by N-OF. Yet they have no commitment to fulfil R-OF, which instead explains that the service of experts amounts to making a contribution to the epistemic progress of their field. This distinction has bearing on the definition requirements as well, on which the second difference between the two notions focuses. Instead of Goldman's truth-linked condition, the definition of an epistemic authority includes the epistemic-position condition (EPC), which differs from the former in at least two relevant ways.[9]

On the one hand, EPC does not require that A be epistemically superior to most people in a domain, rather just to his interlocutor. Thus, one can be an epistemic authority to another about some subject matter without being an expert on that topic. For instance, I might be an epistemic authority for my mother on the history of Scotland simply because I have some vague knowledge of the main battles and events that happened there in the modern era whereas she knows nothing about this topic, but that would

---

[8] This definition is grounded in an alternative definition of an expert proposed by Goldman (2016, 2).

[9] More on the notion of epistemic position can be found in Fricker 2006.

not make me an expert in that domain. Indeed, I could not contribute to the progress of the historical research in this field, as required by R-OF, yet I would still provide my mom with information she lacks and is interested in acquiring and therefore I would fulfil N-OF. On the other hand, EPC does not limit one's epistemic superiority to another to the number of true propositions or core answers one has in a given domain. In fact, A can be better epistemically positioned than B also by having a better understanding of D, by being more intellectually virtuous than B, or simply by having access to more (or better) evidence. Finally, experts and epistemic authorities need to possess different intellectual virtues. Experts should be able to find true answers to the questions arising in their field and therefore need to possess research-oriented abilities. Epistemic authorities, instead, merely have to be sensitive to the interlocutor's epistemic needs, thereby displaying one of the most important novice-oriented abilities.

Let me stress that the pluralistic account of epistemic authority introduced above presents two fundamental advantages over rival views.[10] First, it does not restrict the kind of *practice* that A is entitled to adopt towards B to either imparting information or advising in a more indirect way; second, it does not restrict the *epistemic good* provided by A to either true belief or understanding. Both features are crucial to our argument, in that, first, they allow us to infer that this account of epistemic authority could well include "undertaking paternalistic interferences" as one of the viable ways A can help B achieve epistemic goals in D. Second, they make room for the idea that paternalistic interferences can benefit the interfered-with subject in various ways. Finally, the differences between experts and authorities introduced above highlight that epistemic authorities are good candidates as exemplars of paternalist interferers because they need to possess a fundamental intellectual virtue—namely, the sensitivity to B's needs—that makes A care about discovering what is epistemically better to do in the service of B. For these reasons, we shall consider whether it might be the case that epistemically paternalistic interferences are justified in so far as the interferer is an epistemic authority.

5. Refining the Account: Virtuous Paternalist Interferers

In this section, I first introduce and discuss two objections to the plausible thesis that epistemic authorities are the ideal profile for paternalist interferers in the epistemic realm. I argue that, despite directing us on the right track, this thesis needs to be refined. Then I offer a more compelling account of paternalist interferers.

The first problem affecting this thesis sheds light on a relevant asymmetry between the function requirement of epistemic authorities and the function requirement of paternalist interferers. The asymmetry arises in cases

[10] Compare, in particular, Croce 2017 with Lackey 2018 and Zagzebski 2012.

where an epistemically paternalistic interference can be beneficial to some extent yet is not grounded in A's judgment of what is epistemically better to do in the service of B. Let us consider the following modified version of the example of mathematicians introduced before:

PROF. EVERYT SOLVED*. Suppose again that Joseph is working on Hilbert's third problem. This time, he knows that the problem has already been solved but does not know the solution. Thus, he decides to work on the problem as if it were still unsolved in order to achieve a deep understanding of its structure. Everyt, his supervisor, stops by his desk and, once she notices that he is working on that particular problem, reveals the solution without allowing him to say a word.

This example features a case in which Everyt clearly fulfils N-OF because she has the ability to help Joseph achieve an epistemic good that he lacks: knowledge of the problem's solution. She also displays some sort of sensitivity to the student's needs, as she provides him with some useful piece of information. Nevertheless, I contend that her interference is not justified, because Everyt did not consider the impact of her intervention on Joseph's inquiry, nor has she formed any justified belief about the pros and cons of alternative courses of action that she might have undertaken, as the epistemic-reasons condition requires. As a matter of fact, we expect a virtuous interferer at least to consider that letting Joseph work on the problem on his own would possibly allow him to achieve both knowledge of the solution and understanding of its structure at the same time with small risk, as he could look the solution up online and get to know how Max Dehn solved this problem in 1900 by appealing to invariants of polyhedra.

Thus, the fundamental asymmetry between the two function requirements at play in the definitions of epistemic authorities and paternalist interferers can be highlighted as follows. On the one hand, N-OF is neutral with respect to the epistemic goal Everyt should paternalistically help Joseph achieve. On the other, it is not sufficient that an interferer A has the ability to help B achieve *some* epistemic goods in D, nor that A has the ability to help B achieve *what B aims at* achieving. Paternalist interferers have a more specific service to fulfil: namely, they need to be able to help B achieve *what is epistemically better* for B in D, if that is permitted by the balance of reasons. For the epistemic-reasons condition requires that A intervenes only if he has good epistemic reasons to believe that his interference is going to be more beneficial for B than any other available option.

The second objection challenges EPC by raising the doubt that paternalist interferers need not be better epistemically positioned than interfered-with subjects to successfully provide their service. Consider again Emma's profile in the case of the virtuous colleague. In the last section, I argued that Emma's interference satisfies the conditions of EP introduced in section 2 and that it could constitute a justified paternalistic interference. Nonetheless, some might argue that Emma is not an epistemic authority for Frank, because she is not epistemically superior to him in any relevant sense with respect to the matter at issue. Indeed, both Frank and Emma have worked for decades in the HR department of that company and have already proved to be experienced recruiters. Then we should conclude that EPC is not a necessary condition for one to be justified in undertaking epistemically paternalistic interferences, which would reinforce the thesis that epistemic authorities are not the ideal profile of paternalist interferers.

I am not interested in resisting this conclusion, as I have already argued that the thesis introduced at the beginning of this section needs some refinement. I shall, however, undermine the claim that the notion of a paternalist interferer needs no EPC. On the broad conception of epistemic superiority endorsed here, one can be better epistemically positioned than another in a very local way—for example, by lacking a relevant bias or being able to spot it in other people in a given circumstance. In fact, the interferer, unlike the subject interfered with, displays the virtue(s) of epistemic justice, which enables the interferer to be sensitive to the subject's bias and triggers further intellectual virtues, such as the sensitivity to others' needs and epistemic resources, through which he figures out how to help the subject interfered with.

These objections shed light on the fact that paternalist interferers ought to satisfy more stringent requirements than epistemic authorities, both for what concerns the function requirement and for the intellectual virtues they need to display. As for the former, this section has provided support for the idea that a paternalist interferer needs to be able not merely to provide some kind of epistemic benefit for the subjects interfered with but rather also to figure out what is epistemically better for them to do in given circumstances. A full account of a paternalist interferer's function, though, also requires that the interferer be able to evaluate whether the epistemic benefits his interference is likely to generate are in line with further non-epistemic reasons against intervening that he might have, as required by the alignment condition. To clarify this point, consider the following revised version of Emma's case:

> VICIOUS COLLEAGUE. Suppose again that Emma and Frank are in charge of recruiting twenty new employees for a big company, and that she has recently noticed that he has developed a bias against female applicants. She also knows, however, that he is always suspicious of other colleagues and that her move will raise his worries and undermine his trust in her. Nonetheless, she provides him with two hundred blind CVs, in order to prevent his bias from affecting his judgment, and asks him to select the best forty profiles.

In the example, Emma's interference cannot be justified, because it clashes with the available evidence for what is better to do on behalf of Frank in the given circumstances. Specifically, she lacks a necessary concern with maintaining a relationship of mutual trust among colleagues—that is, a non-epistemic reason that does not align with the epistemic reasons supporting Emma's interference.

Both the function requirement and the definition requirement of a paternalist interferer should reflect Emma's lack of justification. I propose the following account of virtuous paternalist interferers, whose function requirement maintains that a subject A is a virtuous paternalist interferer for a subject B in domain D iff

[N-OF*]   A has the capacity to help B achieve what is epistemically better for B in D when permitted by the balance of reasons.

Thus, I put forth the following definition requirement:

VIRTUOUS PATERNALIST INTERFERER. A subject A is a virtuous paternalist interferer for a subject B in domain D iff

[EPC]   A is better epistemically positioned than B is in D;
[VC]   A's judgment about how to interfere with B's inquiry is the product of A's cognitive faculties; and
[AC**] A deploys a wide range of novice-oriented abilities in judging how to intervene.

As should be evident, this definition differs from the account of epistemic authority in two respects. First, the definition, unlike that of an epistemic authority, includes a *virtue condition* (VC), which ensures that the decision of an interferer to intervene arises out of a competent use of her cognitive faculties. This requirement is necessary to avoid parallel Gettier-style cases, where the fact that A's interference fulfils the epistemic-reasons condition and the alignment condition is simply a matter of luck.[11] Imagine, for example, a case in which a doctor breaks a patient's right not to know the result of a medical test, because she has a justified belief that the patient will benefit from knowing that he is in good health. Unbeknownst to her, someone replaced the result of the test with someone else's. As it turns out, the two tests had identical results. Thus, the reasoning and judgment by the doctor about whether to interfere with the patient's agency would not have been different had she considered the correct results. Yet her beliefs about both the patient's health situation and the best way to intervene are not justified, as they are true simply because of luck. A virtue condition allows us to ensure that a case like this does not become an example of justified EP.

Second, the definition of a virtuous paternalist advisor includes a stronger version of the ability condition, which is meant to accommodate the fact that paternalist interferers have a different, stricter function to fulfil than do epistemic authorities. Indeed, for one to be in a position to accomplish N-OF* it is necessary that one not only be sensitive to another's

---

[11] I thank an anonymous reviewer for pointing this out to me.

epistemic needs but also be able to weigh the epistemic benefit against possible non-epistemic reasons not to interfere—thereby displaying practical wisdom—and to make sure that the subject interfered with is in a position to take advantage of the epistemic good one tries to provide her with—thereby displaying sensitivity to her epistemic resources. Thus, AC** can account for the justification requirements of a paternalistic interference introduced in section 2: practical wisdom will allow a virtuous interferer to fulfil the alignment condition, whereas sensitivity to the epistemic resources of the interfered-with subject, together with sensitivity to her needs and intellectual empathy, will allow him to satisfy the epistemic-reasons condition.

This account explains why Emma is a virtuous paternalist interferer in the first example (the virtuous colleague), while she fails to satisfy the requirements in the second case (the vicious colleague). Specifically, in the former scenario, Emma not only fulfils EPC, as we saw early on in this section, but also VC and AC**, since her judgment about how to help Frank is the product of her cognitive faculties and she proves herself able to make a virtuous use of her novice-oriented abilities by determining that the balance of reasons favours her intervention. For this reason, she proves herself able to accomplish N-OF*, and therefore she can be considered a virtuous paternalist interferer. In the latter scenario, Emma instead fails to fulfil both the function requirement and the definition requirement. For the function requirement, her inability to evaluate whether the epistemic reasons for interfering are aligned with the non-epistemic ones shows that she is unable to figure out what is epistemically better to do in Frank's service. For the definition requirement, although her judgment is the product of her cognitive faculties and Emma is better epistemically positioned than her colleague because she is aware of his bias against female applicants, she does not fulfil AC**. For the fact that she has low concern for the potential harms of her interference indicates a failure to exercise her novice-oriented abilities in a virtuous way—particularly, practical wisdom as well as sensitivity to his needs and resources.[12]

6. Benefits of the Account and the Challenge of Institutional Paternalist Interferers

Before concluding this inquiry into the features of paternalist interferers in the epistemic realm, I want to shed light on several benefits of the proposed account and address one final challenge.

---

[12] A similar story could be told to explain why Everyt, in the case of Prof. Everyt Solved*, is not a virtuous paternalist advisor. Everyt does not fulfil N-OF*, because she fails to display the capacity to weigh the epistemic and the non-epistemic reasons for interfering with Joseph's inquiry. Even though she is better epistemically positioned than Joseph in the domain of Hilbert's problems, she proves to be insensitive to his needs and resources, and she lacks the ability to guide him in the right direction without doing all the work on his behalf.

First, this account of a virtuous paternalist interferer settles the original worry with Goldman's thesis that one can undertake epistemically paternalistic interferences in so far as one is an expert. I showed that Goldman's account of an expert underestimates a fundamental feature of paternalist interferers, namely, that they need to have justified beliefs on what is epistemically better for the subject interfered with to do in given circumstances. Thus, paternalist interferers, unlike experts, need to care about the epistemic well-being of the subject interfered with as well as to display and appropriately exercise what I have called novice-oriented abilities.

Second, the account goes beyond Goldman's and Ahlstrom-Vij's limited veritistic perspective to endorse a broader view of the epistemic well-being that includes both knowledge and understanding as valuable epistemic goods promoted by paternalistic interferences, as suggested by Pritchard (2013).

Third, this inquiry into who can justifiedly undertake epistemically paternalistic interferences accounts for a special way to offer guidance in the epistemic realm and therefore individuates a peculiar way in which an epistemically superior subject may do something in the service of another. This analysis shows that the function of paternalist interferers should not be reduced either to that of experts or to that of epistemic authorities, as paternalist interferers, unlike the others, need to be able to balance epistemic and non-epistemic reasons for intervention on behalf of someone who may not be aware that another is interfering with her own agency.

Despite the benefits of the proposed account of paternalist advisors, one might worry that this view has a very limited scope in that it applies only to one-to-one relationships between two epistemic subjects, one of which is better epistemically positioned and more intellectually virtuous than the other. Any plausible account of epistemic paternalism should, however, take into consideration cases in which groups and institutions undertake epistemically paternalistic interferences towards one or many epistemic subjects. That might be the case, for example, with a state imposing compulsory school age and with a health department mandating the introduction of prediction models for medical diagnosis and prognosis in order to prevent clinicians from overestimating their expertise and clinical abilities. Setting aside whether these particular interferences may or may not be justified, one might contend that the account I endorse cannot explain who would be a virtuous paternalist interferer in similar cases.

In the rest of this section, I want to resist this claim and provide support for the thesis that the virtuous paternalist interferer can be extended to accommodate cases of group and institutional paternalist advisors. I contend that this can be the case because there are available ways to extend EPC and VC to groups, but more importantly because there can be collective and institutional virtues (see, e.g., Fricker 2010; Lahroodi 2007) and there is no principled reason novice-oriented abilities cannot be part of these sets of virtues. I shall also admit that what follows should be considered as a first inquiry into an unexplored issue, rather than a conclusive argument in favour of this model of paternalist advisors in the epistemic domain.

Let us quickly consider the possibility of extending EPC to groups and institutions. All we need to show in this regard is that it can definitely be the case that collective entities—for example, committees, governments, or juries—are better epistemically positioned than other subjects in their activity as collectives and institutional structures. Indeed, the flourishing literature in this branch of social epistemology has already shown that groups intended as collectives can acquire knowledge and understanding.[13] Thus, it can be argued that some groups are better epistemically positioned than others in a given domain by virtue of possessing more knowledge or better understanding. For example, it can be said that a scientific team conducting experimental research on the benefits and the harms of eating red meat is better epistemically positioned on the topic of the impact of food on human health than a farmers' association.

For what concerns the virtue condition and the possibility of extending it to collective epistemic agents, I shall limit myself to mentioning that Kallestrup has recently defended a collective-virtue epistemology along the lines of Sosa's view. More will have to be said on these topics, but what interests us here is the possibility of arguing that a group can have knowledge "when the truth of its belief is a product of its innermost competence … in suitable shape and situation" (Kallestrup 2016, 10), provided that the group forms the appropriate joint intentions (12–13). From the combination of the basics of a collective-virtue epistemology and Kallestrup's remark that the epistemic aims of a group may well extend beyond the acquisition of knowledge (15), it follows that a collective can fulfil VC if its judgment about whether to interfere with someone's inquiry for the person's own epistemic benefit manifests its innermost competence in suitable shape and situation. Thus, there are ways to prevent a Gettier-style case of a collective's epistemically paternalistic intervention into someone's inquiry from being justified.

Let us now focus on how collectives can possess novice-oriented abilities. Fricker has proposed a twofold model for group virtues that includes both motive-based virtues and skill-based virtues. An example of the former is a diligent and thorough research team, whose members behave as follows: "Its members all jointly commit to the motives of diligence and thoroughness; and the team lives up to those motives by proving reliable, over an appropriate span of time and contexts, in achieving their ends. Their research team displays irreducibly collective forms of diligence and thoroughness. They display these virtues as 'a body', or *as one*" (Fricker 2010,

242). As for skill-based virtues, Fricker asks us to imagine a night-watch team of four soldiers who divide their labour so that each of them looks in one direction and performs his task without any specific motive but rather just acts as he is trained to do, thereby displaying the virtue of vigilance as a collective skill on an excellence- or skill-based model of virtue (243).

Similar considerations can be introduced about novice-oriented abilities, depending on whether you want to conceive them as motive-based or skill-based virtues. I shall not take a stand here on this point, particularly because I am inclined to think of novice-oriented abilities as a set that can include both kinds of virtue. Rather, it is important to highlight that, for example, a group of educational scientists working at a reformation of the regional educational policies could—and, in fact, should—as a body be sensitive to the epistemic resources of the youngest generations of students as well as to their epistemic needs; and that a group of statisticians introducing prediction models into a hospital's clinical policies to increase the accuracy of clinicians' diagnoses could—and, in fact, should—possess novice-oriented abilities as well.

Going from group virtues to institutional virtues, however, requires one more step of analysis, as institutions differ from groups in that they have structures and procedures but are not agents and possess no will. Thus, Fricker points out that institutions can possess and exhibit virtues only in so far as the individuals or the groups that create an institution's structures and procedures are virtuous (2010, 249). This model of institutional virtues allows us to contend that a region, a hospital, or a state department can fulfil AC** in so far as (i) the group that works at building the institution's structures and procedures displays novice-oriented abilities as a body, and (ii) the institution's structures and procedures encourage and reflect virtuous behaviour on the part of the aforementioned group.

In conclusion, these considerations show that the three conditions of the virtuous paternalist interferer can—at least, in principle—apply to groups and institutions, thereby reflecting the idea that even a collective can be justified in undertaking epistemically paternalistic interferences in so far as it displays (a) appropriate competence in judging whether to interfere, (b) some sort of epistemic superiority to the subject interfered with, and (c) those virtues that put it in a position to evaluate what is epistemically better to do in their service. The project of extending this account of paternalist advisors in the epistemic domain to institutions should also take into consideration that the bigger the number of the subjects affected by an institution's interference, the more complicated will weighing epistemic and non-epistemic reasons for intervention be. As a matter of fact, it seems reasonable that it takes more for an institution interfering with the agency of hundreds or thousands of people to fulfil the requirements of a virtuous paternalist advisor than it does for subjects like Everyt and Emma in our examples.

7. Conclusion

This essay has explored the fairly new topic of epistemic paternalism from an original point of view: namely, by analysing the requirements that allow one to be considered a virtuous paternalist interferer in the epistemic realm. After introducing the conditions for an interference to be epistemically paternalistic and two prominent strategies for justifying EP (section 2), I argued against Goldman's thesis that experts are the most appropriate candidates as paternalist advisors (section 3). In section 4, I suggested the notion of an epistemic authority—instead of that of an expert—as a plausible ground for an account of a paternalist interferer. As it turned out, the proposed view suffered from several problems, yet it allowed us to shed light on a fundamental feature that virtuous paternalist advisors need to exercise, namely, the capacity to help subjects interfered with achieve what is epistemically better for them in a given situation. Based on this consideration, I proposed a virtue-based account of the paternalist interferer and showed how it accommodates common cases of epistemically paternalistic interferences (section 5). Finally, I highlighted the benefits of the account and showed how it can apply to cases in which the interferer is a group or an institution (section 6).

My ultimate hope is not only that this essay contributes to studying a topic in social epistemology that is still in need of further work but also that it demonstrates how virtue epistemology and, in particular, the study of intellectual virtues can contribute to the research in epistemology as a whole.

Acknowledgments

Earlier versions of this essay were presented in 2017 at the Sixth WFAP Graduate Conference, at the University of Vienna; at the Summer School in Social Epistemology, at the Autonomous University of Madrid; at the New Trends in Epistemology Conference, at the University of Pavia; and at the Third Diaphora Workshop on A-Priori Knowledge, at the University of Stirling. I am grateful to the audiences on these occasions for their helpful comments. Thanks also go to Aidan McGlynn, Duncan Pritchard, Shane Ryan, and an anonymous reviewer. Work on this essay has received funding from the European Union's Horizon 2020 Research and Innovation Programme under Grant Agreement no. 675415.

References

Ahlstrom-Vij, Kristoffer. 2013. *Epistemic Paternalism: A Defence*. Basingstoke: Palgrave Macmillan.
Bird, Alexander. 2010. "Social Knowing: The Social Sense of 'Scientific Knowledge.'" *Philosophical Perspectives* 24, no. 1:23–56.

Brady, Michael. 2016. "Group Emotion and Group Understanding." In *The Epistemic Life of Groups: Essays in the Epistemology of Collectives*, edited by Michael Brady and Miranda Fricker, 95–110. Oxford: Oxford University Press.

Bullock, Emma. 2016. "Knowing and Not-Knowing for Your Own Good: The Limits of Epistemic Paternalism." *Journal of Applied Philosophy.* doi: 10.1111/japp.12220.

Croce, Michel. 2017. "Expert-Oriented Abilities vs. Novice-oriented Abilities: An Alternative Account of Epistemic Authority." *Episteme.* doi: 10.1017/epi.2017.16.

Dworkin, Richard. 2017. "Paternalism." In *Stanford Encyclopedia of Philosophy*, edited by E. N. Zalta, Winter 2017 edition. https://plato.stanford.edu/entries/paternalism/.

Feinberg, Joel. 1986. *Harm to Self*. Oxford: Oxford University Press.

Fricker, Elizabeth. 2006. "Testimony and Epistemic Autonomy." In *The Epistemology of Testimony*, edited by Jennifer Lackey and Ernest Sosa, 225–50. Oxford: Oxford University Press.

Fricker, Miranda. 2010. "Can There Be Institutional Virtues?" In *Oxford Readings in Epistemology*, vol. 3, edited by Tamar Szabo Gendler and John Hawthorne, 235–52. Oxford: Oxford University Press.

Gilbert, Margaret. 2002. "Belief and Acceptance as Features of Groups." *Protosociology* 16:35–69.

Gilbert, Margaret. 2013. *Joint Commitment: How We Make the Social World*. Oxford: Oxford University Press.

Goldman, Alvin. 1991. "Epistemic Paternalism: Communication Control in Law and Society." *Journal of Philosophy* 88, no. 3:113–31.

Goldman, Alvin. 2016. "Expertise." *Topoi*. doi: 10.1007/s11245-016-9410-3.

Jäger, Christoph. 2016. "Epistemic Authority, Preemptive Reasons, and Understanding." *Episteme* 13, no. 2:67–85.

Kallestrup, Jesper. 2016. "Group Virtue Epistemology." *Synthese*. doi: 10.1007/s11229-016-1225-7.

Lackey, Jennifer. 2012. "Group Knowledge Attributions." In *New Essays on Knowledge Ascriptions*, edited by Jessica Brown and Mikkel Gerken, 243–69. Oxford: Oxford University Press.

Lackey, Jennifer. 2014. "Socially Extended Knowledge." *Philosophical Issues* 24, no. 1:282–98.

Lackey, Jennifer. 2018. "Experts and Peer Disagreement." In *Knowledge, Belief, and God: New Insights in Religious Epistemology*, edited by Matthew A. Benton, John Hawthorne, and Dani Rabinowitz, 228–45. Oxford: Oxford University Press.

Lahroodi, Reza. 2007. "Collective Epistemic Virtues." *Social Epistemology* 21, no. 3:281–97.

Pritchard, Duncan. 2009. "Knowledge, Understanding and Epistemic Value." *Royal Institute of Philosophy Supplement* 64:95–111.

Pritchard, Duncan. 2013. "Epistemic Paternalism and Epistemic Value." *Philosophical Inquiries* 1, no. 2:9–37.

Raz, Joseph. 1986. *The Morality of Freedom*. Oxford: Oxford University Press.

Ryan, Shane. 2016. "Paternalism: An Analysis." *Utilitas* 28, no. 2:123–35.

Watson, Jamie Carlin. 2016. "The Shoulders of Giants: A Case for Non-Veritism About Expert Authority." *Topoi*. doi: 10.1007/s11245-016-9421-0.

Zagzebski, Linda. 2012. *Epistemic Authority: A Theory of Trust, Authority, and Autonomy in Belief*. Oxford: Oxford University Press.

CHAPTER 7

NEUROMEDIA AND THE EPISTEMOLOGY OF EDUCATION

DUNCAN PRITCHARD

1. Neuromedia

The technological advances of the past few decades have been staggering, and for many people they have had profound effects on our everyday lives. Moreover, the pace of technological development is, if anything, gaining momentum all the time. I want to explore one particular kind of technological development that might well be right around the corner: *neuromedia*.[1] By neuromedia I have in mind the development of information-processing technology that is so seamlessly integrated with our on-board cognitive processes that the subject is often unable to distinguish between her use of those on-board processes and the technology itself. The relationship of the subject to the technology is consequently no longer one of subject to instrument but rather "feels" like a technological extension of her normal cognitive processes.

In order to see how this might work, consider the recent changes in how we access information. Suppose one needs to know the answer to a specific question, such as how many moons Saturn has. At one time, finding this

[1] For more on neuromedia in a philosophical context, see Lynch (2014, 2016), though since it isn't clear to me that we are using this terminology in quite the same way, the reader should focus on the account of this notion offered here. I also encountered this terminology at a fascinating "impact" workshop that we held at the University of Edinburgh's Eidyn research centre in 2015, as part of the AHRC-funded "Extended Knowledge" project that I was running at the time. This brought academics from several disciplines together with those involved in the development of new technologies at companies such as Microsoft, IBM, and Google. Intriguingly, the consensus among the tech gurus was that neuromedia was imminent (some even thought that it already existed, at least in prototype form), though there was disagreement about what exact form it would take. On this latter point, see also footnote 2.

Connecting Virtues: Advances in Ethics, Epistemology, and Political Philosophy.
Edited by Michel Croce and Maria Silvia Vaccarezza.
Chapters and book compilation © 2018 Metaphilosophy LLC and John Wiley & Sons Ltd.

out might have required a trip to the library, or at least phoning up a more knowledgeable friend (at one point it might have even required being able to design and build a rudimentary telescope). These days, of course, one can just Google this question on one's phone and get the answer within seconds. Technological developments have therefore made it much easier to gain information. Even though looking up an answer on your phone is a far easier way of finding something out than visiting a library, one's relationship to the phone is still one of subject and instrument. You are conscious, after all, of using the phone to find this out; that it was the phone that communicated to you the answer to your question.

Imagine, however, that one was technologically augmented in such a way that when a question like this occurs to one, the answer becomes immediately present to mind (we don't need to worry just now about how this is done). In particular, imagine that the accessibility of the answer and the associated phenomenology involved are just like remembering this answer yourself. If technology could be made to work in this fashion, then this would be neuromedia in the sense that I have in mind. In particular, one's relationship to the technology would not now be essentially one of subject and instrument (even though one is in fact using an instrument, in effect), in that one might not even be aware that one is employing the technology.

Neuromedia, if it happens, will constitute a transformational shift in our relationship to technology. A wealth of factual knowledge—if knowledge is what it is; we will return to this point—will potentially be at our fingertips, phenomenologically on a par with knowledge that we have personally acquired. Moreover, a range of skills that are currently prized will start to become redundant, as they are offloaded onto technology. After all, many of our current skills—whether navigational, memorial, arithmetical, linguistic, and so on—are such that they will be more effectively managed via the neuromedia. If this happens, it will have seismic effects on our society.

For the remaining sections of this essay I am going to assume that neuromedia is on the horizon in order to explore its philosophical implications, especially in epistemology, the epistemology of education in particular. But to start with I want to make some brief remarks about this kind of technology and flag some broader issues that it raises.

First off, notice that there is more than one way that this kind of cognitive augmentation could happen.[2] One might imagine that this would be achieved via technological implantment—that is, the *cyborg* route. The very name "neuromedia" implies this, since it suggests that one is adding technological media to the cognising subject. One difficulty with this route, however, is that it may be prohibitively expensive, as the augmentation needs to be replicated for every subject. Indeed, one could imagine a dystopian

---

[2] I was made aware of this distinction regarding two competing technological models for neuromedia, and the associated terminology to describe it, by speaking to technology industry delegates at the event described in footnote 1.

future in which only the superrich are cognitively augmented in this way, and hence are a class apart from everyone else not only in terms of their wealth but also in terms of their cognitive powers.[3]

Another way for neuromedia to develop is by embedding subjects within high-tech adaptive environments (though this will often involve some degree of individual cognitive augmentation as well, albeit of a lesser degree to that found with the cyborg route). This is sometimes referred to as the *Minority Report* route because it mirrors how the technology works in that film (which is now famous for predicting lots of new technological developments). The thought is that if one's environment is enriched with technology that is responsive to cognitive subjects, thereby providing each subject a "bespoke" cognitive environment, then this lessens the need for individual cognitive augmentations. (In the film, for example, the environment would recognise the subject when present and offer information that it thought would be relevant for that particular person.) This option may prove cheaper overall, but it also has a lot of downsides (some of which are depicted in *Minority Report* itself). After all, it is unlikely to be the state that creates this structural environmental technology for its citizens, in which case it will be in the hands of corporations that may not have individual citizens' best interests at heart. (In the film this technology essentially gives people individually tailored adverts, of the kind one is now familiar with on, say, Facebook.)

This last point reminds us that even if we can overcome the technological hurdles facing the development of neuromedia, there may be other barriers to its implementation. For example, there might be legal concerns. If subjects are unable to know when they are relying on their on-board cognitive resources rather than the technology, this is likely to have important implications when it comes to issues like legal liability. For example, if it is the technology that is guiding one's calculations and this has a bug that leads to a mistake with important legal consequences, then in what sense are *you* liable for this error (why not the company that installed the technology)? Or, to take another example, if I testify to something under oath and it turns out that the source of this information is (unbeknownst to me) the technology rather than my biological memory, then have I misled the court? Relatedly, should technology-assisted testimony even count as admissible evidence in court?

There are also obvious political concerns regarding the misuse and regulation of this kind of technology. It can clearly be used to deceive us, and thereby deny us epistemic goods, as much as it can be used to cognitively enhance us. And if cognitive enhancement is available, who is to receive it? We've already noted the dangers of a specifically cognitive inequality,

---

[3] Of course, the rich already have cognitive advantages over the poor in terms of such things as their access to good education and cognitively useful technology, so this would be an *additional* layer of cognitive privilege.

whereby there emerges a cognitive underclass. But is it even feasible to provide such augmentations to everyone? Could one have a *right* to be cognitively augmented (in the way that many hold that one has a right to access to a good education, to good health services, and so on)? And what about those who don't want to be cognitively augmented? Could we imagine a society that obliges everyone to be cognitively augmented, so that no-one is left behind?

These are all fascinating questions, but I will be setting them to one side in what follows. Our focus will instead be on understanding the epistemological ramifications of neuromedia, especially with regard to the epistemology of education. In particular, I will be assuming that neuromedia will constitute a genuine cognitive augmentation of the subject (that is, not be used to manipulate or deceive us, and so forth).

2. Extended Cognition

Neuromedia is a form of *extended cognition*.[4] Indeed, I submit that it is the *most* plausible candidate for this title. According to extended cognition, the cognitive processes of a subject can extend beyond her brain and central nervous system; indeed, can extend beyond her skin and skull. So, for example, features of the subject's environment could be employed in such a way that they become genuine parts of the cognitive process itself (that is, they become part of the *vehicle* for cognition, which is why this view is also sometimes called *vehicle cognition*). Note that our focus will be on factors external to the subject's brain and central nervous system that are specifically information processing, such that the idea is that at least some of the information processing that is part of the wider cognitive process is taking place outside the subject's brain and central nervous system.[5]

The standard criterion for extended cognition (the "parity argument") is that an extended cognitive process is one that is functionally on a par with a comparable on-board cognitive process, in virtue of how it is seamlessly integrated into the subject's cognitive character, leading to rich feedback loops in its employment. Neuromedia clearly fits the bill on this score.

[4] The locus classicus for discussions of extended cognition is Clark and Chalmers 1998, but see also Clark 2008.
[5] For two prominent critiques of extended cognition, see Adams and Aizawa 2008 and Rupert 2009. Note that extended cognition can also have a social aspect, as when the extended cognitive process is socially distributed. I will set this aside in what follows here but have explored the particular features of this kind of extended cognition in Palermos and Pritchard 2016. See also Hutchins 1995, which is a seminal work on socially distributed cognition. Note too that the way I have described extended cognition treats embodied cognition as a form of extended cognition (sometimes the former is defined in such a way as to distinguish it from the latter). This is when features connected to one's embodiment play a constitutive role in one's cognitive processes. Again, I will be setting this type of extended cognition to one side for our current purposes, but for further discussion of embodied cognition, see Noë 2004, Chemero 2009, Rowlands 2009, and Shapiro 2011.

Indeed, neuromedia seems to constitute a far more compelling example of extended cognition than the usual cases that are offered in the literature. The original example offered of an extended cognitive process is that of the dementia sufferer "Otto," who makes up for his failing memory by employing a notebook that he carries around with him (see Clark and Chalmers 1998). The thought is that if Otto always has the notebook with him, and regularly uses it to, say, navigate his environment, then this would constitute an extended cognitive process.

But this isn't all that plausible. For one thing, the technology does not seem especially seamless and integrated in its use, and the feedback loops are somewhat thin, given the limitations of the media in play. In particular, is Otto's use of the notebook really as seamless as his employment of his biological memory (when it is working anyway)? Relatedly, Otto's use of the notebook is arguably phenomenologically very different to his use of his biological memory.[6] One experiences consulting one's notebook as using an external instrument; this is not the case when we retrieve our biological memories. That is, the relationship of Otto to the notebook is very much one of subject and instrument, unlike his use of his on-board cognitive resources.

Things look a bit better if we shift our attention from notebooks to wearable tech, like an Apple Watch. Since it's wearable, one can imagine that it does start to become seamlessly integrated into one's cognitive practices over time, perhaps to the point that one is no longer always conscious that one is employing it. The sophisticated nature of the technology also means that there is more scope for rich feedback loops on a number of fronts. Looking at the watch might provide information, which in turn stimulates biological memories, which in turn might influence what you do next, thereby generating new information, and so on. So we have one's on-board cognitive resources working in an integrated fashion with the technology.

I grant that a case like this could, over time, pass the test for being a case of extended cognition, in the sense of being functionally on a par with corresponding instances of on-board cognition. Neuromedia would be a much more convincing example of extended cognition, however. After all, even with wearable technology there is nevertheless an inevitable sense in which one's relationship to the technology is still, at least phenomenologically, one of subject and instrument, such that they are (quite often, anyway) not phenomenologically on a par. In contrast, it is built into the very idea of neuromedia that our interactions with the technology can be so seamless

---

[6] Proponents of extended cognition are usually happy to grant that there are phenomenological differences of this kind, though they might also insist that they are overstated. For them the focus is a functional equivalence between the extended cognitive process and a corresponding non-extended cognitive process, and that's held to be compatible with there being some differences at the level of phenomenology. In any case, what everyone will surely agree with is that cases of extended cognition that involve both functional equivalence and a similar kind of phenomenology would be more compelling cases of extended cognition.

that we are not always even aware that we are employing technology, so it will be a much clearer-cut case of extended cognition than, say, an Apple Watch or a pair of Google Glasses.[7]

Neuromedia is also an interesting case to focus on because, unlike other potential forms of extended cognition, there is a sense in which it needn't be a technological adaption that is external to the skin and skull of the subject (it is thus in one sense an "internal" form of extended cognition). In particular, if the neuromedia is developed along the cyborg route described above, then the technology may well be completely within the skin of the subject (although it will still be in a sense "external" to the subject's brain and central nervous system, even if it is somehow embedded within it). That the technology is "hidden" in this way is of course part of what helps to make one's use of it so seamless, as one is not physically interacting with the technology at all.

Note that even if one grants the possibility of extended cognition, it is a further question whether such cognition generates epistemic states like knowledge (that is, whether there is *extended knowledge*). Perhaps only the subject's on-board cognitive processes are able to generate the epistemic pedigree required for knowledge. I've argued elsewhere that on the most plausible accounts of the nature of knowledge—roughly, *virtue epistemology*, broadly conceived—there is no inherent reason to be sceptical about extended knowledge (see Pritchard 2010, 2017, 2018).

According to virtue epistemology, a necessary condition on knowledge is that one's cognitive success is significantly attributable to one's manifestation of cognitive agency.[8] The crux of the matter is that so long as the

[7] Note that I am not saying that there is any difference in kind here between neuromedia and other putative cases of extended cognition, only that there is a difference in degree. For example, there will likely be cases where one is aware that one is employing technology even in the neuromedia case, as when one finds oneself "remembering" something that one is aware one can't possibly have known in this way (for example, an extremely complex mathematical theorem). Of course, neuromedia might develop in such a way that subjects do not become aware that they are using technology in such cases (for example, in terms of the case just considered, perhaps they are also "fed" information to suggest that they are mathematically adept), but remember that our interest is in neuromedia as a bona fide cognitive augmentation rather than as something epistemically malign. There are interesting issues here about whether certain kinds of epistemic paternalism, of a kind that would mirror the scenario just described whereby subjects are "fed" faulty information for supposedly their own epistemic good, are permissible. For more on the nature and justification for epistemic paternalism, see Goldman 1991, Ahlstrom-Vij 2013, and Pritchard 2013a.

[8] Indeed, some virtue epistemologists—for example, Sosa (1991, 2007, 2009, 2015), Zagzebski (1996, 1999), and Greco (2003, 2007, 2008, 2009, 2012)—think that a condition of this kind is in fact sufficient for knowledge, a position I have elsewhere christened "strong" or "robust" virtue epistemology (e.g., Pritchard, Millar, and Haddock 2010, chaps. 1–4). My own view, however, is that it is not sufficient, in that we also need a distinct way of eliminating certain kinds of epistemic luck/risk (e.g., Pritchard 2012, 2013a). In any case, since the necessity claim is the more liberal of the two, in that it captures a broader range of virtue-theoretic proposals about knowledge, it will function very well for our purposes.

extended cognitive process is suitably integrated within the subject's cognitive character (which it needs to be if it is to count as an extended cognitive process in the first place), then it will count as one of the subject's extended cognitive processes. Thus any target cognitive success that results from this process will be significantly attributable to the extended cognitive subject (i.e., her cognitive character as a whole, including the extended cognitive process). This would be extended knowledge.[9]

One question we might ask about extended knowledge is whether it is in some sense second-grade knowledge when compared with unextended knowledge. One rationale for this is that we are epistemically dependent upon the technology for our knowledge, rather than being self-reliant. There is certainly something to this thought, in that our reliance on technology brings with it a kind of epistemic vulnerability, in that we run the risk of being cognitively impoverished were the technology to fail us (such is the premise of many a disaster movie). But the mere fact that we are dependent on technology for our knowledge is not itself an obvious worry. In fact, it is quite common for our knowledge to be dependent upon external factors that, alongside our (unextended) cognitive abilities, play a significant explanatory role in our cognitive success. This is what I have elsewhere called *epistemic dependence*.[10] Nonetheless, there is an important issue here, concerned with the distinctive value of certain epistemic traits, to which we will return.

3. The Epistemic Aims of Education

Education has many goals, some of them *social* (for example, to help students to get along with each other), some of them *practical* (for example, to enable students to have certain useful skills, like good handwriting), some of them *political* (for example, creating good citizens), and so on. But one core goal of education is specifically *epistemic*. That is, we want to confer epistemic skills and states onto students, so that they are good inquirers, know useful information, can reason well, and so on.

I've argued elsewhere that the overarching epistemic goal of education should be to promote *intellectual character* rather than bodies of information/knowledge or the development of mere cognitive skills. In particular, intellectual character essentially involves the development of a specific kind of cognitive skill: *intellectual virtue* (see Pritchard (2013b, 2014b, 2016b). (Related to this, I also claim that education should be geared towards promoting understanding rather than mere rote knowledge. We will come back to this point in due course.)

---

[9] For more on this point, see Pritchard 2010, 2017, 2018.

[10] See Pritchard 2013a. Note that this is very much a term of art, and so what I mean by it is not what, for example, Hardwig (1985) means by it in his influential article on epistemic dependence (though inevitably there are some overlaps).

Intellectual virtues—such as *conscientiousness* and *open-mindedness*—are distinct from mere cognitive skills along several axes.[11] The list of differences is in fact very long, but let's focus on some of the key divergences. To begin with, intellectual virtues involve distinctive *motivational states* that are constitutive of possessing the virtue. In general terms, the motivational state associated with an intellectual virtue is a love of the truth. But such motivational states are not a constitutive part of mere cognitive abilities. Indeed, one can manifest a cognitive ability such as one's rational faculties even while having no particular concern for the truth. Perhaps, for example, one is a lawyer who simply wants to develop a strong case for the prosecution, even though one's personal view is that the defendant is innocent, and one simply doesn't care what the truth of the matter is, only what kind of compelling case can be presented to the court. In this case one is manifesting a high level of cognitive ability but is not manifesting intellectual virtue, as the cognitive ability is reflecting one's instrumental goals rather than a love of the truth.[12]

Like other virtues (arguably, at any rate), intellectual virtues have the property of *lying between two vices*: one of excess and one of deficiency. One can be lacking in conscientiousness (deficiency), in which case one lacks this intellectual virtue. But one can also be unduly conscientious (excess), perhaps by obsessively attending to every detail, no matter how trivial, in which case one will also lack this intellectual virtue. Mere cognitive abilities are not like this. One's perceptual faculties may be very reliable, but they can always be more reliable, and if they are then this is a good thing. For cognitive abilities the general rule is that we evaluate them in terms of their reliability, and the more reliable they are, the better. If that's right, then there is no vice of excess when it comes to cognitive ability.

Intellectual virtues have a *distinctive kind of value* that contrasts them with mere cognitive abilities. They are to be prized regardless of their practical worth, for example, whereas mere cognitive abilities are usually only evaluated in terms of whether they serve our instrumental goals. Relatedly, intellectual virtues are also held to be constitutive parts of a life of flourishing, and thereby have a kind of non-instrumental, final, value (on account of the fact that the life of flourishing is meant to be valuable for its own sake). In contrast, mere cognitive abilities are axiologically evaluated in terms of how useful they are. For example, if a mere cognitive ability is no longer practically useful, then there would be nothing intellectually amiss in

[11] For more on the intellectual virtues, see Zagzebski 1996, Baehr 2011, and Battaly 2014.

[12] Most real-life cases of legal advocacy are likely to be more complex on this front, in that even while the lawyer might be advocating for a viewpoint that she doesn't personally endorse, she is nonetheless manifesting intellectual virtue. That is, one can care about the truth but also be willing to advocate for something other than what one knows is the truth for legitimate non-epistemic reasons, as might be the case in a legal context where one's ultimate concern is a free trial. The example just given is not of this kind, however, in that the lawyer is by stipulation only ultimately motivated by purely strategic, rather than epistemic, concerns.

a subject choosing to let this ability wane. Crucially, however, this is not so of an intellectual virtue, in that the intellectually good person would recognise the inherent value of an intellectual virtue and strive to maintain it.

Following on from this point, intellectual virtues are distinct from mere cognitive abilities in terms of their *acquisition* and *cultivation*. Mere cognitive abilities can be innate, such as our cognitive faculties, like memory, and they can also be acquired unreflectively, such as by one being continually exposed to the relevant stimuli. But intellectual virtues, like virtues more generally, are not like that. They need to be acquired in a *reflective* fashion, such as by emulation of someone who already has the intellectual virtues. Moreover, once they are acquired one needs to cultivate one's intellectual virtues, since if they are not cultivated they are lost (again, this is in contrast to mere cognitive abilities, which are often not lost once acquired, even if not cultivated).

The intellectual virtues promote *epistemic autonomy*, where this is the ability to develop and cultivate one's own viewpoints on matters of interest, and to determine what matters in the first place. One's mere cognitive abilities may enable such epistemic autonomy, but this is more like a side-effect than being central to the kind of abilities that they are. Relatedly, the intellectual virtues promote *active knowing* where this involves an inquiry/curiosity-driven approach to knowledge and understanding. This is in contrast to *passive knowing*, where one's knowledge is simply passively received and is not the product of thirst for it, of a seeking out of it.[13]

This feature of the intellectual virtues also explains why an account of the epistemic aims of education in terms of the development of intellectual character dovetails with a view according to which education should promote understanding rather than mere fact/skill retention, or rote knowledge. This is because understanding is by its nature an active epistemic state, unlike mere knowledge, which can be passively acquired. One can know something just by being told it, for example. But to understand something—a mathematical principle, say—it's not enough that one truly believes it via a good epistemic source (such as testimony from an expert). Rather, one needs to grasp why this principle is true, how the different aspects of the principle relate to one another. Moreover, one needs to be able to employ this principle appropriately, where this means more than just asserting it when asked to do so. That is, one manifests one's understanding by being able to do things with what one understands. All these features make understanding essentially an active epistemic standing, which is why developing intellectual character naturally leads to creating inquirers who seek to understand, not merely know.[14]

---

[13] For more on the importance of active knowing in the context of epistemic autonomy, see Pritchard 2016d. See also Pritchard 2016c.

[14] For more discussion of this point about the difference between knowledge and understanding, see Pritchard 2009 and 2014a and Pritchard, Millar, and Haddock 2010, chap. 4.

Finally, the intellectual virtues perform a *managerial role* in one's cognitive architecture, in that they are employed to govern the use of cognitive skills rather than vice versa. One's intellectual virtues will determine what one cares about from an epistemic point of view, and thus determine the nature of the inquiries that one undertakes. In this way the intellectual virtues will marshal one's other epistemic resources, such as one's mere cognitive skills and one's body of knowledge, to promoting these ends. One consequence of this feature of intellectual virtues is that they have a more general focus than mere cognitive abilities. The latter are usually, if not always, an ability to do something quite specific, whereas intellectual virtues are general capacities that can be implemented in lots of distinct ways (think, for example, of the multiple ways in which being intellectually conscientious can manifest itself).

I think that once we understand how the intellectual virtues function in our cognitive lives, and understand their inherent value, then the claim that the epistemic goal of education ought to be the development of intellectual character ceases to be controversial. There may be facts and mere cognitive skills that every person ought to have, in which case education should instil them. But this will be just a starting point in the educational process. What we really want is to develop the intellectual character of students so that they have a body of intellectual virtues that enables them to inquire well, and thereby to employ their mere cognitive skills and body of knowledge to intellectually valuable ends. There is so much more, from an epistemic point of view, to education than merely instilling skills and facts into the subject.[15]

4. Neuromedia and the Epistemology of Education

How will neuromedia affect our educational practices? One effect is that it will make a lot of our current educational practices redundant. Knowledge and skills that might hitherto have needed to be taught can be technologically engineered instead. Whereas students might have previously acquired knowledge using their own on-board cognitive resources, they will now be able to draw on their extended cognitive processes too. Why would we want students to remember large bodies of factual information using their biological memory, when they can draw on their extended memory and its vast resources? The same goes for lots of our basic cognitive skills. Why teach

---

[15] A related issue in this regard is that on most conceptions of the virtues, one cannot develop the intellectual virtues of subjects without thereby developing their moral and practical virtues too, given how interrelated they all are (on this score, see also our prisons education project, discussed below, and also in footnote 19, which while focused on the development of the intellectual character of the prisoners also developed their character more generally). This means that the epistemic goal of education in developing intellectual character would go hand in hand with a conception of the broader goal of education to develop the subject's virtuous character in general.

people to learn a foreign language if anyone can, via the technology, simply speak any language they want immediately?

It thus seems that there is a lot less for the educator to do in a world where neuromedia is common, and that's because many of our cognitive processes can be offloaded onto the new technology. So one might well wonder what the epistemic point of education would be in such a scenario. In particular, is there anything left for the educator to do, or can the whole educational enterprise be offloaded onto the technology? Crucially, however, while our cognitive abilities can be extended via neuromedia, the idea that our intellectual virtues can be extended in this fashion is somewhat implausible. If that's right, then while neuromedia will drastically reduce the need to educate people for basic knowledge and cognitive skills, it's primary epistemic function—that of developing intellectual virtue, and thus intellectual character—will remain (albeit in a slightly altered form, for reasons that I explain in the next section).

In order to see why the intellectual virtues cannot be simply offloaded onto technology like other kinds of cognitive ability, let's look at an intellectual virtue alongside a comparable (mere) cognitive ability. For example, let's consider the intellectual virtue of being observant with the mere cognitive ability involved in having good perceptual abilities. For instance, we could contrast the exceptional observational skills manifested by Sherlock Holmes with the merely good perceptual abilities of his sidekick Watson.

Being observant involves so much more than merely having good perceptual faculties, as the contrast between Holmes and Watson makes clear, as there is such an epistemic gulf between them on this score. Faced with the very same visual scene, for example, Holmes is able to extract vast quantities of useful information, unlike Watson. This reflects the fact that perception is just a cognitive ability but being observant is an intellectual virtue. Accordingly, the two traits differ along the axes noted above.

Perception is often passive, for example, but being observant is essentially active, in that one is actively inspecting the scene before one for information. Thus, being observant reflects one's epistemic autonomy. Relatedly, being observant involves a motivation to find the truth, something that could be completely lacking in one who merely has good perceptual faculties. One is not born an observant person but needs to acquire and cultivate this trait, and that will require one to reflect upon one's exercise of it. In contrast, one can simply have good perceptual faculties and may not need to do anything to ensure that they are retained. They can also be reliably exercised in a completely unreflective manner.

The intellectual virtue of being observant also lies between two vices, though this might not be immediately obvious. Doesn't Holmes have this trait in excess, and if so, doesn't that mean that he lacks this virtue? I don't think that's right, and this becomes clear once we reflect on what it would mean to be excessively observant. This is not to have acute observational skills like Holmes but rather to obsess about irrelevant details. This is why Holmes, even while being exceptional in this regard, nonetheless still retains the virtue, as he is attending only to the details that matter and not merely every possible detail, regardless of its import. In any case, we don't evaluate perceptual abilities in this way. If one's vision, say, is drastically improved, then that's always a good thing from an epistemic point of view. There's no such thing as having vision that's "too good" to count as a genuine cognitive ability.

Notice too how while perception can very easily, and passively, lead to knowledge of one's environment, being observant enables one to actively understand things as a result of one's perception. Watson surveys the crime scene in front of him and immediately comes to know facts of various kinds, such as that the victim is such-and-such, that the window is open, that there is a revolver on the mantelpiece, and so on. But Holmes does not merely come to know all these facts, he also appreciates their significance and thereby comes to understand something—for example, that this murder scene has been faked, that such-and-such a person cannot be the murderer, that such-and-such must be involved in this crime, and so on.

Finally, recall our point about how the intellectual virtues play a managerial role in our cognitive economy. Holmes is putting his knowledge and other cognitive skills, such as his perceptual skills, at the service of his intellectual virtue. It is his intellectual character, composed of his intellectual virtues, which is determining the lines of inquiry that he takes, and which employs his vast body of knowledge and his exceptional cognitive skills. Notice that this is an essentially reflective process, just as the cultivation of one's intellectual virtues is, in that the process involves deliberation and judgment. It is not the kind of thing that can "just happen" (which is precisely how perception often occurs).

I don't think that it is controversial that many of Watson's perceptual abilities could become cognitively extended via neuromedia. Take eyesight, for example. One could certainly imagine cognitive augmentations of this faculty that enabled Watson to do incredible things with his vision, to be able to see far into the distance, or focus in on a particular detail before him at high magnitude. Moreover, such an augmentation could, over time, be so integrated within his other cognitive abilities that his employment of it is completely seamless, such that it doesn't even feel as though he is relying on technology at all but rather just using "his" cognitive abilities.

Could we do the same with Holmes's intellectual virtue of being observant? I don't see how. Holmes may well employ technology in lots of ways to assist his observational powers, as when he uses his famed magnifying glass to inspect the crime scene before him. But notice that this is technology that is being reflectively brought into service to serve his intellectual virtues. Similarly, even if Holmes is fitted with the same neuromedia to enhance his vision that we just hypothetically attributed to Watson, it is still employed only under the guidance of his intellectual virtue.

Indeed, what would it even *mean* for an intellectual virtue to be cognitively extended? One's intellectual virtues, and one's intellectual character more generally, are constituted by being reflective, managerial traits that guide one's employment of one's cognitive abilities (extended or otherwise) and one's knowledge (again, extended or otherwise). This means that it is built into these traits that they are manifestations of one's unextended cognitive character. Technology, even in the form of neuromedia, is only ever a tool that one can virtuously employ in reaching one's intellectual goals; it is never a substitute for the intellectual virtue itself.

If that's right, then while a great deal of "lesser" educational tasks will not be necessary in a world of neuromedia, the core epistemic goal of education—that of developing good intellectual character, and thus promoting the intellectual virtues—will remain intact. Moreover, one could argue that in an age of neuromedia we need intellectual character more than ever. Consider some of the challenges that neuromedia poses that we looked at above, such as how it can be used just as much to misinform as to inform. The intellectually virtuous will be far better placed to handle such difficulties.

I think this point is also relevant when it comes to our increasing reliance on technology, something that I noted above seems problematic. The intellectually virtuous person will be reliant on technology, including neuromedia, in a very different way to someone who is lacking those virtues. For one thing, having intellectual virtues means having very general cognitive skills, as opposed to the way in which mere cognitive abilities tend, as I noted above, to be devoted to specific cognitive tasks. This means that they are very practically useful in terms of helping one to develop further mere cognitive skills and obtain new knowledge. As a consequence, in a situation where the technology is suddenly no longer available the intellectually virtuous will be in a good position to know what to do, in particular to adapt to the new epistemic environment.

In addition, the intellectually virtuous person is someone who will be careful about his reliance on technology in the first place. After all, these extended cognitive processes are, for him, a mere epistemic resource, and it is part of what it is to be intellectually virtuous that one employs one's epistemic resources wisely. Accordingly, the intellectually virtuous person will make sure that he is not unduly reliant on technology, and in particular that he has the means available to him to function adequately were the technology to no longer be available.

5. Intellectual Character and Technology

It is important to note that denying that the intellectual virtues cannot be cognitively offloaded onto technology does not entail that technology can't be used to enhance one's employment of the intellectual virtues, or even that it can't play a role in the acquisition and cultivation of the intellectual virtues. The first point is obvious. Sherlock Holmes, our exemplar of intellectual virtue (albeit an exemplar who is often somewhat lacking in some of the non-intellectual virtues), frequently uses technology to aide his employment of his intellectual virtue (whether it is the magnifying glass from the original novels or the advanced tech found in contemporary presentations of the detective).

The second point—that technology can play a role in developing intellectual virtue, and thus intellectual character—is perhaps not so obvious. I want to spell out what this might involve by describing: (i) an actual project that we undertook, using technology to develop intellectual character; and (ii) a possible app that would help students enhance their intellectual character. As we will see, in both cases we have technology at the service of the goal of enhancing intellectual character, but in neither case is it leading to instances of extended cognition. Moreover, turning the technology in question into neuromedia won't make a difference.

The first example I want to focus upon is a project that I was involved with, and am still involved with, that brought philosophy—more specifically, critical thinking—into prison education. The goal of the project was to enhance the intellectual character of the prisoners.[16] To that end, they were aided by two factors. The first was an (offline) version of the MOOC (Massive Open Online Course) entitled "Introduction to Philosophy" that we had created, along with supporting educational materials (for example, handouts to go with each topic, a set of critical thinking problems, discussion topics, and so on).[17] The MOOC was designed to introduce people to philosophical topics without presupposing any philosophical background, and so was ideal for this educational setting. The second was a series of seminars using a particular way of teaching philosophy/critical thinking, known as "Community of Philosophical Inquiry," or CoPI for short.[18] This approach has been widely and effectively used in educational contexts, and it also has the advantage that, like the MOOC, it doesn't presuppose

[16] This project was hosted by the University of Edinburgh's Eidyn research centre but was a collaboration between Eidyn, the Moray House School of Education (also at the University of Edinburgh), colleagues at New College Lanarkshire involved in prison education, and the Scottish Prison Service. Two prisons were targeted, a male prison (Low Moss) and a female prison (Cornton Vale). A second run of this project has just been completed, with more runs planned for the future. For more details about the project, see http://eidyn.ppls.ed.ac.uk/project/philosophy-prisons.

[17] Note, by the way, that the reason the MOOC they used was offline is that in the Scottish system prisoners are not allowed access to the Internet. The version they used was nonetheless functionally equivalent to the online version, albeit without the online discussion forums. Incidentally, the MOOC in question has been enormously popular, with well over two million enrolments worldwide. For more details about this course, go to: https://www.coursera.org/learn/philosophy.

[18] The particular version of CoPI that we employed was pioneered by Catherine McCall, who also advised us on the project. See McCall 2009 for details of this approach. See also earlier work by Lipman (1991), which is a precursor to this model.

any previous knowledge of philosophy (which is why this technique is often used in philosophy in school programmes that target younger children).

The project had a demonstrable effect on the prisoners' intellectual character. At the start of the project, the prisoners struggled to articulate their reasoning, struggled to understand other people's reasoning (or even grasp different points of view), very easily gave up on problems they found difficult, were unwilling to collaborate with others in solving problems, showed very little creativity in problem solving, and so on. These traits are all indications of a lack of intellectual character, and in particular they showed that the prisoners—like many of us—have many intellectual vices. But on all these fronts the prisoners showed marked improvement as the project went on. For example, they became much better at articulating their reasoning and grasping the reasoning of others. This meant that they could now engage in a genuine reasons-based debate with each other, rather than simply dismissing each other's opinions from the start. Their intellectual tenacity improved, in that they stuck with difficult problems for longer, often engaging collaboratively with others in trying to solve the problem. Relatedly, they were more intellectually creative in their attempts to answer problems, employing novel approaches rather than sticking only to the same strategies. These are all indications of the development of intellectual virtue and thus of the development of intellectual character.[19]

Note that I say that the project *developed* the prisoners' intellectual character and thus their intellectual virtues, which is not to say that they were suddenly intellectually virtuous after the project—that would have been an incredible educational feat, given that the project only lasted a few months. The prisoners were instead just a lot closer to being intellectually virtuous as a result of the project, in that they had mastered some important intellectual skills, such as being able to articulate their reasoning, that are necessary to acquire intellectual virtue. More importantly, now that they had these skills they were in a position to further develop their intellectual character themselves.

The technology employed in this project—essentially, the MOOC—certainly enhanced the effectiveness of the educational techniques employed. Moreover, one could imagine running versions of this project that employed even more technology, including neuromedia. Perhaps neuromedia is used as a replacement for watching the MOOC, and instead of educators in the room running the CoPI sessions, one could imagine a kind

---

[19] The results from the project, and their evidential basis, are detailed in Bovill and Pritchard manuscript. A summary of the project and its results is available here: https://www.ed.ac.uk/education/rke/making-a-difference/philosophy-in-prisons. Note that one of the results of the project, which on reflection is unsurprising given standard conceptions of the virtues, is that in developing the intellectual character of the prisoners we also seemed to develop their character more generally (for example, their self-esteem, their respect and concern for others, and so on).

of technologically "scaffolded" environment that delivered prompts to the prisoners to help them master these techniques. But no matter how much of a cognitive role in this process is played by the technology, there is no way of simply technologically engineering the prisoners' intellectual virtue. Even in the most technologically enhanced version of this project that one could imagine, one is at most using the technology to enable the development of certain basic intellectual skills that are crucial to a good intellectual character, such as learning more creative ways of problem solving. Such skills are vital to the development of intellectual virtue, but they are not yet intellectual virtues, in that they lack many of the features of the intellectual virtues noted above. But as we saw above, turning them into intellectual virtues will require the subject to manifest all kinds of dispositions—for example, distinctive motivational states, reflecting on one's intellectual performance, actively rather than passively knowing, and so forth—and these dispositions are not of a kind that can simply be cognitively offloaded onto technology. Instead, the manifestation of genuine intellectual virtue will always involve the technology becoming a mere instrument for the intellectually virtuous person to employ.

Now consider an idea for a possible educational app. Think of how one these days finds the answer to a question one has: we simply Google it. This puts a wealth of information right at our fingertips, and if neuromedia becomes a reality then it will be closer still (that is, phenomenologically akin to our biological memory). But the intellectually virtuous person is not satisfied with merely getting an answer to a question. Rather, she will engage in intellectually virtuous *inquiries*, where this will involve an interesting series of questions being answered. Imagine an app that tries to cultivate this trait within a student, such that the student doesn't merely ask a question of Google and get an answer but thereafter follows through with a train of inquiry. How might it be constructed?

The problem, of course, is how to have a way of determining a good inquiry in advance of having a fixed account of what constitutes a good inquiry in this context. But there are ways of resolving this difficulty. Suppose one starts with an educational pilot, whereby pupils are asked to develop a chain of inquiry based on an initial question and then are graded on how intellectually stimulating this inquiry is. This is obviously a thin data set, but nonetheless one could use the data to start "weighting" certain inquiries over others, in terms of whether the person doing the inquiry has been judged to have done good inquiries in the past. If one could get the relevant algorithm right, then over time by repeating this process with more and more pupils and educators, one could get a way of rating inquiries. Pupils could be given a score as an inquirer, depending on what kind of inquiry route that they took, so that it is not just inquiry paths that are rated but also inquirers. In the beginning, this would involve lots of evaluation from the educators, but over time this would become a self-regulating process (at least if the algorithms are done well), in that one could have "good" inquirers rate the inquiries of others (perhaps anonymized to ensure that there is no bias entering the system). Over time, one could develop a data set for particular questions that picked out lines of inquiry that were distinctive of good inquirers and also picked out good inquirers.

With this data set in play, such an app could go beyond the developmental stage and actually play a role in the cognitive development of pupils, by offering a way of helping them to enhance their core critical skills involved with critical inquiry, skills that are essential to the development of intellectual virtue. Note that expanding the initial run to a broader set of pupils also substantially expands the data set, and thereby helps to refine the algorithm in place to determine good inquiries, and thus good inquirers. We now have a bigger set of pupils rated by their educators as being good inquirers (because their inquiries have been rated as good), and we now have data about how inquirers are rating each other (weighted in terms of how good an inquirer one is).

Suppose that one now takes this basic model, gleaned from the specifically educational context, and makes it available wholesale. One could imagine, for example, that instead of doing a simple Google search, one has the option of doing instead a "Schmoogle search" (or whatever it might be called). This would involve getting to see where "good" inquirers went next in terms of their inquiries originating with this search. This way one would get to see what good inquirers did next, as opposed to simply getting a closed answer to a closed question.

More interestingly, however, moving the model to a wholesale scale affords a number of additional advantages. Previously we had the educators as experts, with a weighed rating as a result. Imagine now that inquirers are rating each other en masse. An algorithm needs to be developed to ensure that raters are weighted accordingly (for example, in terms of their past inquiries and how they fit with inquiries previously judged to be "good," and in terms of whether their ratings of inquiries fit with the ratings from "good" evaluators). With the right algorithms in place, there will be a way of inquirers ranking others and being ranked themselves that promotes good inquiry. One can even imagine that, over time, inquirers will not merely Google search but actively Schmoogle search instead, and even that inquirers who are rated as "good" via this process are lauded, with their particular searches followed by others.[20]

This is all highly hypothetical, of course, but the point of the exercise is to demonstrate how technology could be employed to help people enhance their intellectual character. As with the prisoners, however, all that is on offer here is an *enabler* of the development of intellectual character—the technology cannot all by itself ensure that pupils develop the suite of

---

[20] Indeed, one could even envisage that, over time, the app would become more nuanced in its evaluations, such that inquiries are evaluated along several axes (such as originality, novelty, and so forth).

intellectual virtues distinctive of a good intellectual character. What is being developed are some basic cognitive skills that are necessary for the development of cognitive character. But for these cognitive skills to develop into intellectual virtues the subject is going to have to manifest the dispositions listed above—such as being suitably reflective, being guided by the right kind of motivational states, being an active rather than passive knower, and so on—that can't be offloaded onto the technology. Again, we see that there is a place for technology to aid the development of intellectual character, but it cannot be a substitute for it.

6. Concluding Remarks

Were neuromedia to become a reality, much of our knowledge would likely be replaced by extended knowing, and many of our cognitive skills would likely end up being extended cognitive skills. But this doesn't pose any challenge to the epistemic goal of education, since this was never about the development of (mere) cognitive skills or the instillation of (mere) knowledge. Instead, the epistemic goal of education is that of developing intellectual character, and thus the intellectual virtues that comprise a good intellectual character. This goal would be no less important in an age of neuromedia, because, as we have seen, intellectual virtues are by their nature non-extended cognitive traits. If anything, it is *more* important to inculcate intellectual character in an age of neuromedia. In any case, while technology might have a role to play in aiding the development of intellectual character, it cannot play any more of a role than that.

Acknowledgments

An earlier version of this essay was presented at a conference on the Philosophy of Education at the University of London in May 2017, and I am grateful to the audience members for their feedback on the talk. Thanks also to Mary Bovill, J. Adam Carter, Michel Croce, Andy Clark, Chris Kelp, Andrea English, Aaron James, Catherine McCall, Orestis Palermos, John Ravenscroft, and especially Michael Lynch. Thanks too to an anonymous referee from *Metaphilosophy* and David Mott from IBM's Emerging Technology team. This essay has benefitted from four grants, all of them for projects hosted at the University of Edinburgh's Eidyn research centre. The first is the AHRC-funded "Extended Knowledge" project (AH/J011908/1). The other three are all funded by the John Templeton Foundation. These are: (i) the "Virtue Epistemology, Epistemic Dependence and Intellectual Humility" project, which was part of the wider "Philosophy and Theology of Intellectual Humility Project" hosted by Saint Louis University; (ii) the "Intellectual Humility MOOC" project; and (iii) the "Philosophy, Science and Religion Online" project.

References

Adams, Fred, and Ken Aizawa. 2008. *The Bounds of Cognition.* Oxford: Blackwell.

Ahlstrom-Vij, Kristoffer. 2013. *Epistemic Paternalism: A Defence.* London: Palgrave Macmillan.

Baehr, Jason, 2011. *The Inquiring Mind: On Intellectual Virtues and Virtue Epistemology.* Oxford: Oxford University Press.

——, ed. 2015. *Intellectual Virtues and Education: Essays in Applied Virtue Epistemology.* London: Routledge.

Battaly, Heather. 2014. "Intellectual Virtues." In *Handbook of Virtue Ethics*, edited by Stan van Hooft, 177–87. London: Acumen.

Bovill, Mary, and Duncan H. Pritchard. Manuscript. "Philosophy in Prisons: Critical Thinking and Community of Philosophical Inquiry." Unpublished manuscript.

Chemero, Anthony. 2009. *Radical Embodied Cognitive Science.* Cambridge, Mass.: MIT Press.

Clark, Andy. 2008. *Supersizing the Mind: Embodiment, Action, and Cognitive Extension.* Oxford: Oxford University Press.

Clark, Andy, and David Chalmers. 1998. "The Extended Mind." *Analysis* 58:10–23.

Goldman, Alvin. 1991. "Epistemic Paternalism: Communication Control in Law and Society." *Journal of Philosophy* 88:113–31.

Greco, John. 2003. "Knowledge as Credit for True Belief." In *Intellectual Virtue: Perspectives from Ethics and Epistemology*, edited by Michael DePaul and Linda Zagzebski, 111–34. Oxford: Oxford University Press.

——. 2007. "The Nature of Ability and the Purpose of Knowledge." *Philosophical Issues* 17:57–69.

——. 2008. "What's Wrong with Contextualism?" *Philosophical Quarterly* 58:416–36.

——. 2009. *Achieving Knowledge.* Cambridge: Cambridge University Press.

——. 2012. "A (Different) Virtue Epistemology." *Philosophy and Phenomenological Research* 85:1–26.

Hardwig, John. 1985. "Epistemic Dependence." *Journal of Philosophy* 82:335–49.

Hutchins, Edwin. 1995. *Cognition in the Wild.* Cambridge, Mass.: MIT Press.

Lipman, Matthew. 1991. *Thinking in Education.* New York: Cambridge University Press.

Lynch, Michael P. 2014. "Neuromedia, Extended Knowledge, and Understanding." *Philosophical Issues* 24:299–313.

——. 2016. *The Internet of Us: Knowing More and Understanding Less in the Age of Big Data.* New York: W. W. Norton.

McCall, Catherine. 2009. *Transforming Thinking: Philosophical Inquiry in the Primary and Secondary Classroom*. London: Routledge.
Noë, Alva. 2004. *Action in Perception*, Cambridge, Mass.: MIT Press.
Palermos, S. Orestis, and Duncan H. Pritchard. 2016. "The Distribution of Epistemic Agency." In *Social Epistemology and Epistemic Agency: De-Centralizing Epistemic Agency*, edited by Patrick Reider, 109–26. Lanham, Md.: Rowman and Littlefield.
Pritchard, Duncan H. 2009. "Knowledge, Understanding and Epistemic Value." In *Epistemology: Royal Institute of Philosophy Supplement* 64, edited by Anthony O'Hear, 19–43. Cambridge: Cambridge University Press.
———. 2010. "Cognitive Ability and the Extended Cognition Thesis." *Synthese* 175:133–51.
———. 2012. "Anti-Luck Virtue Epistemology." *Journal of Philosophy* 109:247–79.
———. 2013a. "Epistemic Paternalism and Epistemic Value." *Philosophical Inquiries* 1:1–37.
———. 2013b. "Epistemic Virtue and the Epistemology of Education." *Journal of Philosophy of Education* 47:236–47.
———. 2014a. "Knowledge and Understanding." In *Virtue Scientia: Bridges Between Virtue Epistemology and Philosophy of Science*, edited by Abrol Fairweather, 315–28. Dordrecht, Netherlands: Springer.
———. 2014b. "Virtue Epistemology, Extended Cognition, and the Epistemology of Education." *Universitas: Monthly Review of Philosophy and Culture* 478:47–66.
———. 2016a. "Epistemic Dependence." *Philosophical Issues* 30:1–20.
———. 2016b. "Epistemic Risk." *Journal of Philosophy* 113:550–71.
———. 2016c. "Intellectual Virtue, Extended Cognition, and the Epistemology of Education." In *Intellectual Virtues and Education: Essays in Applied Virtue Epistemology*, edited by Jason Baehr, 113–27. London: Routledge.
———. 2016d. "Seeing It for Oneself: Perceptual Knowledge, Understanding, and Intellectual Autonomy." *Episteme* 13:29–42.
———. 2017. "Extended Virtue Epistemology." *Inquiry*. Online First, DOI: 10.1080/0020174X.2017.1355842.
———. 2018. "Extended Knowledge." In *Extended Epistemology*, edited by J. Adam Carter, Andy Clark, Jesper Kallestrup, S. Orestis Palermos, and Duncan H. Pritchard, 90–104. Oxford: Oxford University Press.
Pritchard, Duncan H., Alan Millar, and Adrian Haddock. 2010. *The Nature and Value of Knowledge: Three Investigations*. Oxford: Oxford University Press.
Rowlands, Mark. 2009. *The Body in Mind: Understanding Cognitive Processes*. New York: Cambridge University Press.
Rupert, Robert D. 2009. *Cognitive Systems and the Extended Mind*. Oxford: Oxford University Press.

Shapiro, Larry. 2011. *Embodied Cognition*. New York: Routledge.

Sosa, Ernest. 1991. *Knowledge in Perspective: Selected Essays in Epistemology*. Cambridge: Cambridge University Press.

——. 2007. *A Virtue Epistemology: Apt Belief and Reflective Knowledge*. Oxford: Oxford University Press.

——. 2009. *Reflective Knowledge: Apt Belief and Reflective Knowledge*. Oxford: Oxford University Press.

——. 2015. *Judgment and Agency*. Oxford: Oxford University Press.

Zagzebski, Linda. 1996. *Virtues of the Mind: An Inquiry into the Nature of Virtue and the Ethical Foundations of Knowledge*. Cambridge: Cambridge University Press.

——. 1999. "What Is Knowledge?" In *Blackwell Guide to Epistemology*, edited by John Greco and Ernest Sosa, 92–116. Oxford: Blackwell.

CHAPTER 8

EPISTEMIC VICE AND MOTIVATION

ALESSANDRA TANESINI

Intellectual character vices involve non-instrumental motives to oppose, antagonise, or avoid things that are epistemically good in themselves.[1] In short, intellectual vice comprises a motivation actively to turn away from the epistemic good. This view, or something like it, has recently come under attack (Cassam 2016; Crerar 2017). In this essay I argue that arguments denying that such epistemically bad motivations are necessary to character vices neglect an important distinction between two kinds of explanation of action and belief. The first rationalises them by offering motivating reasons in their support; the second makes these beliefs and actions intelligible in terms of reasons that explain them. Both kinds of explanation invoke motives. Opponents of motivational accounts of vices focus their discussions on motivating reasons but fail to consider the motives presented in mere explanations of actions and belief.

There are, as is well known, two approaches to virtue in epistemology. Virtue reliabilists think of virtues as cognitive faculties or capacities, such as memory or perception, that are in ordinary circumstances reliable (Sosa 2007). Virtue responsibilists claim that virtues are character traits with their distinctive motivations (Zagzebski 1996). In its clearest example, which is found in Zagzebski (1996, 2003), the view states that each intellectual virtue is individuated by its distinctive proximate motivation. These virtues, however, also share one ultimate motive, which is love of truth or of cognitive contact with reality. This is a motivation to seek non-instrumentally,

---

[1] In this essay I treat "intellectual vice" and "epistemic vice" as synonymous expressions. Intellectually vicious individuals also possess other non-instrumental motives that are not epistemic in character. For instance, they may be motivated by power or self-interest. Human actions are often done for more than one motive, including more than one that is not instrumental. I set these issues aside here.

Connecting Virtues: Advances in Ethics, Epistemology, and Political Philosophy.
Edited by Michel Croce and Maria Silvia Vaccarezza.
Chapters and book compilation © 2018 Metaphilosophy LLC and John Wiley & Sons Ltd.

something that is epistemically good in itself.[2] It is therefore natural to ask whether bad motivations may be essential to intellectual vices in the same way in which good motives are said by responsibilists to be defining of virtue. There is a small but growing literature addressing this issue either directly or indirectly. Heather Battaly has suggested, for example, that vices may have distinctively bad motivations (2016, 2015), while Linda Zagzebski (1996) at times indicates that vice is defined by the absence of good motivations. Finally, Quassim Cassam (2016) and Charlie Crerar (2017) have defended the view that individuals may possess epistemic vices despite having some good motivations. In this essay I argue that once the notion of motivation is properly understood, the objections against the view that intellectual vices have characteristic bad epistemic motivations can be shown to be ill founded. Further, I show that the view that epistemic vices have these distinctive motives can be independently motivated. There is, however, an important disanalogy between virtues and vices because there is no ultimate motive that is common to all vices.

The essay consists of three sections. The first details some counterexamples to the view that epistemic character vices require epistemically bad motives, or at least the absence of good motivations. The second section shows that once the motivations involved in these hypothetical cases are properly understood, all of these examples involve non-instrumental aversion to epistemic goods. Hence, the challenge to motivational accounts of vices based on them is shown to fail. In the third and final part of the essay, I distinguish motivating from explanatory reasons for belief and action. I argue that once it is accepted that explanatory reasons can be motives, our epistemic practice of vice attribution supplies some evidence in favour of motivational accounts of vice.

1

May intellectual character vices require non-instrumental motives to oppose, avoid, or antagonise things that are epistemically good in themselves?[3] There are intellectual vices that seem to involve such motives: epistemic malevolence, for example. Jason Baehr characterises this vice as the

---

[2] Zagzeski's formulates two distinct accounts of the value of motivations. The first is eudaimonic. Motivations are good because they are aimed as something that is good since it is a constituent of the good life. The second is motivation based. It identifies some motivations which are good in themselves and whose goodness confers value on their ends. Other virtue responsibilists are not so clear on these points. They are also often unclear about the source of the goodness of good motivations. When they use the term "intrinsic" to refer to good motives, it is often unclear whether they are referring to things that are good in themselves or to things that are valued non-instrumentally. See Kosgaard (1983) for a clear statement of this distinction.

[3] My sole concern here is with character vices such as laziness and arrogance. Intellectual vices may not be restricted to character traits, since they may include habits of thought such as wishful thinking (Cassam 2016, 160). In this essay I set this issue aside.

opposition to the epistemic good as such (or for its own sake) in all its incarnations or to others' share in it (2010, 192, 204). He defines such opposition in volitional terms. The person who is epistemically malevolent acts out of an ill will. He is driven by the motive universally to antagonise, block, or prevent what he regards as epistemically good, or to put obstacles in the way of the acquisition by some person of her share of this good. That is to say, malevolent motives may target specific people, or they may be directed impersonally to the epistemic good itself.[4] A person may be malevolent for malevolence's sake. He may be ill willed toward others for no further purpose than seeing their share in epistemic goods languish and decline. It is also possible to harbour malevolent motives for instrumental purposes. For instance, an individual may, out of arrogance, want to acquire some epistemic goods for herself that she is not prepared to share with others. Hence, she may also malevolently keep other people ignorant as a means to her goal of becoming intellectually superior to them.

Baehr seems to think that a motive is either final or instrumental, but not both (2010, 192). If this is his view, it is mistaken. It is possible for one person to be at the same time motivated by malevolence for its own sake and as a means to a further end. The person who initially behaves malevolently for the sake of feeling intellectually superior to others may eventually love being malevolent for malevolence's sake. When this happens, his actions may be simultaneously motivated both non-instrumentally and instrumentally by antagonism to the epistemic good.

Baehr discusses some fictional and actual examples of epistemic malevolence such as O'Brien in George Orwell's *1984* and Sophie Auld as described in Frederick Douglass's autobiography. The latter, after having taught Douglass the rudimentary elements of reading, is transformed into an epistemically malevolent individual by the corrupting influence of her husband. Hence, she starts to oppose angrily and actively impede the attempts by Douglass to read and acquire knowledge, whilst openly displaying her contempt for him and his pursuit of self-education.

Ill will toward others' intellectual flourishing is necessary for the vice of epistemic malevolence.[5] The person who blocks, antagonises, or actively prevents other people from acquiring epistemic goods is not best thought malevolent if he does not act out of ill will. To see why this is the case consider the example mentioned above of an intellectually arrogant person

[4] Baehr explains being opposed to the epistemic good in itself for its own sake in terms of making the epistemic good one's enemy (2010, 193–94). He also thinks that malevolence may not always be a vice, because its characteristic motive may co-exist with a sufficiently good ultimate epistemic motivation (2010, 190, n. 2). I find this deeply implausible but shall not pursue it here.

[5] Here and throughout this section I rely on what I hope are shared intuitions about whether an individual is vicious. There are some worrying limitations to this methodology. I adopt it here because it has been used in the arguments against the motivational account of vice that I wish to oppose.

who behaves malevolently out of a desire to be intellectually superior to other people. In so far as this person attempts to block others' access to epistemic goods, he behaves in the same way as a malevolent person would. He may, however, not be malevolent himself.

He may instead think of people that they are a threat to his quest for intellectual superiority. But, if they were not a threat, he would have no interest in denying them access to the epistemic good. Hence, he considers them to be obstacles rather than his enemies. Therefore, this person does not seem to harbour malevolence toward others; rather, he tries to crush them only when they are in his way. If he has nothing to gain from putting them down, he will leave them alone. It is plausible to conclude that we would not characterise this person as malevolent, because he harbours no ill will toward these people, although we would think of him as viciously arrogant. Thus, here we have an intellectual vice that requires the presence of a non-instrumental motive to oppose the epistemic good as such. Ill will may also be sufficient for epistemic malevolence, since it is plausible to think of an ill-willed person who ineptly ends up promoting the acquisition of epistemic goods as being epistemically malevolent, even though ineffectual.

I have argued that the possession of a non-instrumental motive to make the epistemic good one's enemy is both necessary and sufficient for malevolence. For the purpose of a defence of the motivational view, it is also important to note that this is a motive that is bad in itself, rather than merely because of its effects or contributions to something else that is bad. The motive of malevolence is bad in itself because it is the enemy of what is in itself epistemically good.[6]

The view that intellectual vice requires non-instrumental epistemically bad motivations has its supporters. The clearest pronouncements in this regard have been offered by Battaly, who has often stated that there is a plausible (responsibilist) conception of epistemic vices according to which they are "partly composed of bad epistemic motives" (2016, 106; 2017b, 226). She explicitly models this account of intellectual vice on a responsibilist theory of epistemic virtues according to which motivations to pursue non-instrumentally epistemic goods are essential to virtue.[7]

I have suggested that the purely motivational theory of epistemic vice is plausible with regard to the vice of epistemic malevolence. If, however, the theory is to be of interest, it must offer a plausible account of all intellectual vices or at least of all those vices that are character traits. Once we think of

---

[6] This characterisation of malevolence presupposes that malevolence is a bad motive because its aim is to oppose something that is independently good. Alternatively, one could argue that being ill willed is bad in itself. It is the badness of ill will that would make antagonising the epistemic good a bad thing.

[7] Battaly's notion of an epistemically bad motive is not wholly clear. It at least requires that it is a non-instrumental motivation to pursue something that is bad (either in itself or because of its effects).

the theory as having a general application, we can readily think of seeming counterexamples.

For instance, Crerar has argued that the eponymous main character in Goncharov's novel *Oblomov* is intellectually vicious despite lacking epistemically bad motivations of the sort required by motivational accounts (2017, 5).[8] Oblomov shows no interest in anything. He loafs on his sofa because nothing, in his view, is worth his efforts.[9] In this characterisation he is shown as lacking that deep concern for cognitive contact with reality that is sometimes said to be essential to every intellectual virtue (cf. Zagzebski 1996). His apparent lack of good motives alone, as should be obvious, does not make him a counterexample to the motivational account.[10] Instead, what must be shown is that, first, Oblomov is intellectually vicious and, second, he has no relevant epistemically bad motivations. The latter point is arguably disputable.[11]

We may support the first claim that Oblomov suffers from intellectual vices by our describing his behaviour as flowing from epistemic laziness.[12] Oblomov, so characterised, has no interest in the acquisition of epistemic goods; therefore, he lacks curiosity and shows no inclination to initiate inquiry or to persevere with it when a question pops into his mind. Once his situation is described in these terms, it is open to the supporter of the motivational account to agree that Oblomov is vicious but to deny that he has no epistemically bad motivations. Instead, one may claim that his vice stems from those epistemically bad motivations—whatever they may be—that are characteristic of the vice of epistemic laziness.

Opponents of the motivational view have an immediate response to this argument. They may retort that although there may be some bad epistemic motives that are associated with intellectual laziness, these are not the kind of motive required by motivational accounts. That is, they are not non-instrumental motives that actively oppose or avoid things that are epistemically good in themselves. Instead, to be lazy is primarily to lack the good motives that would be required for virtues like inquisitiveness and

---

[8] Crerar is not committed to the view that Oblomov has no motivations that are in some sense epistemically bad. He is instead committed to the claim that these motivations are not bad in the sense required by motivational accounts.

[9] Oblomov is also discussed by Gabriele Taylor (2006, 19–21), who describes him as the archetype of sloth and indolence.

[10] An individual, for instance, may have an instrumental concern for the truth without being intellectually vicious.

[11] One may also take issue with the description of Oblomov as intellectually vicious. In the book he is often described as being riven by anxieties. He is confined to his bed because of his inability to prioritise. So described, he appears to be not slothful but akratic. He may care for the truth but against his better judgement finds himself unable to regulate his mental activity in line with his motivations.

[12] Kidd (manuscript) provides an account of intellectual laziness. Battaly's (2017a) vice of capitulation is also closely related to laziness and indolence. See also Baehr (2011, 19, 70) and Zagzebski (1996, 152) for some brief remarks.

perseverance.[13] This response is plausible since there is a ring of truth to the thought that to be lazy is to lack the motivation to make an effort. Despite its plausibility, I argue in section 2 that this conclusion is ultimately mistaken.

One may concur that this example shows that epistemically bad motives are not necessary for intellectual vice. Nevertheless, one may also think that motivations are important. For instance, one may claim that these vices are characterised by an absence of the good motivations required by virtue. This position has widespread support since it can be plausibly attributed to Baehr (2010), Montmarquet (2000, 138), and Zagzebski (1996).

A deeper challenge to the motivational view of intellectual vice is presented by fictional examples of individuals whose motivations appear to be epistemically good but who display a range of seemingly vicious behaviours. Crerar discusses two cases. Since these are similar, I limit my discussion to the first. It concerns a scientist—Galileo—who is motivated to seek the truth for its own sake but who is also arrogant (2017, 7).[14] Out of his sense of intellectual superiority Galileo underestimates the intellectual abilities of his interlocutors and so takes no notice of their comments. Thus, Galileo is intellectually vicious despite possessing the kind of motivation that is common to all intellectual virtues.

Analogous to the Galileo case is the example of Oliver the conspiracy theorist (Cassam 2016, 162–63). Cassam describes him as a person who is genuinely motivated to find out the truth but is gullible and easily led astray by the Internet. Crerar questions whether Oliver is best described as intellectually vicious or as possessing limited cognitive abilities (2017, 8). Be that as it may, it is possible to conceive of a conspiracy theorist—Olivia—who seems to be motivated by the truth and yet is intellectually vicious. Olivia does not want to believe conspiracies, come what may; she only wants to believe them if they are true. She may be perseverant and curious. She may even be better informed than most on the topic.[15] In some sense, however, she also wants the conspiracies to be true, and it is this motivation that guides her inquiries. Hence, she has a blind spot; she is closed-minded about the falsity of her pet theories. In short, she displays many of the behaviours that are characteristic of virtue, and she is motivated to believe only what is true. She is, however, not equally motivated to find out whether her favourite theories are false.

There is also another kind of counterexample to the motivational theory of intellectual vice. It concerns individuals who turn vicious trying to compensate for a defect that they attribute to themselves. Montmarquet,

---

[13] See Watson (2015) for an account of inquisitiveness and Battaly (2017a) for perseverance.

[14] Crerar borrows this example from Roberts and Wood (2007, 254).

[15] That is to say, she may have more true beliefs on the topic than most people. Of course, she also has more false beliefs than most. This fact alone does not make her ill informed. Presumably, anybody who cares about a given subject has more false beliefs than those who have not given it any thought.

for instance, imagines a person who becomes dogmatic out of fear that she is too gullible (1993, 25). This person—call her Gail—out of a concern for what is intellectually good attempts to correct for what she perceives to be a defect in her character. This endeavour leads her, however, to develop a tendency not to listen to contrary views, because she fears that she might too easily believe them. Unfortunately, she ends up overcompensating and thus turns herself into a dogmatic person. She seems to be exclusively motivated in the right ways but nevertheless ends up acquiring an intellectual character vice.

If all of this is right, then epistemic bad motivations are not a defining feature of intellectual vice. While some character vices such as malevolence may require them, and others necessitate an absence of good motives, there are other vices that can be had even though one is exclusively driven by good motivations of the kind required for intellectual virtue. There would, therefore, be nothing of significance to say in general about the relation of intellectual character vices to motivations.

There are reasons, however, not to rest happy with this negative conclusion. The proposal that vices have non-instrumental motives to avoid, oppose, or antagonise things that are in themselves epistemically good is intended to do much explanatory work as part of an account of the nature of vice. First, the proposal provides an account of what makes vices bad and thus grounds criticisms directed toward those who have these features. Vices would derive their disvalue from the disvalue of their motivational component.[16] Second, the proposal offers a criterion for the individuation of individual vices, since each one of them has its distinct motivations. Third, it helps to distinguish vices from other kinds of intellectual shortcoming, such as incapacity, cognitive malfunction, and lack of ability or skill. The only intellectual shortcomings that are vices are those that have bad motivational states of the requisite kind among their components. If we abandon the motivational account of vice, it becomes at best unclear what else could take its place in these explanations.

2

In this section I argue that non-instrumental aversion to epistemic goods is at play in all the examples considered above. These, therefore, do not refute the motivational account of vice. In the next section I offer some independent reasons in support of such a view.

Crerar focuses on Oblomov's lack of motivation (2017, 5). Further, although Crerar leaves it open that Oblomov may possess some bad motives, he claims that his viciousness precisely consists in his indifference for what is intellectually good and therefore in the absence of the kind

[16] Further motivations may be the ultimate source of disvalue or they may be bad because they oppose or avoid that which is epistemically good in itself. It should be noted that explanations that ground the badness of vice on something other than motivations are also possible, since attributions of blame may not require bad motivations.

of motivation required by epistemic virtue. There are, however, reasons to doubt this characterisation. Oblomov, if he is lazy rather than akratic, must in some sense choose not to bother with inquiry. He has opportunities to acquire epistemic goods that he does not take because he abhors making the required effort. So understood Oblomov is an agent who regulates his mental activity. His behaviour is guided by his motivations rather than by external forces. Oblomov's ultimate motive is to avoid making any effort. This motivation itself is not epistemic; it is also not always bad, since effort is not unqualifiedly a good. Oblomov, however, also possesses other motivations, some of which are plausibly described as epistemic since they guide his intellectual conduct.

Oblomov is an irresponsible epistemic agent. He is not guided by the evidence; he is negligent in his belief formation; he shows a lack of due care when thinking about any topic.[17] He acts in this manner because his behaviour is driven by an aversion to making any intellectual effort. It is this aversion that also explains his indifference to the truth. Thus, although it is accurate to describe Oblomov as lacking virtuous motivations, what is most telling about his character is the presence of the motive actively to avoid whatever may require intellectual effort or application. This is the characteristic bad motivation that is necessary for intellectual laziness. It is a non-instrumental motivation to avoid intellectual labour.

It may be objected, however, that this motivation is not of the kind demanded by motivational accounts, because aversion to intellectual labour is not bad in itself since what is being avoided is not something that is good in itself. It is true that effort is not always valuable. There are many domains in which effortless success is preferable to having to labour for the same outcome. As Zagzebski also notes, there are many goods whose goodness does not depend on having to work to get them (2003, 20). These are goods that are desirable and include epistemic goods, such as true belief. But there are other goods whose goodness requires that we work for it. These are goods that are admirable and that, arguably, include knowledge. It is also plausible to think that intellectual work or effort is epistemically good in itself. We do admire people who apply themselves in the pursuit of intellectual inquiry, and our appreciation of them is not wholly dependent on the success of their endeavour. In conclusion, although much more would need to be said to establish the point, in the epistemic domain doing the work required by inquiry is epistemically good in itself because it warrants admiration. What is characteristic of epistemic laziness is aversion rather than indifference to effort. This aversion to application is the bad epistemic motivation that explains Oblomov's behaviour.

Having rebutted the example purporting to show that some vices are characterised by an absence of good motives of the right kind, I turn my attention to three cases intended to show that one may be vicious despite

---

[17] See Cassam (2016, 166) for a characterisation of the obligations of responsible inquiry.

possessing intellectually virtuous motives. Below I cast doubt on attributing to these fictional characters the motivation to love the truth for its own sake. But for now I shall not challenge the coherence of the examples and grant, for the sake of argument, that these individuals have virtuous motivations.

Galileo, in the example under consideration, cares for the truth, but he is also arrogant. Further, his arrogance leads him to become closed-minded. It is important to distinguish clearly this case from another in which a Galileo-like figure—Copernicus—makes an honest mistake. He believes that he is intellectually superior to other people around him. Consequently, he may not give to their views the credit they deserve. He, however, would not be arrogant or closed-minded; he would be misguided.[18] Therefore, this is not the case that we are being asked to consider, because Galileo in our example is supposed to be both arrogant and closed-minded.

What is the difference between Galileo and Copernicus? I submit that a crucial difference lies in their motives. Suppose that they both dismiss out of hand a criticism raised by an opponent. If we ask why they behave in this way, however, our answers differ. Copernicus may think that the opponent's claim is not a genuine challenge, Galileo may find any criticism to be an affront to his intellectual standing. But even if these are not precisely their motives, their similar actions will have different psychological explanations. Whatever these may be, it is plausible to think that those who are arrogantly closed-minded are motivated to preserve their sense of superiority by trying to do others down.

The contrast with Copernicus supports this point. Copernicus has the right motivation without also having bad motives such as envy. He is, however, not plausibly classified as vicious. Galileo is *ex hypothesi* vicious and has good motivations. An explanation is needed, however, for his behaviour. His actions are intelligible if we think of Galileo as being driven by a desire to preserve his sense of superiority by doing others down. This motive is an aversion to, or strong dislike of, other people's epistemic achievements that is also manifested as a delight in, and an enjoyment of, their failures.

It is plausible to think that Galileo is non-instrumentally averse to others' achievements. He sees other people's successes instrumentally as obstacles, but he is also simply opposed to them for no other reason than that he dislikes the idea that others have achievements to their name. Further, since epistemic achievements are good in themselves, it is plausible to think that a motive of aversion to them is an epistemically bad motivation.

---

[18] For defences of this position see Tanesini 2016, 516, and Roberts and Wood 2007, 243. Crerar has commented in a private communication that he does not envisage Galileo to be epistemically selfish. I think what he has in mind is a person who cares for the truth and wrongly but honestly thinks he is intellectually better than other people. Such a person in my view would not count as being arrogant. Hence, he would not be a counterexample to the motivational approach.

One can run a parallel argument to address Olivia's case. Olivia has desire for the truth, but she also wants some beliefs of hers to be true. She is therefore closed-minded, dogmatic, and prone to wishful thinking. But Oliva is not Oliver. She is not easily swayed because of limited cognitive abilities. She has mixed motivations. She cares for the truth but, because she is dogmatic, she is unwilling to engage with views alternative to her own (Battaly forthcoming). This unwillingness is the manifestation of a disposition actively to ignore evidence. This motive exemplifies an opposition to an epistemic good that is a component of epistemic responsibility: namely, the careful consideration of evidence. Further, if Olivia has become genuinely dogmatic rather than someone who has a blind spot for conspiracy theories in particular, it seems plausible to think of her as being averse to the careful consideration of evidence non-instrumentally, because she would find such evidence challenging. She does not ignore evidence exclusively as a means to achieve her goal of holding on to her favourite theories.

If the above is correct, these cases are not even challenges to the view that the presence of motivations actively to turn away from things that are epistemically good in themselves is both necessary and sufficient for intellectual vice. They would, however, undermine the view that good motivations of the requisite sort are sufficient for intellectual virtue. It is thus worth pointing out that the claim that Galileo and Olivia are motivated in the right way by the truth is at least open to question.[19]

Since we are dealing with thumbnail examples, the psychologies of these fictional characters are largely under-described. Of course, one may make it a matter of stipulation that Galileo is motivated by the truth for its own sake. For these stories to be effective counter-examples, however, they must possess a degree of psychological plausibility. Given that Galileo is described as arrogant and also as closed-minded as a result of his arrogance, it is extremely implausible that he would be motivated by a desire that the truth be discovered no matter by whom, and that he simply thinks he is best placed to discover it. Believing this, truly or falsely, does not make one arrogant or closed-minded. Thus, at the very least Galileo is only motivated to acquire truths for himself. He is not prepared to sacrifice the amount of truth he has access to for the greater epistemic good of the community.

This characterisation, however, does not really fit Galileo. He is not motivated to discover as many significant truths as possible for the truth's sake. The fact that he does not value the truth for its own sake is illustrated by the fact that he would be bitterly disappointed if he were not the one to discover it. One may object that his psychology may not fit this description. In response, I would argue that we need to be told more about his character than the sketchy characterisation offered by those who use the example to attribute to Galileo only epistemically good motivations. I would also

---

[19] For reason of space I develop the point only with regard to the Galileo example.

add that a psychologically realistic way of filling in the picture is to portray him as not caring for the truth for its own sake but only caring that he is the one that discovers the truth. If I am right, Galileo is only instrumentally motivated by a desire for epistemic goods; he desires the truth because being the one who discovers it enhances his epistemic standing in his own and others' eyes. He is ultimately motivated by a desire to further inflate his own inflated self-conception. This fact would explain his arrogance and closed-mindedness and his apparent drive to discover truths.

The final alleged counterexample to the motivational account is structurally different from the cases discussed above. Gail does seem to have genuinely and exclusively good motivations. Having discovered a temperamental weakness, she resolves to counteract it to become a better inquirer. Unfortunately, she ends up overdoing it and thus starts ignoring objections that she should address. In my view it is not altogether clear that she suffers from an epistemic character vice. If we ask her why she behaves as she does, she would make reference to her gullible temperament, which requires her to be particularly active in counterbalancing this tendency. Thus, she would not be dogmatic, although she behaves in seemingly dogmatic ways. Her behaviour would, instead, be indicative of a series of misjudgements about what it takes to be receptive to others' views without being too easily swayed.

This characterisation of Gail, however, may not ring true to some. It is psychologically plausible also to think of her as acquiring the vice of dogmatism through repeated acts of overcompensation. But if we think of her in these terms, she appears as someone who first develops an instrumental motive for not listening to other people's views to fulfil her end of avoiding false beliefs. Over time, however, she turns herself into a dogmatic person, because the motive for closing her mind to opposing views becomes an end in itself. In short, it makes sense to think of her as possessing a vice rather than a weakness, if we think of her actions as constituting a process of habituation into the vice of dogmatism. Such a process leads Gail to act out of the motives for dogmatism automatically. Thus, her dogmatic responses are the result of motives that are automatically engaged.[20] Therefore, Gail no longer considers whether the dogmatic response would serve the further purpose of acquiring epistemic goods. She has become dogmatic because she is averse to careful consideration of the relevant evidence. Hence she ends up acquiring the same bad motivation as Olivia, even though the processes by means of which she acquires it are different.

3

There is something unsatisfactory in my dispute against those who claim that motivation of the right kind is neither necessary nor sufficient for vice

[20] For an account of automaticity see Rees and Webber (2014).

since we simply appear to trade in intuitions. I am sure that those who oppose motivational theories of vice may provide alternative accounts of the examples described above. Therefore, we appear to have reached a stalemate. In what follows I provide some independent support for the idea that vices require non-instrumental motivations to avoid, oppose, or antagonise things that are in themselves epistemically good. My argument begins by considering the purpose of charging or, more neutrally, attributing vices to other people (Kidd 2016). It proceeds by deploying some distinctions that are standard in the philosophy of action to suggest that there is a plausible conception of vice according to which it is part of the very concept of vice that it is correctly attributed only to individuals whose non-instrumental motivations include aversion to things that are in themselves epistemically good.

We can approach questions about the nature of intellectual vice by considering the use of vice attributions to explain people's actions. Cassam (2015) describes these attributions as intellectual vice explanations. He characterises them as explanations of another person's beliefs or activities that are intended to undermine that belief or action as lacking any rational grounds and being merely a reflection of personal idiosyncrasies.[21] That is to say, the attribution of a vice explains, in the sense of making it intelligible, a person's belief or action by showing it to flow from a psychological state of that person. The attribution also entails that there are no reasons that would support holding the belief or carrying out the action.

While I agree with Cassam that its ability to play this explanatory role is an important feature of the concept of vice, I have a quibble with the idea that explanations in terms of vice are explanations of belief and action as a result of individual idiosyncrasies. Or at least I find myself in disagreement if these are understood as akin to quirks or eccentricities. Sometimes we do explain people's activities in terms of their idiosyncrasies. Thus, we may say of the person who uses only a specific brand of sugar in her coffee that this behaviour is one of her quirks. Nonetheless, by saying so we would not be taking ourselves to criticise this person or attribute any particular vices to her.

To clarify the thought that vice plays an essential role in some explanations of people's beliefs and actions, it is helpful to borrow from the philosophy of action a distinction between three kinds of explanation: justifications, rationalisations, and mere explanation. An explanation justifies an action or a belief when it adduces considerations in its favour. These considerations are normative reasons, which is to say facts that provide rational grounds for the belief or the action. A rationalisation adduces the reasons that the agent takes to support her beliefs or actions. These reasons are known as motivating reasons; they are the considerations that

---

[21] Cassam focuses exclusively on explanations of belief, but attributions of vice are used as often in explanations of behaviour.

EPISTEMIC VICE AND MOTIVATION

the agent takes to offer rational support for her actions and beliefs and that as a result motivate her to believe and behave as she does.[22] A mere explanation supplies reasons that make the agent's actions or beliefs intelligible without either justifying or rationalising them. Both rationalisations and mere explanations are psychological explanations, while justifications are not.

An example I borrow from Maria Alvarez will help to clarify this distinction. Consider the killing of Desdemona by Othello. There are no normative reasons in support of his action. For which, therefore, there is no justifying explanation. Othello has a reason for his action, though. His reason is the putative fact that Desdemona was unfaithful to him.[23] This is the consideration that motivates Othello to act. Hence, there is a rationalising explanation for his killing. Othello murders Desdmona because he thinks that she is unfaithful. Finally, one may also supply another explanation that makes his action intelligible. Othello is jealous. His jealousy explains why he forms the belief that Desdemona is unfaithful, and thus why he kills her. The motive of jealousy is not what he takes to be his reason for his behaviour. It is not something that rationalises his behaviour. Nevertheless, it is the psychological state that explains both his deliberation and his actions. It is a motive without being a reason (Alvarez 2010, 2016).[24]

Vice explanations are psychological explanations. One may wonder whether they could be rationalisations or whether they always function as mere explanations. Cassam's discussion is not clear on this matter. In my view there may be some rationalisations that undermine the belief or action as lacking rational support because the adduced motivations are plainly bad from a normative point of view. Actions that manifest epistemic malevolence exemplify this structure. We can explain why a person blocks others' access to epistemic goods by adducing her motivating reasons. These may include the fact that she opposes their epistemic well-being. This is the consideration that rationalises her actions because it specifies her reasons for acting as she does. It also explains her actions, since it presents the motivations that make these activities intelligible.

More typically, however, vice explanations make someone's actions or beliefs intelligible by supplying psychological motives that explain, but do not rationalise, them. An agent is typically unaware of possessing these motives, since bringing them to consciousness would make her realise that she has no reason that rationalises her actions. For instance, an

[22] I leave it an open question whether normative and motivating reasons are essentially the same kind of thing—putative facts—or whether they are different because motivating reasons are psychological states.

[23] Alternatively, one may say that the belief that Desdemona was unfaithful is Othello's motivation reason. If one adopts this stance, one takes motivating reasons to differ in kind from normative reasons. Nothing in my essay hangs on this issue.

[24] Not all psychological explanations of action invoke motives. Some, for example, may explain actions in terms of impairments.

intellectually arrogant person may silence other people out of defensiveness.[25] His defensiveness explains his deliberations and actions, but it is not the reason he acts as he does. Nevertheless, defensiveness may be an underlying motivation of his activities.

The discussion so far indicates that if we are prepared to take seriously our use of the vocabulary of vice when criticising people for their beliefs and actions, then vices constitute psychological states that make actions intelligible and also on occasion rationalise them. These psychological states are the motives underlying individuals' beliefs and activities that may be said to reflect or manifest them. It is also part of our practice of vice charging that an explanation of a belief or an action as reflecting a vice implies that this belief or action lacks any justification. It also presupposes that the person who believes or behaves in this way is a legitimate target of criticism.

There is a sense in which anyone who believes or does something that she has no (normative) reason to believe or do is falling short of what is normatively required. We do not, however, criticise or blame people who make honest mistakes or whose reasoning falls short of what is normatively required due to temporary or permanent impairments of their cognitive capacities. In these cases we may be critical of their beliefs or actions but are not critical of these individuals themselves.[26] In this regard vice attributions are different. Explaining a person's belief or action as reflecting a vice entails taking this person to be a legitimate target of criticism.[27]

These considerations raise the question of what may warrant such criticism. I contend that the most plausible answer is that criticism is legitimate because of the badness of the psychological states from which the individual's beliefs and actions flow. Thus, what grounds criticism of vicious people are the psychological states that motivate their behaviours, even though these states are not their reasons for their actions. The states are the motivational components of vice. These are bad because they are noninstrumental motives actively to turn away from things that are epistemically good in themselves.

If it is granted that our practices of vice attributions presuppose that vices involve psychological states, which supply bad motivations without always being reasons for action, we can settle my disagreement with those

[25] See Tanesini 2016 for a discussion of the plausibility of defensiveness as a deep motive for arrogance.

[26] It might be claimed instead that we do criticise these people, even though we do not blame them. For this view see Montmarquet (2000, 132). Be that as it may, we are more critical of people for their vices than for their cognitive defects.

[27] I wish to set aside here the further question whether we also think vice attributions warrant blaming the person for her viciousness and the behaviours that flow from it. Battaly (2016), for instance, has argued that we may not always want to blame people for their intellectual vices. Cassam (manuscript, chap. 1) also considers this.

who claim that epistemically bad motivations are not necessary or sufficient for vice.

The distinction between motivating and explanatory reasons sheds light on Oblomov's motivational architecture. It is plausible to attribute to Oblomov a paucity of motivating reasons. He does not think that anything is worth doing. Therefore, he has no reasons that motivate him to act. Nevertheless, it is possible to explain his behaviour in terms of his underlying motivations. We intuitively think that Oblomov is intellectually lazy or indolent because he is motivated to avoid effort. This motivational architecture explains why he does not see the value of seeking the truth, and why he always gives up too soon. His opposition to epistemic work is the ultimate epistemic motive that explains his epistemic conduct.

The same distinction between two kinds of reason also explains the viciousness of Galileo. His ultimate motivation is one of self-enhancement, but his deepest epistemic motive is an aversion to others' epistemic achievements. This motive explains why Galileo is arrogant; it also explains his rationalisations of his actions. He takes his reasons to be a love for the truth. But he is mistaken. The motives of self-enhancement and envy of others' achievements bias his thinking and guide his behaviour. In short, Galileo does not really have epistemically good motives. Rather he is self-deceived, since his rationalisations hide the true motivational structure behind his activities.[28]

In sum, if it is granted that our practice of charging people with vice is genuinely explanatory, it follows that we take vice to be at least in part constituted by a psychological state that explains people's beliefs and actions without justifying them but normally also without rationalising them. Further, there is a respectable notion of motivation that identifies the motives for believing or doing something with the psychological states that explain why one believes or acts in that manner. Hence, the idea that vices have motivations as one of their constituents is part and parcel of our practice of vice attribution. I have not argued here that our practice is in order; I have assumed that it is. Hence, it is open to my opponents to argue that there is something mistaken with our folk practice.

However, and I take this to offer substantial support for my view, if we do go along with our practice and deploy the distinction between justifications, rationalisations, and mere explanations, we are able to offer richer and psychologically plausible accounts of the psychology of vice. The richness of these descriptions, when contrasted with the sketchiness of the accounts of those who claim that motivations are neither necessary nor sufficient for vice, is evidence for the motivational account. The arguments offered here do not show that bad motivations are sufficient for vice, but—I hope—they do provide evidence that they are necessary.

---

[28] This fact explains the stealthiness of arrogance (Cassam 2015). It is because arrogance always involves a kind of self-deception that it is hard to cure oneself of.

Acknowledgments

I would like to thank audiences at the University of Reading and at the 2016 Genoa conference on Connecting Virtues for their suggestions. Thanks also to Jonathan Webber and Ian Kidd for their comments on earlier versions of the essay. My deepest gratitude to Charlie Crerar, whose incisive criticisms have really helped me to become clearer on these issues.

References

Alvarez, Maria. 2010. *Kinds of Reason: An Essay in the Philosophy of Action*. Oxford: Oxford University Press.

———. 2016. "Reasons for Action: Justification, Motivation, Explanation." In *Stanford Encyclopedia of Philosophy*, edited by E. N. Zalta (Winter 2016 edition). Retrieved from https://plato.stanford.edu/archives/win2016/entries/reasons-just-vs-expl/.

Baehr, Jason. 2010. "Epistemic Malevolence." *Metaphilosophy* 41, nos. 1–2:189–213.

———. 2011. *The Inquiring Mind: On Intellectual Virtues and Virtue Epistemology*. Oxford: Oxford University Press.

Battaly, Heather D. 2015. *Virtue*. Cambridge: Polity Press.

———. 2016. "Epistemic Virtue and Vice: Reliabilism, Responsibilism, and Personalism." In *Moral and Intellectual Virtues in Western and Chinese Philosophy*, edited by Chienkuo Mi, Michael Slote, and Ernest Sosa, 99–120. New York: Routledge.

———. 2017a. "Intellectual Perseverance." *Journal of Moral Philosophy* 14, no. 6:669–97.

———. 2017b. "Testimonial Injustice, Epistemic Vice, and Vice Epistemology." In *The Routledge Handbook of Epistemic Injustice*, edited by Ian J. Kidd, José Medina, and Gaile J. Pohlhaus, 223–31. London: Routledge.

Battaly, Heather D. Forthcoming. "Closed-Mindedness and Dogmatism." *Episteme*.

Cassam, Quassim. 2015. "Stealthy Vices." *Social Epistemology Review and Reply Collective* 4, no. 10:19–25.

———. 2016. "Vice Epistemology." *Monist* 99, no. 2:159–80.

———. Manuscript. *Vices of the Mind*.

Crerar, Charlie. 2017. "Motivational Approaches to Intellectual Vice." *Australasian Journal of Philosophy*, 1–14. doi:10.1080/00048402.2017.1394334.

Kidd, Ian J. 2016. "Charging Others with Epistemic Vice." *Monist* 99, no. 2:181–97.

———. Manuscript. "The Vices of Epistemic Laziness."

Korsgaard, Christine M. 1983. "Two Distinctions in Goodness." *Philosophical Review* 92, no. 2:169–95.

Montmarquet, James. 1993. *Epistemic Virtue and Doxastic Responsibility*. Lanham, Md.: Rowman and Littlefield.

——. 2000. "An 'Internalist' Conception of Epistemic Virtue." In *Knowledge, Belief, and Character: Readings in Virtue Epistemology*, edited by Guy Axtell, 135–47. Lanham, Md.: Rowman and Littlefield.

Rees, Clea F., and Jonathan Webber. 2014. "Attitudes and Virtuous Automaticity." In *The Philosophy and Psychology of Character and Happiness*, edited by Nancy Snow and Franco V. Trivigno, 75–90. New York: Routledge.

Roberts, Robert C., and W. Jay Wood. 2007. *Intellectual Virtues: An Essay in Regulative Epistemology*. New York: Oxford University Press.

Sosa, Ernest. 2007. *A Virtue Epistemology: Apt Belief and Reflective Knowledge*, volume 1. Oxford: Clarendon Press.

Tanesini, Alessandra. 2016. "Teaching Virtue: Changing Attitudes." *Logos and Episteme* 7, no. 4:503–27.

Taylor, Gabriele. 2006. *Deadly Vices*. Oxford: Clarendon Press.

Watson, Lani. 2015. "What Is inquisitiveness?" *American Philosophical Quarterly* 52, no. 3:273–87.

Zagzebski, Linda. 1996. *Virtues of the Mind: An Inquiry into the Nature of Virtue and the Ethical Foundations of Knowledge*. Cambridge: Cambridge University Press.

——. 2003. "The Search for the Source of Epistemic Good." *Metaphilosophy* 34, nos. 1–2:12–28.

PART 3

POLITICAL PHILOSOPHY

CHAPTER 9

SENSES OF HUMOR AS POLITICAL VIRTUES

PHILLIP DEEN

1. Introduction

While a sense of humor is praised in others, it is not often thought of as a moral or intellectual virtue, much less a political one. Among the central political virtues are sociability, prudence, and justice. A well-ordered community, its citizens, and its leaders must all be able to get along with one another, exercise good judgment, and ensure that people get what they deserve. It's not clear that a sense of humor would help with any of these. Humor can divide, it often mocks the social order, and comedians are virtually the opposite of prudent persons, as evidenced by the fact that they decided to disappoint their parents and commit to a career where they try to amuse drunks in exchange for half-price nightclub chicken wings. Others have highlighted the dangers of comedy in the public square. As the famed 1960s British satirist Peter Cook remarked, we are "in danger of sinking giggling into the sea," while, as Ben Schwartz put it recently, political humor has been "satirized for your consumption," and citizens and politicians alike have become a nation of class clowns (Schwartz 2015).[1]

In what follows, I argue that a sense of humor is a secondary virtue conducive to the cardinal political virtues of sociability, prudence, and justice. I survey the recent debate over a sense of humor as a type of excellence, including the finding from recent psychological research suggesting that different forms of humor are associated with different virtues. Extending that idea, I argue that prudence and sociability are served by benevolent humor that (a) cultivates an awareness of the limits of politics and of the need to overcome our self-serious attempt to bend reality to our ideology

---

[1] No, not the Ben Schwartz who played Jean-Ralphio Saperstein on TV's *Parks and Recreation*.

Connecting Virtues: Advances in Ethics, Epistemology, and Political Philosophy.
Edited by Michel Croce and Maria Silvia Vaccarezza.
Chapters and book compilation © 2018 Metaphilosophy LLC and John Wiley & Sons Ltd.

and (b) promotes connections and sympathy between citizens. Whereas benevolent forms of humor lead to prudence and sociability, more cutting forms of humor such as satire are conducive to the virtue of justice. Satire exposes and condemns the intellectual and moral vices of hypocrisy, ignorance, and pride, particularly among the powerful. While citizens generally should be gentle in their treatment of each other, they must not be afraid to use pointed humor to condemn vice and the abuse of political power. To make this more concrete, I use the case study of the current absurd joke by the United States on itself and the world: Donald Trump.

One clarification: I do not make the claim that it is impossible to live an excellent life without a sense of humor. Though personally I am tempted to believe that a life without a sense of humor is less than fully excellent and, therefore, that a sense of humor is essential to a good life, I do not attempt to make the case here. Rather, for present purposes, I have set the bar lower. I argue that a sense of humor is *instrumental* to already acknowledged political virtues, not that it is a political virtue *in itself*.

2. Sense(s) of Humor as Virtuous

If you were to ask people what they want in a friend or a lover, it is very likely they would include a sense of humor. "Funny" is often right at the top of the list with "caring" and "honest." We want those close to us to be not only reliable and supportive but also delightful to be around, able to handle life's troubles, and willing to "get over themselves." And virtually all of us want to believe that we have a good sense of humor. Franklin Moore Colby observed wryly, "Men will confess to treason, murder, arson, false teeth, or a wig. How many will own up to a lack of humor?" (1926, 1). A 1986 study found that 94 percent of people believe that their sense of humor is better than average, which necessarily entails that at least 44 percent of people are in a state of denial (Lefcourt and Martin 1986). Indisputably, not everyone has a good sense of humor, but the fact that almost everyone would claim to indicates the importance we place on it. A person without humor is widely believed to be deficient in some way, though it is not clear whether that deficiency is moral.

Our easy judgment that it is better to have a sense of humor is complicated by the fact that a sense of humor is difficult to define, as it may mean a general temperament of cheerfulness or bemused distance, a set of skills or talents such as joke telling, an activity such as laughter or a passive capacity to appreciate others' humor, and so on (Ruch 2008, 20–54). There is, however, a cluster of ideas and tests to categorize and measure it. A person with a sense of humor habitually: (a) comprehends jokes, (b) expresses humor and mirth, (c) creates humorous content, (d) appreciates humor, and/or (e) uses humor to cope, among other things (Martin 1998, 16). Thankfully, for the present argument it is not necessary to reach a high level of precision; this cluster of concepts joined to an everyday understanding is sufficient.

Contrary to Colby's claim, a sense of humor has historically been condemned in Western philosophy and religion, so perhaps there have been a number of scolds throughout history who have happily denied having a sense of humor. For millennia, humor has been accused of being hostile, immoderate, idle, hedonistic, irrational, insincere, and anarchic. It is said that humorists delight in vice and the suffering of others, while failing to control their base emotions (Morreall 2009a, 90–110). There is some support for the belief that humor arises from a dark place. The clown who is secretly crying on the inside is a well-known cliché, but it is perhaps one with a measure of truth. The comedian Chris Rock has said that comedy is the blues for people who can't sing. One study of seventh graders found that children who were more likely to joke around and to be found funnier by their peers tended to have lower self-esteem. Being funny was perhaps a way of getting affirmation (cited in Martin 1998, 28). Humor can also clearly be a form of aggression. We laugh more easily and heartily when it denigrates those of whom we have a negative opinion. Comedians have even been found to have higher degrees of psychotic tendencies (Ando, Claridge, and Clark 2014).

A sense of humor has, however, had its defenders. It is associated with being humble, exposing vice, and providing comfort to those who are suffering. Particularly regarding the last, humor is strongly correlated with the ability to transcend life's troubles. It enhances feelings of self-esteem and confidence in the face of threats and allows people to cope when faced with social limitations, such as the demand to conform to others' expectations or the sheer absurdity of existence. As the psychologist of humor Rod Martin notes, "Individuals with a sense of humor, as compared to their more serious counterparts, tend to be more nonconformist and iconoclastic, taking a more playfully rebellious approach to the most serious and sacred aspects of life, while continuing to embrace life despite its injustice, hypocrisy, and foolishness" (1998, 41). People with a sense of humor are less anxious and less likely to feel helpless in stressful situations, resulting in greater job success and marital stability. A sense of humor correlates with a person's general satisfaction with life (Ruch 2008, 47).[2] If this is true, then a sense of humor is perhaps either virtuous in itself or conducive to virtue.

A divide between vicious and virtuous forms of humor was delineated among increasingly egalitarian seventeenth- and eighteenth-century Britons as they turned against the prevailing belief that humor reflects the amusement felt at one's superiority over others. The malicious glee at putting others down, of ridiculing them, was distinguished from pro-social

[2] A survey of studies regarding the correlations between humor and stable self-conception, self-evaluation without dysfunction, optimism, and stress moderation found, however, that the strength of correlation varied widely. The link was found to be strong in cases of autonomy, optimism, and environmental mastery, and weak in cases self-esteem, negative affect, and fear of being negatively evaluated (Kuiper and Martin 1998).

forms of humor. Hence, they elaborated a distinction between (Continental) wit, which was vicious and not properly amusing, and (British) humor (Schmidt-Hidding 1963).[3] One's sense of humor, then, was virtuous insofar as it found pleasure in pro-social comedy and vicious insofar as it was cutting. But this is too simple.

Perhaps the reason it is so difficult to determine whether a sense of humor is virtuous is that we have oversimplified both halves of the equation. Taking a clue from Beermann and Ruch's work on everyday perceptions of the virtue or viciousness of humor and its uses, we might be better off rejecting the notion that there is a unified Sense of Humor that is or is not a unified Virtue. Rather, each is plural, and certain senses of humor correspond to certain virtues (Beermann and Ruch 2009 and 2008). Put another way, a sense of humor is not necessarily vicious if witty, and not necessarily virtuous if humorous. Rather, each form of comedy is virtuous in its own way and depending upon its context.

Drawing from Peterson and Seligman's classification of virtues, which lays out the six major areas of virtue—wisdom, courage, humanity, justice, temperance, and transcendence—Beerman and Ruch asked what sorts of humor and uses of humor correlated with these various virtues. They found that a sense of humor was most closely associated with wisdom, humanity, and transcendence—that is, with (a) using knowledge for good purposes, creativity, curiosity, judgment, and perspective, (b) empathy, kindness, and social understanding, and (c) hope, appreciation of beauty, gratitude, and a sense of one's place in a larger whole. They also found that people are more likely to use humor in cases that call for the expression of humanity and wisdom.

As a result, while seen to have a connection to sociability and transcendence, a sense of humor was not typically associated with the central political virtue of justice, which deals with fairness and the qualities that sustain the community. Justice is less about love and acceptance than it is about ensuring that people get what they deserve, either through the distribution of rights and goods or through retribution for their wrongdoing. The benevolent, "virtuous" humor would then seem to miss out on the core political virtue of justice. But that is not the only type of humor there is. Beerman and Ruch found that justice was linked most closely to malevolent or derisive humor. Following Schmidt-Hidding, they note that malevolent humor in the form of satire "aims to decry the bad and foolish, and at the general 'betterment of the world'" (Beermann and Ruch 2009, 399). Even humor that is sarcastic, derisive, and cutting is seen as virtuous if targeted correctly. Significantly, among those surveyed, justice was described as the most important virtue, along with humanity, whereas the humor associated with it was seen as the most suspect.

---

[3] For an artistic expression of this split within the French prerevolutionary court, see the film *Ridicule*.

I find this quite interesting, and relevant to the question of whether a sense of humor is a political virtue. Rather than asking this singular question of the connection between humor and political virtue, we should be asking many questions. What senses of humor are politically virtuous, with the understanding that there are many political virtues?

3. Political Virtues of a Sense of Humor

John Morreall has discussed the virtues and vices of humor generally and political humor specifically (2009a, 90–124; 2009b). He focuses on two facets. First, he draws attention to humor's capacity to decommit speakers from what they say. Comedy, like other art forms, is not bound by rigorous requirements of truth and morality. Comedians are not necessarily asserting truths or moral beliefs as they slacken their everyday commitments for the sake of aesthetic amusement. It is sometimes immoral, however, to slacken those commitments. Morreall's general moral principle is that "we should not laugh at someone's problem when compassion is called for" (2009b, 71). This concern is heightened when we turn to Morreall's second facet when analyzing political humor: who has the power. Politicians have enormous power and responsibility. Accordingly, we must be vigilant that they do not laugh in the presence of their constituents' suffering or make light of serious matters of public concern in order to escape criticism and maintain power. Morreall then seems to come very close to saying that a sense of humor is virtuous when it is found among the citizens but not among the politicians, which would be an error.

I would like to constructively critique Morreall's analysis by adding further complexity. As noted above, we may divide humor roughly into two types, benevolent humor and malicious wit, with each corresponding to different political virtues of sociability, prudence, and justice. Humor aligns with the political virtues of sociability and prudence, while wit serves justice. The questions of whether humor is appropriate, or in the right hands, then depend on the type of humor being used and in service of what end.

3.1 Trump as Anti-Exemplar

Perhaps the best way to understand when a sense of humor is a political virtue is to examine the living embodiment of when it is vicious: the current U.S. president, Donald Trump. Since his campaign began, a robust conversation has arisen concerning the relation between Trump and comedy. Jimmy Fallon tousled candidate Trump's hair on the *Tonight Show*, and *Saturday Night Live* had Trump on as a host, raising the concern that comedians were complicit in the normalization of a white nationalist, incompetent, and proudly sexually assaulting demagogue. In the immediate wake of his election, a number of comedians openly asked if their social role had changed, demanding they all be satirists (while also asking whether satire even had the capacity to provoke political resistance). In this section, I focus on three other questions: Does Trump have a sense of humor? If so, of what sort? What does it matter if he does?

Some have charged that the president has no sense of humor, implying that there is something profoundly wrong with him, either psychologically or morally. Former senator Al Franken, who entered public life as a writer and performer on *Saturday Night Live*, observed Trump's performance at the Al Smith dinner, when politicians typically engage in a roast of sorts, and noted that "Donald Trump never laughs....He smiled, but didn't laugh. I don't know what it is" (Leibovich 2016).[4] Franken is not the only one to observe this. Chuck Todd, who has interviewed Trump many times on NBC, says the same. In the *Nation* and the *Atlantic* we find articles entitled "Have You Ever Seen Donald Trump Laugh?" (Savan 2016) and "Does Trump Know How to Laugh?" (Wagner 2016; on the other hand, see Gray 2016). The *Huffington Post*'s behind-the-scenes account of Comedy Central's *Roast of Donald Trump* provides further evidence. While most would imagine that participating in a roast, in which friends and comedians lovingly mock the guest of honor, is proof of Trump's sense of humor. Those involved, however, claim that he seemed to lack a sense of what is funny. "He would poll the people around him if they thought it was funny. He never really seemed to have a grasp on what was funny and why it was funny. He was always looking at others to validate if it was funny" (Libit 2016). To be fair, any nonprofessional would be nervous about how his or her performance were playing, but the problem seems deeper. Trump failed to understand the basic workings of jokes, such as the notion of a punchline and its importance. When reviewing the proposed jokes, he would think that some jokes were made funnier by removing the punchline itself. And when he was being roasted and one would typically laugh along in a self-deprecating manner, he did not. Instead, he grimaced or presented a tight-lipped smile that lacked the mirth found in the "Duchenne face" when a person is spontaneously and genuinely amused.

Of course, there have been those who have claimed he has a great sense of humor, but such claims are suspect. In the most notable example, Hope Hicks, White House spokesperson and eventual communications director (who subsequently stepped down), issued a statement asserting that the current president has a great sense of humor. In itself, this is already an extremely odd thing for the White House spokesperson to assert. Further, this is the statement of an employee about her employer, and therefore it lacks credibility. But the most damning material surrounds it: "President Trump has a magnetic personality and exudes positive energy, which is

[4] Franken resigned from the Senate because of a history of unwanted sexual advances. In one of these, he "jokingly" pretended to grope the breasts of a sleeping woman. He admitted that it was a failed attempt at humor, which is no justification. In his autobiography published soon before this, *Giant of the Senate*, he ironically discusses his hard-learned lesson that what strikes him as funny does not always make for good politics.

infectious to those around him. He has an unparalleled ability to communicate with people, whether he is speaking to a room of three or an arena of 30,000. He has built great relationships throughout his life and treats everyone with respect. He is brilliant with a great sense of humor ... and an amazing ability to make people feel special and aspire to be more than even they thought possible" (Borchers 2017). Prima facie false in many ways, this statement resembles the praise heaped by functionaries upon their Glorious Leader. One expects Hicks to continue by claiming that Trump eats the sun and drinks the sky. Others have claimed that, in less formal settings, Trump is quite charming and funny, but they have not provided any examples or other concrete evidence.

It is not true, however, to say Trump has no sense of humor. It is more accurate to say that he has a type of sense of humor that is particularly troubling for those in power. He did veto jokes at the Comedy Central roast. He insisted that there be no jokes about his bankruptcies, his level of wealth, or his hair—sources of personal pride, or at least insecurity. He is not willing to laugh at himself. According to observers, his primary concern is his self-aggrandizement. He needs to be the center of attention, not the butt of a joke. Recall his abiding fear that Mexico and China, among others, are laughing at us. This gelatophobia both motivates his foreign policy and allows Trump to appeal to the justified sense of social dismissal among his rural and working-class voters and unjustified sense of the same among white voters. Some have speculated that it was his revulsion at being laughed at by President Obama and the audience at the 2011 White House Correspondents Dinner that compelled him to run for president and regain his pride. (Trump denies this, however.)

Though Trump may fear others' laughter, he has no problem with being the one who mocks. His humor consistently comes from ridiculing others, crafting simple yet effective insults like Little Marco Rubio, Little Adam Schiff, Liddle Bob Corker, Crooked Hillary, Pocahontas (Elizabeth Warren), Rocket Man (Kim Jong Un), and Lyin' Ted Cruz. When he did pitch jokes for his roast, they were crass and aggressive, more direct insults than jokes exhibiting any craft or conceptual incongruity. The one confirmable case of his genuinely laughing in the past two years—and yes, people have searched—was when, at a campaign rally, a dog barked and someone in the crowd joked that it was Hillary Clinton. Trump does not laugh as an expression of the humility and sociability that is the mark of benevolent humor. His is only the scathing wit—or "wit," in this case—targeting women, the socially marginal, and those who criticize him. This sort of humor is quite dangerous in the hands of the powerful. But it does appeal to those who share his grievances and target the same marginal people.

There is another point regarding the current president's sense of humor that is important for the present argument. Humor allows for decommitment. By making something into a joke, we distance ourselves from what is being said. Jokes are not assertions of the truth, nor do they necessarily present the moral beliefs of the joker. This may be laudable, as it clears out a space solely for aesthetic pleasure not burdened by serious commitments or provides temporary distance from life's troubles. But this may be used to protect the ego of the joker. When jokers receive criticism or rejection, they can always say, "I was just joking." This tactic has been used frequently by the Trump administration in the face of criticism. To survey only some of the times that Trump has used this strategy during his first year in office, we find "jokes" that: Obama was the literal founder of ISIS (while explicitly stating that he was not joking), the Russian government should hack the Clinton campaign (which happened), U.N. ambassador Nikki Haley was easily replaceable, Health Secretary Tom Price would be fired if repeal of Obamacare failed (which happened), intelligence agencies leaking information was comparable to the situation in Nazi Germany, mocking a physically disabled reporter at a campaign rally, we need a "Second Amendment solution to Hillary Clinton," power allows men to grab women by their genitals without consequences, Putin had done the United States a favor by expelling our diplomatic officials, the police should rough up subjects when taking them into custody, and Democratic congressmen who did not applaud his State of the Union speech were committing treason (Graham 2017; Merica 2017a and 2017b; Merica and Acosta 2018). After receiving warranted criticism regarding the truthfulness or moral rightness of the claim, the president or his representatives walked it back with a "just joking" explanation or an assertion that it was just "locker room talk."[5] A particularly blunt example is when, after reportedly being called a "fucking moron," Trump challenged Secretary of State Rex Tillerson to a test of IQs. Despite the fact that there was no indication of humor, and a documented history of Trump both touting his purportedly high IQ and of seriously challenging people to IQ contests, Press Secretary Sarah Huckabee Sanders claimed that it was just a joke and chastised reporters, saying they "should get a sense of humor" (Shuham 2017).

In each case, the offered explanation provides an escape hatch through which those in power can avoid accountability to those they govern (Bump 2017). As nicely put by Dahlia Lithwick (2017), "'It was only a joke' has become the GOP and Donald Trump's equivalent of 'the dog ate my homework,' a catch-all defense for genuine gaffes and even for potential criminal obstruction of justice." Trump's administration, then, readily commits the sin that John Morreall warned us about: using (the claim of) humor to decommit the powerful from their own assertions in order to avoid criticism.

[5] Perhaps inspired by the president's "locker room talk," a politician in Greenwich, Connecticut, named Chris von Keyserling allegedly crowed that in this new world he no longer had to be politically correct, pinched a town employee in her groin, and informed her that no one would take her word over his. Once caught, he told a detective that he regretted his actions. He also, however, claimed that it was all just a joke and didn't understand why she would be offended (MacEachern 2017).

Such decommitment is particularly vicious when it conceals an underlying, ongoing, and shameful sincerity. Consider only one of the list of supposed jokes: Trump's speech to law-enforcement officers at Suffolk County Community College in which he said, "Like when you put somebody in a car and you're protecting their head, you know, the way you put their hand over? Like, don't hit their head and they've just killed somebody—don't hit their head. I said, you can take your hand away, okay?" (Merica 2017b). Taken literally, the head of state is encouraging police to engage in illegal brutality against untried suspects. This signals that police officers are not bound by the law. Of course, his spokespeople claimed that Trump was merely joking and should not be taken literally, but the administration's weakening of restrictions on law-enforcement officers, such as consent decrees, and a general rejection of established laws and norms belie the administration's claim of joking. It is a serious initiative wrapped in the decommitting appearance of a joke (Cobb 2017).

When the powerful play this game, it undercuts the notion that there are intersubjectively valid truths that ground politics. Consider yet another example. After touting unemployment figures early in the Trump administration at a March 10, 2017, press conference, Press Secretary Sean Spicer was asked how this fit with Trump's frequent dismissal of unemployment figures as "fake" when they spoke well of the Obama administration. How was is possible to know if Trump's assertions were true or sincere? Could the president be trusted? Spicer replied that the figures were no longer "phony" and that the president could always be trusted "if he's not joking, of course" (Graham 2017). Those in power cannot be trusted if they can unilaterally revoke anything they say after the fact by claiming they were joking, despite the fact that it is abundantly obvious that they never were. The problem, it was said of candidate Trump, was that the press (and other critics) were "taking him literally, but not seriously; his supporters take him seriously, not literally" (Zito 2016). Perversely, assuming the literal truth of a presidential candidate's statements had become a political liability and a sign of naiveté. This strategy is particularly powerful because those who express outrage or demand that truth be the foundation of social life are dismissed as humorless prigs. This is described as a "finger trap" that holds tighter the more one struggles against it. The only winning move then is not to play (Nussbaum 2017).

Having provided an example of when a sense of humor is politically vicious, let me now try to derive some general propositions about when it is politically virtuous.

3.2 Sociability and Humor

One of the distinguishing markers of a politically vicious sense of humor, then, is ridiculing fellow citizens and the socially marginal. Building social bonds, however, is one of the central functions of humor, understood in the narrow eighteenth-century British sense. This humor is affiliative humor. The sharing of a laugh makes people feel part of a shared activity. It produces a feeling of acceptance and equality. Consider the many times in life when laughing with others weakens social barriers and cultivates a sense that we are engaged in a common social life or common struggles. Affiliative humor nurtures a sense that we are laughing *with* rather than laughing *at*, and this is essential to social bonding. The capacity for certain styles of humor to promote such sociability is politically virtuous.

Aristotle dedicated sections of both the *Nicomachean Ethics* and the *Politics* to friendship (*philia*), a broad term ranging from application to those engaged in a common project to the more robust idea of those who genuinely delight in the virtue of a second self. One of the central questions of Aristotle's virtue ethics is whether it is possible to live an excellent life without friends, and he concludes that it is not. We are social beings who can exhibit virtue only in a robust community and with others who exhibit similar virtue. Interestingly, Aristotle asserts in one passage that friendship is a precondition of justice. We cannot discuss the just distribution of power and honor if the people are not first bound together in a community. And Aristotle further identifies the virtue of wittiness (*eutrapelia*), your ability to make others feel well without either compromising your dignity or being so attached to your dignity that you are unable to attend to others. He identifies the specific capacity of entertaining and kind words to serve sociability. Wittiness is conducive to friendship (which is a precondition for justice).

It is no coincidence that the delineation of humor from wit, and elevation of the former, arose during a period of rising egalitarianism. A prosocial bonhomie was seen as better suited to a time when political virtue included shared participation and mutual respect. Such humor is opposed to the hierarchy and competition believed to be present in the more cutting, and European, wit. As we still live in a liberal democracy, humor that supports liberal virtues of toleration and sociability are, then, of great value. It does not identify and vilify the other but shows us as fundamentally "in it together." In a time of stark political opposition among the citizenry and political elites (abetted by the mass media), in which bipartisanship or mutual respect is sorely lacking, the idea of laughing together has great appeal.

Though sociable humor is generally virtuous, it depends on the situation at hand. It can also be the foundation of perverse communities, as on sub-Reddits in which aggrieved or simply bored and angry young men mock fellow citizens just "for the lulz." This sort of humor is akin to a middle schooler who thinks it is funny to hold the finger near another's eye and repeatedly say "I'm not touching you" for the sole purpose of irritating the other. "Ironic" Nazis claim to reside in the country of "Kekistan" and engage in "shitposting" in which they harass people and derail conversations supposedly just for the joy of mocking established decencies. When met with resistance they ask, "U mad bro?" and claim to be surrounded by a world full of people with no sense of humor. This humor is affiliative, but in a way that ridicules and mocks anyone outside their community.

Therefore, one way that a sense of humor may be virtuous is when it cultivates a sense of equality and mutual affection among the citizenry. It is vicious when it establishes hierarchies and other artificial distinctions that undercut an environment of common purpose and mutual toleration. While this is particularly vicious when done by those in power, as it has greater effect, it is vicious between lay people as well. A Trumpian sense of humor that is harsh, divisive, and disingenuous is vicious, even when it is expressed in everyday interactions between citizens.

3.3 Prudence and Humor

While the central liberal political virtue is toleration, the central conservative one is prudence. Edmund Burke, the founder of modern conservatism, celebrated prudence in the wake of the Terror following the French Revolution. In his diagnosis, the Terror was the triumph of ideology over prudence—the practical wisdom that comes of a respect for both the limits of human reason and the historically proven institutions that would restrain and shape our fallen nature. We are ambitious by nature and need the "cloak of culture" to keep us from inflicting horror. Prudence is demanded particularly of political elites, who must see themselves as caretakers of an intergenerational trust.

Humor, admittedly, is not often seen as prudent. It is taken to be inherently foolish or disrespectful of the past and of established institutions and elites. It is more likely to be celebrated as a means of undercutting the powerful, not respecting them. It may, however, still be conducive to prudence as a political virtue. As highlighted above, humor (in the narrow sense) is closely associated with the virtue of transcendence. It allows us to cope with the struggles and indignities of life. It gives us a sense of perspective, a recognition that "this too shall pass" or "it could have been worse." A sense of humor also allows one to have a sense of perspective about oneself, to understand the limits of one's own power and the frequent foolishness of one's desires. Aided by the affiliative, social aspect of humor, we are able to see that we are not alone in our struggles and that others have survived. Humor has a critical role to play in self-transcendence, in "getting over ourselves." It is a form of humility.[6]

This awareness is conducive to prudence. Ideologues are not able to distance themselves from their own worldview, to see it wryly. If Burke is correct, politicians who would describe denying tens of millions access to health care as a celebration of freedom need to recognize both their underlying ambition and the limits of their own understanding (concealed as

---

[6] For more on a sense of humor and the virtue of self-transcendence, see Roberts 1988 and Lippitt 2005.

an ideological commitment to liberty). Of course, citizens and elites alike should fight for what they believe to be true, but they must also be able to have perspective—to acknowledge a world larger than their own ideology and to respect the ways that others and historical experience push back. Classical conservatism is then an anti-ideology, a recognition of concrete realities against philosophical abstractions.

Even those who are deeply committed to the truth of their beliefs must have the capacity to laugh at themselves, to overcome a dangerous self-seriousness. True political leaders understand that they are the custodians of an ongoing intergenerational covenant and their job is both to preserve and to incrementally change the fragile web of culture that reins in human ambition. Contrast this humility and prudence with the humor of the current U.S. president, whose sense of humor has no room for self-mockery.

Insofar as one's sense of humor leads one to disrespect established constitutional norms such as the separation of powers and universal suffrage, or democratic norms such as mutual respect and a commitment to moderate debate oriented toward truth, they have cast off Burke's cloak of culture that holds our democracy together. People who lack the capacity to laugh at themselves do not recognize their own limits; nor do people who cannot laugh at life's struggles. Therefore, a sense of humor that expresses the virtues of humility and transcendence is then politically virtuous insofar as it is conducive to prudence. If one's sense of humor is contemptuous of established norms, or if one lacks the ability to laugh at oneself, one will not be a good citizen or shepherd of the political community. This virtue is particularly important for someone in power.

3.4 Justice and Wit

The claim that pro-social humor is instrumental to political virtue is less controversial than the one that cutting, malicious, or dark forms of humor are. If humor promotes social bonds and respect for established institutions and the limits of one's desires and beliefs, wit and sarcasm do not. As I noted above, however, malicious humor can be turned to just ends in the form of satire, the form of humor that targets vice, typically in the form of ignorance or hypocrisy. While it is generally politically vicious to show malice toward fellow democratic citizens, institutions, and norms, it is sometimes essential if we are to protect them or force citizens and politicians to nurture them.

Unlike humor (narrowly defined), satire targets, excludes, and condemns in the interest of rooting out vice and improving the political community. While we would want citizens to be able to get over themselves, there are limits. We would not want them to shake their heads in bemusement when facing injustice. We want those in power to be held to account and citizens who have threatened the body politic to receive justice. Cutting humor has the critical role of enforcing social boundaries and calling rightful attention to wrongs. While we should not take excessive pleasure in punishing the vicious, cutting wit has a critical role to play in securing the essential political virtue of justice: ensuring that people get what they deserve. When political elites use humor, or claim that they were just joking, perhaps the most effective countermeasure is a wit that demands accountability. In the wake of Trump's election, the comedians have asked themselves what is demanded of them when political elites act without respect for democratic norms, or when they are unwilling to question themselves. It is no coincidence that there has been an explosion of viewership for satirical programs. In addition to the stalwart *Daily Show*, there are the unofficial spin-offs *Full Frontal* with Samantha Bee and *This Week Tonight* with John Oliver. The *Late Show with Stephen Colbert*'s ratings have spiked as Colbert has returned to the territory of the *Colbert Report*. Seth Meyer's "A Closer Look" segments on the *Tonight Show* target the current administration and have gone viral. Meanwhile, anodyne late-night hosts like Jimmy Fallon and James Corden have fallen behind. Satire has a vital role to play in ensuring that those who exhibit moral and intellectual vices like ignorance and hypocrisy, particularly those who would misuse humor to avoid accountability to citizens, must be called out (though satire is often misunderstood in a way that protects its targets from its sting, as when *Colbert Report* viewers were found to believe that Colbert was actually on their side, despite all evidence to the contrary).

This is not only the case for citizens speaking truth to power. The virtue of sociability or collegiality may lead to a welcome bipartisanship, but we also need former comedian and senator Al Franken's dedication of a chapter of his *Giant of the Senate* to his abiding hatred of his fellow senator Ted Cruz. We would want elites to use scathing humor in the defense of the marginal, as we see in the hilarious but caustic debates in the British Parliament. This bile, however, is kept in check by a sense of sociability and respect for long British tradition.

Wit, then, is not necessarily vicious. Even humor infused with anger or a desire to humiliate is politically virtuous when it has the right target. When it targets the innocent, particularly those on the margins of society, it is corrosive; but to expose and punish those who truly deserve to be is conducive to the primary political virtue of justice. Justice is often violent, but it is permissible so long as it is fair. A tendency of character to use humor in the appropriate way is then virtuous.

4. Conclusion

Humor, then, is conducive to political virtue in contrary ways, making it impossible to claim summarily that humor is or is not virtuous. Rather, there are various styles of humor that may be instrumental to certain political virtues under certain circumstances. Wit must not aggrandize the powerful and further marginalize the powerless. If a political elite uses cutting humor to mock a disabled reporter, it is not virtuous, as the target is undeserving of mockery, but it may be virtuous if turned on Ted Cruz. The capacity of affiliative humor to build social bonds is virtuous when it builds a tolerant political community, but not when it binds together alt-right Redditors and "ironic" Nazis. Humor is valuable when it allows us to recognize our own limits and to refrain from forcing others to submit to our ideological commitments, but not when it leads us to ignore injustice. In short, as with all discussions of virtue ethics, it comes down to practical wisdom—the ability to learn from experience and to judge the concrete situation at hand in its particularity. As Aristotle noted, the politically virtuous mean—where one's sense of humor genuinely is sociable, prudent, or just— is set by the context and the people at hand. Unless we are talking about Ted Cruz—then have at it.

References

Ando, Victoria, Gordon Claridge, and Ken Clark. 2014. "Psychotic Traits in Comedians." *British Journal of Psychiatry* 204, no. 5:341–45.

Beermann, Ursula, and Willibald Ruch. 2008. "How Virtuous Is Humor? What We Can Learn from Current Instruments." *Journal of Positive Psychology* 4, no. 1:528–39.

——. 2009. "How Virtuous Is Humor? Evidence from Everyday Behavior." *Humor* 22, no. 2:395–417.

Borchers, Callum. 2017. "This White House Statement on Trump's 'Positive Energy' Reads Like a Parody." *Washington Post*, May 30. Online at: https://www.washingtonpost.com/news/the-fix/wp/2017/05/30/this-white-house-statement-on-trumps-positive-energy-reads-like-a-parody/

Bump, Philip. 2017. "Out: Literal vs. Serious Interpretations of Trump's Comments. In: Joking vs. Not." *Washington Post*, March 13. Online at https://www.washingtonpost.com/news/politics/wp/2017/03/13/out-literal-vs-serious-interpretations-of-trumps-comments-in-joking-vs-not

Cobb, Jelani. 2017. "Donald Trump Is Serious When He 'Jokes' About Police Brutality." *New Yorker*, August 1. Online at: https://www.newyorker.com/news/news-desk/donald-trump-is-serious-when-he-jokes-about-police-brutality

Colby, Frank Moore. 1926. "Satire and Teeth." In *The Colby Essays*, 1:1–8. New York: Harper and Brothers.

Graham, David. 2017. "How Can You Tell Is Trump is Serious?" *Atlantic*, March 14. Online at https://www.theatlantic.com/politics/archive/2017/03/how-can-you-tell-if-the-white-house-is-serious/519564/

Gray, Freddy. 2016. "Donald Trump's Sense of Humour Might Win It for Him." *Spectator*, November 4. Online at https://blogs.spectator.co.uk/2016/11/donald-trumps-sense-humour-might-win/#

Kuiper, Nicholas, and Rod A. Martin. 1998. "Is Sense of Humor a Positive Personality Characteristic?" In *The Sense of Humor: Explorations of a Personality Characteristic*, edited by Willibald Ruch, 159–78. Berlin: Walter de Gruyter.

Lefcourt, Herbert M., and Rod A. Martin. 1986. *Humor and Life Stress: Antidote to Adversity*. New York: Springer.

Leibovich, Mark. 2016. "Al Franken Faces Donald Trump and the Next Four Years." *New York Times Magazine*, December 13, sec. MM, 50.

Libit, Daniel. 2016. "The Inside Story of Donald Trump's Comedy Central Roast Is Everything You Thought It Would Be." *Huffington Post*, October 16. Online at: https://www.huffingtonpost.com/entry/the-inside-story-of-donald-trumps-comedy-central-roast-is-everything-you-thought-it-would-be_us_57fbed42e4b0e655eab6c191

Lippitt, John. 2005. "Is a Sense of Humor a Virtue?" *Monist* 88, no. 1: 72–92.

Lithwick, Dahlia. 2017. "Constitutional Crisis of Comedy." *Slate*, May 25. Online at http://www.slate.com/articles/news_and_politics/jurisprudence/2017/05/mike_birbiglia_on_how_donald_trump_is_killing_comedy.html

MacEachern, Frank. 2017. "Cops: Greenwich Republican Insulted Town Worker, Then Pinched Her Groin." *Greenwich Daily Voice*, January 12. Online at http://greenwich.dailyvoice.com/police-fire/cops-greenwich-republican-insulted-town-worker-then-pinched-her-groin/696124/

Martin, Rod A. 1998. "Approaches to the Sense of Humor: A Historical Review." In *The Sense of Humor: Explorations of a Personality Characteristic*, edited by Willibald Ruch, 15–60. Berlin: Walter de Gruyter.

Merica, Dan. 2017a. "Inhofe: Trump's Reference to Nazi Germany Shows His 'Sense of Humor.'" CNN, January 12. Online at http://www.cnn.com/2017/01/12/politics/jim-inhofe-donald-trump-nazi-germany/index.html

———. 2017b. "Spokeswoman: Trump 'Joking' When He Told Police to Be 'Rough' on Suspects." CNN, July 31. Online at: http://www.cnn.com/2017/07/31/politics/white-house-police-tough-suspects/index.html

Merica, Dan, and Jim Acosta. 2018. "Trump Was 'Joking' When He Accused Democrats of Treason White House Says." CNN, February 6. Online at: https://www.cnn.com/2018/02/06/politics/treason-donald-trump-joking/index.html

Morreall, John. 2009a. *Comic Relief: A Comprehensive Philosophy of Humor*. Malden, Mass.: Wiley-Blackwell.

———. 2009b. "Humour and the Conduct of Politics." In *Beyond a Joke: The Limits of Humor*, edited by Sharon Lockyer and Michael Pickering, 63–78. Basingstoke: Palgrave Macmillan.

Nussbaum, Emily. 2017. "How Jokes Won the Election." *New Yorker*, January 23.

Roberts, Robert. 1988. "Humor and the Virtues." *Inquiry* 33, no. 2:127–49.

Ruch, Willibald. 2008. "Psychology of Humor." In *The Primer of Humor Research*, edited by Victor Raskin, 17–100. Berlin: Walter de Gruyter.

Savan, Leslie. 2016. "Have You Ever Seen Donald Trump Laugh?" *Nation*, September 26. Online at https://www.thenation.com/article/have-you-ever-seen-donald-trump-laugh/

Schmidt-Hidding, Wolfgang. 1963. *Humor und Witz*. Munich: Hueber.

Schwartz, Ben. 2015. "Satirized for Your Consumption." *Baffler* 27. Online at: https://thebaffler.com/salvos/satirized-consumption

Shuham, Matt. 2017. "White House: Trump IQ Test Challenge to Tiller-son was a 'Joke.'" *Talking Points Memo*, October 10. Online at http://talkingpointsmemo.com/livewire/sanders-trump-joke-iq-test-tillerson

Wagner, Alex. 2016. "Does Trump Know How to Laugh?" *Atlantic*, September 28. Online at https://www.theatlantic.com/politics/archive/2016/09/does-trump-know-how-to-laugh/501875/

Zito, Salena. 2016. "Taking Trump Seriously, Not Literally." *Atlantic*, September 23. Online at https://www.theatlantic.com/politics/archive/2016/09/trump-makes-his-case-in-pittsburgh/501335/

CHAPTER 10

CITIZENS' POLITICAL PRUDENCE AS A DEMOCRATIC VIRTUE

VALERIA OTTONELLI

Political prudence has an uneasy place in the theory of democracy. The rise of the democratic ideal in modern times has gone hand in hand with the recognition that the people at large were entitled to rule the polity, including those who had been kept in a state of political minority, like women and manual workers. Since Rousseau's famous dictum that only a "nation of Gods" could govern itself democratically, however, the history of democratic theory has also been punctuated with caveats about the actual ability and entitlement of the democratic people to jointly exercise executive powers. This seems to leave no room for vindicating the capacity of the members of a democratic public to exert political prudence, that is, act with the sense of opportunity, responsibility, and political insight that is the typical virtue of the statesmen who occupy executive positions. As a result, while the political prudence of democratic political leaders continues to be theorised, the exercise of political prudence by the ordinary citizens who compose a democratic public—let us call it "citizens' prudence"—has been almost completely neglected.[1]

This lack of theorisation about citizens' political prudence is problematic, as I argue in this essay, for at least three reasons. First, it provides a truncated account of democratic agency and of the responsibilities of a democratic people. Second, it fails to acknowledge the deep respect that democratic institutions as we know them pay to "ordinary citizens" as capable of political agency and of the kind of skills and virtues that in autocratic regimes are bestowed upon the few. Third, it makes us blind to

[1] Among the works theorising the political prudence of democratic political leaders, see Ackerman 1991; Ruderman 1997b; Rawls 1999; Philp 2007; and Overeem and Bakker 2016.

Connecting Virtues: Advances in Ethics, Epistemology, and Political Philosophy.
Edited by Michel Croce and Maria Silvia Vaccarezza.
Chapters and book compilation © 2018 Metaphilosophy LLC and John Wiley & Sons Ltd.

the possible curtailments of the institutional space and opportunities that we currently enjoy for exercising citizens' political prudence.

In order to find citizens' prudence we need to look in the right place. If the citizen of a large democracy is to exercise political prudence, it cannot be the same sort of virtue that is cultivated and theorised when government is conceived as a game for the few. Democracy is rule by the many. Indeed, a fundamental requirement and function of prudence in a democratic polity consists in taking into account the thoughts, actions, and feelings of millions of other people. Thus, political prudence, as exercised by the ordinary citizen of a democratic polity, will not have the decisionist, peremptory traits of the prudence of the solitary leader. Nevertheless, the exercise of citizens' prudence is a form of statesmanship, in that it pertains to political action properly understood and to the judgments and character traits required to find the most timely and responsible way to act in the circumstances of politics.

In this essay I aim to vindicate the importance of a theory of citizens' political prudence and try to sketch its main traits. I follow a reconstructive method, looking at the full range of powers and decisions that are enabled by democratic rights, and the kinds of activities that are usually performed by citizens under the protection of such rights, in order to show that there is room for the exercise of political prudence by ordinary citizens. By the same method, I also reconstruct the main traits and manifestations of citizens' prudence in the everyday politics of our democracies.

In the first section of the essay, I explain why we need a theory of citizens' political prudence by pointing at quintessentially democratic activities and rights that are otherwise left untheorised. In the second section, I rely on Weber's characterisation of the three components of the ethics of statesmanship—*passion, sense of proportion* and *responsibility*—in order to illustrate the place, uses, and importance of citizens' prudence in a democratic polity. In the third section, I defend the feasibility and relevance of a theory of citizens' political prudence. In the fourth and final section, I point to some important ways in which citizens' political prudence can be failed, both by institutions and by citizens.

Making Room for Citizens' Political Prudence in Democratic Theory

Political prudence is the eminent virtue attributed to the enlightened states-man by a long tradition of thought including Aristotle, Cicero, St. Thomas Aquinas, Edmund Burke, Thomas More, Max Weber, and many others (Dobel 1998; Coll 1991). In this tradition, political prudence does not sub-stitute for the speculative use of reason in theorizing about justice and the common good (Ruderman 1997a) but constitutes instead its pragmatic counterpart. The enlightened statesman who exercises political prudence, in fact, must be guided by an idea of justice and the good, but also must take action, by devising the proper means and ways to further justice and the common good in the troubled and capricious circumstances of political life (Nelson 2004). Therefore, political prudence is concerned not with what is absolute and universal but with what is best given a specific context and circumstances, including the feelings and actions of all the actors involved.

As already mentioned, this important tradition of thought about political prudence as the eminent virtue of statesmanship is still alive and well in current normative theories of democracy; however, notwithstanding the assumption that in a democracy it is the people who rule, theories of democratic prudence are almost exclusively concerned with the behaviour and responsibilities of professional politicians, rather than those of ordinary citizens.

The lack of theorisation about citizens' prudence can best be explained by three seemingly good reasons for adopting an economizing strategy in accounting for the virtues of democratic citizens. The first is a concern for feasibility. More than any other normative ideal, democracy must be feasible here and now; therefore, it cannot require citizens to possess virtues too difficult to cultivate or exercise. A second, related, reason is that modern democracies are complex representative regimes that call for a division of political labour along two main axes: first, between citizens as electors and their representatives; and, second, between law-making powers (exercised through representative institutions) and the powers exercised by those appointed in executive positions. Consequently, it may be felt that citizens need not themselves exercise the virtues that can be expected in professional politicians. Finally, an important reason for adopting an economizing strategy in accounting for the virtues of democratic citizens is a presumption against perfectionism that is shared by much contemporary political theory. An account of democracy that calls for special virtues, or—even worse— that is centred on those virtues as a fundamental component of human flourishing, risks alienating all those who want to keep democracy as open as possible to different lifestyles and conceptions of the good.

Of course, no normative theory of democracy can completely do without an account of ordinary citizens' virtues. Democratic rights protect forms of power and agency. Therefore, a theory of democracy, to the extent that it accounts for democratic rights, must provide some description of what citizens *do* in exercising those rights. And any such description must assume a picture of the pertinent forms of agency and of the virtuous ways of exercising them. Most current normative theories of democracy, however, do not count political prudence among the virtues of democratic citizens but rely instead on a seemingly less demanding, and more parsimonious, list of character traits and activities.

This exercise of parsimony, though, has a downside. In fact, if we look at how democratic government actually works in our societies, and at the full content of democratic rights and the activities that they enable, we may soon come to realise that such parsimonious theories of ordinary citizens' virtues are gravely incomplete.

Consider, for example, the popular account according to which democratic political rights are meant to enable citizens to have a say about their own good and goals (their "best interests," broadly understood) whenever decisions of collective relevance need to be made (Dahl 1989, 100). Following an established tradition in political philosophy, we could call the agency and skills thus protected a form of practical *rationality*, meaning by this the capacity to form and pursue a conception of the good. Such an account of the typical activities of a democratic citizen is parsimonious and uncontroversial, since it appeals merely to the virtues involved in the exercise of personal autonomy, as protected by civil rights. If, however, we think of the content of political rights and of what citizens do when they, for instance, exercise their right to vote, we realise that this kind of account leaves too much unexplained. If democracy were simply about exercising authoritative competence over one's own interests and goals when a decision of collective relevance needs to be made, voting rights or the other rights of political participation would seem utterly superfluous. A hearing procedure might suffice, such as a panel appointed with the task of consulting with all the affected parties and then making decisions based on the parties' declarations about their relevant interests and goals. Political rights, evidently, protect forms of action and decision making that exceed the mere authoritative expression of one's interests and goals (Richardson 2002, 63).

Indeed, some other theories of democracy provide a more ambitious account of what citizens do when they exercise their democratic rights. According to these theories, when democratic citizens vote, participate in public discussions, and otherwise affect the results of collective decision making, they are not simply authoritatively affirming their own ends and interests but are also entrusted with the task of devising a just balance between all the interests, goals, and values involved. Deliberative theories of democracy are especially well suited to account for this dimension of democratic agency. According to these accounts, in a democracy citizens are called to exercise not only rationality but also adequate "deliberative virtues" (Aikin and Clanton 2010; Grönlund, Setälä, and Herne 2010; Talisse 2007)—virtues that are essential to form judgments about what is just and in the interest of all, such as openness, reasonableness, concern for the common good, empathy, and charity.

Although much richer than the account of democratic rights as merely protecting the exercise of citizens' rationality, however, an account focused on the virtues that are needed for democratic deliberation still leaves out a host of activities, commitments, and decisions that are typically protected and made possible by democratic political rights. In a well-known essay on the democratic aspects of politics that exceed democratic deliberation, Michael Walzer has provided a rich list of activities that pertain to this further dimension of political agency (2005, 90–109). They include educating other people to a political faith; organizing campaigns, strikes, and other political events; mobilizing and "calling to arms" other people; demonstrating and other forms of political protest; lobbying; campaigning; fund-raising; and the work done by the rank and file engaged in party mobilisation. These are important ways in which the citizens of a democratic polity *act* when they fully exercise their political rights, as opposed to just declaring their own personal goals or debating about what is just and where the common good lies.

I suggest that we think of such activities as the proper space for the exercise of a form of political prudence. When engaging in them, citizens are called to make decisions about the right time, place, and manner of acting in the pursuit of their ideals of justice and the common good, taking into account all the relevant circumstances and facts that will affect the outcomes of their actions.

There are many authoritative characterisations of political prudence. In the next section, in order to illustrate how this notion can be applied to the ordinary citizens of a democratic polity, I rely on the famous account provided by Max Weber in his *Politics as Vocation* (Weber 2004).[2] Of all the classical accounts of political prudence, in fact, Weber's is one that most closely relates to the institutions of modern democracies, having been devised precisely in the context of an analysis of the transformations of political power in Western representative governments. Still, in Weber's account, as in most earlier theories of political prudence, there seems to be no room for the exercise of such virtue by ordinary citizens. In fact, Weber's analysis is exclusively centred on the conduct that should be expected from democratic political leaders. This makes the confrontation with Weber's account especially relevant for the purpose of advocating for the role of ordinary citizens' political prudence in the life of our democracies.

In the end, his lack of attention for citizens' prudence depends on the view Weber has of the nature of political power in a democratic society, which basically rules out the possibility of citizens participating in the steering of the polity (Breiner 1996; Shaw 2008; Klein 2017). In response to this stance, some critics have called for a deep transformation of democratic institutions in order make room for more participatory and direct forms of democracy (Warren 1988; Dryzek 1994; Breiner 1996). Instead, I want to suggest that Weber's account underappreciates the weight and significance of the already existing forms of political power that are institutionalised and exercised through democratic rights as we know them. Once we focus on such rights and the activities that they make possible, we naturally find room for the exercise of citizens' political prudence and realise that Weber's insightful analysis can also be applied to the citizens of our existing democracies; or so I shall argue.

[2] For recent readings of Weber's discussion of politics as a vocation as the expression of an ethical concern, see Cherniss 2016 and Satkunanandan 2014.

Ordinary Citizens as Statesmen: A Weberian Analysis

Weber's account of the virtuous traits of the prudent politician comprises three main qualities. The first is *passion* (Weber 2004, 76). Political passion is principled, genuine, and not self-interested. It is true devotion to a cause. Weber describes the appropriate passion as "down-to-earth," however; it is a steady commitment to a cause that can be translated into significant political action, as opposed to the "sterile excitement" of those in thrall to romantic vagaries or utopian thinking. We can see how passion, as Weber describes it, would be a virtuous trait of the professional politician. But how can we recognise this trait in the political action of ordinary citizens?

As a matter of fact, we do not need to look too far. At a basic—though far from trivial—level, this sort of political passion is displayed by the millions of citizens, in every democratic country, who cast a ballot in every political election or referendum. It is well known that this behaviour—especially in those countries where no sanctions for not voting are in place—cannot be explained by mere self-interest or short-term calculations about the impact of one's vote.[3] Instead, we can make sense of why people go out to vote if we assume that by voting people exhibit their commitment to their political ideals, along with their awareness that in a democracy changing the course of political events is a collective enterprise that can be achieved only by playing a cooperative game. In other words, it is only commitment to a cause and the sense of the appropriate kind of action that is needed to further it that can explain this apparently odd fact about democratic politics. As various scholars have recently remarked,[4] although much normative political theory appeals to the calm operation of citizens' deliberative reason, partisan spirit and adversarial confrontation between different voices in the political arena (Manin 2011; Leydet 2015) is in fact the salt of democratic politics. So, in short, it is a kind of Weberian passion that drives those citizens who join a party or a political movement, take part in political protests and demonstrations, or spend their time and resources in other ways meant to further the political goals they believe in.

All the forms of action that manifest this commitment to a political cause are made possible and protected by democratic rights, such as the right of association, freedom of speech and press, freedom of assembly, and the right to strike. It is important to note that all these are *freedom* rights, which leave up to citizens whether, when, and how to exercise the forms of political action the rights cover. This means that the relevant forms of action must be sparked by the initiative and passion of citizens themselves and can only be sustained if people cultivate their political passion with discipline, method, and a sense of what it takes to make their passion effective in the circumstances in which they live.

[3] For an insightful discussion, see Brennan and Lomasky 1989.
[4] Muirhead 2006; Rosenblum 2008 and 2014; White and Ypi 2016; Bonotti 2017.

The second Weberian virtue is a *sense of proportion* (Weber 2004, 77). What Weber had in mind is the ever-present danger that politicians, consumed with their passion and their sense of empowerment, might leave their vanity unchecked and forget that the political space is populated by other actors as well (Cherniss 2016). I suggest that the same sense of proportion, or perhaps an even more refined one, is exercised by the citizens of a democracy when they act in the public sphere. The sense of proportion, thus understood, is good judgment about when and by which means we can press a demand for justice or fight against our political opponents. It is not just a matter of strategic prudence; rather, it is inspired by other values and concerns, such as the worry that too aggressive an approach may be detrimental to peaceful coexistence within the political community, or that certain groups might feel humiliated or alienated by our political action. The exercise of this virtue by democratic citizens implies a consideration of the history of past relations between social and political groups and the sense that when we act in the public sphere, in a democracy, we usually do so as members of larger groups and as representatives of a political identity.

There are cases in which a just cause needs not to be pressed too harshly or needs to be postponed, because doing otherwise would disrupt a hard-earned equilibrium with other social forces or because it would steal the scene from legitimate demands coming from other social groups, thus undermining their chances of success (Rawls 1999, 328). On the other hand, there are also times when the citizens of a democratic society need to decide that it is time to act and demonstrate their commitment to a cause, even if this is going to spark social conflict or is likely to be fruitless in instrumental terms (Boxill 1976). In both cases, political action should be guided not only by one's sense of justice only but also by due reflection about one's own political position within the polity and relations to political allies and opponents (LaVaque-Manty 2002, 165–66). In this sense, political action requires detachment and a sense of proportion.

One might think that this political quality pertains exclusively or primarily to a few prominent political characters, such as the leaders of social movements, trade unions, and organised advocacy groups, who can initiate a protest and coordinate it. This, however, obscures the fundamental fact that such prominent characters may call for political action but it is up to ordinary citizens, individually, to decide whether they will answer the call. The democratic rights of association, assembly, and speech give citizens the power to decide how, when, and where they want to step up and make their claims heard, under which political identity they want to do so, and which political partners they want to associate with. In these actions democratic rights recognise and make possible the exercise of this important component of political prudence.

Finally, the third important trait of statesmanship, according to Weber, is *responsibility* (2004, 83). As is well known, the sense of responsibility Weber advocates accounts for an essential moral dimension of politics;

however, it rejects the morality of absolute principles in order to take into account the implications of one's actions in the world as it is, with all of its complexities and imperfections, and above all the presence of other actors with their own goals and ends. One might think that the exercise of this sense of responsibility is only proper among those who are in power and hold institutional roles, and therefore are entrusted with important and immediate executive decisions. But in fact if we think of the power political rights bestow on citizens, we realise that citizens are recognized as having an enormous responsibility in steering the course of political events. Typically, for example, when we decide for whom to vote we have in view not only our own preferences and values but the overall consequences of electoral results as well. We need to be careful, for instance, not to "waste" our vote on irrelevant political parties when it could be more efficiently employed otherwise; and, conversely, we need to be careful not to leave important political claims unvoiced only because of the risk of the "wasted vote." We need to consider not only what our values and preferences are, and even not only what would be the best for our polity, but also the expectations and possible reactions of other political actors, including foreign countries that have a stake in our internal political order. Finally, we need to keep an eye on the balance of political power among different political parties. Even when, in a given election, one of the candidates or programs is obviously better than the others, voters may not give all their votes to the best one, not only because of entrenched political loyalties but also because that would give the winning party enormous power and might upset the balance within the polity (Cox 1997, 196).

The right to vote and other political rights are designed to make the exercise of this sense of responsibility possible. During political campaigns, citizens collect and exchange information about the best strategic use of their vote, that is, data that help them decide not only what is best from the point of view of absolute justice or their personal goals but also what is best all things considered and taking into account other people's actions. In this sense, citizens vote strategically in most elections: their vote does not reflect their genuine preferences and their "ethics of principles" but reflects what they think will be the best result overall (Cox 1997, 80–96, 11–21). Political parties and other forms of political mobilisation play an essential role in making this strategic action possible: they are essential agents of coordination and a source of information about other people's intended actions (Dewan and Myatt 2007).

Two important points should be made about citizens' political prudence. First, democratic political agency displays a special and distinctive feature that should be taken into account in adapting Weber's analysis to our purposes. Being focused on the virtues of professional politicians, Weber's account does not consider the complex problems of coordination and collective action that democratic citizens need to face and solve in exercising their democratic rights. Modern democracy is a game played by the masses, in which individual actors can have a relevant role only to the extent they can coordinate their actions with those of millions of others or are able to influence the way those others act. Therefore, although citizens' prudence is a virtue exercised by individuals, it calls each one to take into account the actions and feelings of large numbers of others. This adds an important and distinctive element of complexity to all three components of political prudence. Democratic citizens can only develop political passion in association with others and by relying on shared meanings and values (Kingston 2011); they can only exercise a sense of proportion as members of larger social and political groups that can have an impact on the political scene; and the exercise of their sense of responsibility, for example when they vote, requires the capacity to forecast the actions of large numbers of people and to coordinate one's actions with theirs.

A second and related remark is that although citizens' prudence concerns a central dimension of political agency in a democratic society, it does not substitute for the other virtues and forms of agency allowed by the exercise of democratic rights that we mentioned earlier, that is, the selfregarding rationality exercised in issuing authoritative judgments about one's well-being and interests, and the reasonableness and other virtues exercised in democratic deliberation. Rather, it shapes their meaning and exercise. In fact, citizens' prudence concerns, among other things, the right time, manner, and place for engaging in fair-minded reasoning or for pressing one's interests within the public sphere. This means that it would be wrong to oppose citizens' prudence to the virtues exercised in democratic deliberation or the pursuit of one's interests. Instead, citizens' prudence guides and constrains the exercise of the other dimensions of democratic political agency.

The Relevance of Citizens' Political Prudence for Democratic Theory

The reconstruction of the exercise of political prudence by ordinary citizens offered in the last section is not meant to provide a full-fledged and complete theory, only to point to some obvious and relevant ways in which such a virtue manifests itself in the life of democratic polities and demands our theoretical attention. If we look at these activities and uses of democratic political powers by ordinary citizens, we realise that they call for subtle, skilful, and difficult deployments of epistemic faculties and practical reason in the challenging circumstances of politics, which surely exceed the simple use of rationality or of the "deliberative virtues" that are needed if citizens are to participate in discursive exchanges in the public sphere. Yet, it is important to stress that a theory of democratic political prudence, though surely more complex and demanding than the accounts based on rationality or deliberative reasonableness, does not need to overlook the legitimate reasons for caution that were recalled at the beginning of our discussion: namely, the concern for feasibility, the acknowledgment of the division of powers in a modern representative democracy, and the need to avoid perfectionism.

In fact, the exercise of citizens' prudence considered in the last section must surely be feasible, because it is experienced in the everyday life of existing democracies. This does not mean that ordinary citizens are always exercising the virtue of political prudence; it means instead that there is room for exercising it even in the actual circumstances of democratic politics, although such an exercise, as happens with all virtues, can be difficult and requires training and education.

The exercise of citizens' political prudence is also compatible with the division of political labour in modern democracies, since it does not imply that citizens appropriate the powers of their representatives or of the members of the executive bodies of government. In fact, citizens' prudence pertains to the places and circumstances in which citizens exercise their political rights and the powers they have qua "ordinary" citizens.

Finally, the analysis above does not involve a commitment to a perfectionist view of democratic politics, nor to political activism as a worthwhile task per se. Surely, citizens' prudence requires a certain dose of political passion among citizens without which democratic institutions could not survive, as also many non-perfectionist liberal theories have come to acknowledge. This does not imply, however, that politics is a fundamental component of human good, nor does it automatically translate into a strict mandate of civic engagement at all times. In fact, the appeal to citizens' political prudence, as compared with the usual lists of duties and imperatives addressed to the citizens of a democratic polity, broadens the scope of the considerations that citizens are meant to take into account in deciding how to act in the exercise of their political rights. Among the things that citizens are left to decide, given the leeway granted by political prudence, is how much engagement in politics is required in given circumstances and with consideration of their other interests and goals.

Even if citizens' prudence is neither unduly demanding nor unrealizable nor disruptive of the democratic division of political labour, we may still be left with two other reasons for worrying that theorizing such virtue might just be an idle exercise. The first worry is that there might be no need for a unified theory that collects all the forms of political agency considered in the last section under the one and common label of "political prudence." Could not we just say that citizens need, for example, passion in pursuing their ideals of justice, respect for other political agents, and mindfulness in exercising their right to vote in a referendum? In response to this question, two answers can be offered. The first is that to the extent that citizens' prudence can be seen as a special kind of political prudence, it must be conceived as a single—although complex—virtue. As Weber's analysis clearly illustrates, the various components of political prudence (passion, sense of proportion, and responsibility) can be conceptually separated for the sake of analytical clarity, but they need to operate in close connection to one another. Where they do not operate in a coordinated manner, they may not even be virtuous. This is the reason they must be seen as components of a unified virtue, rather than as a collection of separate virtues. The second reason for seeing political prudence as a single virtue is that applies to a specific and unified sphere of action, that is, the exercise of democratic political rights. This also points to what is distinctive of political prudence as opposed to other virtues that we exercise in the social sphere, including those that are essential to the life of a democratic society, like integrity, honesty, open-mindedness, and a certain degree of benevolence. Unlike these other important civic virtues, citizens' prudence specifically pertains to the exercise of citizen's institutional political rights and powers. It concerns citizens as rulers, rather than simply as members of the polity.

A second worry is that citizens' prudence might be only contingently required, given the actual configuration of democratic political rights, while being substantially endogenous to the democratic ideal. In other words, it might simply *happen* that in our democracies people have room to exercise political prudence, but perhaps different institutional and electoral arrangements could spare them this effort while still—or better—fulfilling the goals that a democracy is supposed to serve. Of course, the response to this objection essentially depends on the conception of democracy one wants to embrace. There is, however, a fundamental reason for thinking that the room that is currently available for the exercise of citizens' prudence is not just an accidental feature of existing democratic regimes. In fact, democracy has emerged as the political regime that recognises all the members of the polity as not only entitled to but also capable of political rule. The progressive advancement of democracy in modern times has been marked by the extension of the franchise and other political rights to categories of subjects—such as women, manual workers, and the propertyless—that in earlier times were seen as incapable of the wisdom and independence of judgment required for governing. This is to say that the fact that democratic political rights, as they are currently shaped in advanced democracies, leave ample room for the exercise of political prudence is not a contingent fact about actual democratic regimes; rather, it is one way in which they instantiate the ideal of democracy as the exit from a "state of political minority" for all members of the polity.

How Citizens' Prudence Can Fail to Be Properly Exercised

Theorizing citizens' political prudence is important not only because it makes us see its value and relevance in the life of a democratic polity but also because it allows us to detect and acknowledge cases in which it fails to be properly exercised, which cannot be accounted for simply in terms of a lack of adequate civic virtues, deliberative competence, or rationality.

A recent, striking example of a failure in the exercise of citizens' prudence is the voting behaviour of some sectors of the United Kingdom public in the Brexit referendum. Of course, whether the decision to exit the European Union was a good one is a matter of controversy, but we can leave this question aside for our purposes. What is directly relevant, instead, is that right after the vote, apparently, many people regretted their decision (Dearden 2016). Some of those who did not show up at the polls, and some of those who voted "leave" as a form of protest, confessed that they had wrongly underestimated the chances that "leave" could win (Allegretti 2016). But some of those who voted "remain" likewise repented, after realising that in the aftermath of the election the high percentage of remain votes gave rise to political unrest and a sense of deep division in the people (Piggott 2016). In sum, many British voters felt that they should have had a better grasp of the political climate and of the feelings of their fellow citizens, because they miscalculated the impact of their own vote. This cannot be accounted for in terms of a failed judgment about their own interests or as a failure of their virtues of reasonableness as participants in democratic deliberation; the virtue they failed to adequately exercise is instead political prudence.[5] Typical examples of the same kind of failure can be seen in cases of hung parliaments and other circumstances in which an elected assembly, due to the existing balance of political forces, cannot operate. Recently, for example, Belgium was left without government for almost two years, and Spain had to repeat elections twice, in 2015 and 2016, because of the impossibility of forming a stable executive. These circumstances are often commented upon as though they were simply due to the political makeup of the nation, to a malfunctioning electoral system, or to the short-sightedness of political parties. Many cases, however, might also be viewed as major failures of political prudence by citizens who did not manage to cast their votes in a way that could have ensured greater political stability.[6]

Other patent failures of citizens' prudence concern the capacity of citizens to realise the right time, and the right way, to mobilise for their cherished political goals. A recent case in point is a sudden campaign against surrogate pregnancy that was sparked by some women's associations in Italy in 2015, at a time when a very troubled law on the rights of gay couples was being debated in the Italian parliament (Cuzzocrea 2015). No matter what one thinks about the issues at stake, the timing of the campaign was unfortunate. The two issues, which in the intentions of the advocacy groups involved had to be kept separate, became inextricably intermingled in the public debate, and the veto on surrogate pregnancy ended up being

---

[5] As I mentioned earlier, although the effects of imprudent voting behaviour are cumulative in that they depend on the actions of large numbers of people, the burden of exercising political prudence still falls on each and every individual voter, as evidenced by the feeling of personal regret that people sometimes feel after elections.

[6] I am assuming here that in these circumstances political instability is not a welcome result. Of course, we may conjecture that there are also cases in which political prudence suggests promoting political instability.

perceived as a way to hinder the passing of the law on the legal status of gay couples. The history of social movements in Western democracies contains many examples of the same sort, in which bad timing and formulation of political protest create troublesome oppositions between minorities in the public space, to the detriment of all parties involved.[7]

Citizens' prudence can fail in its exercise not only on the side of citizens but also, and even more importantly, on the side of political institutions, to the extent that they reduce the room for its exercise or undermine the conditions necessary for exercising it.

Consider, for example, the case of compulsory voting (Hill 2011; Elliott 2017). It is difficult to explain what gets lost when this measure is adopted if we rely only upon the idea that by voting people give voice to their interests and goals, or exercise their deliberative virtues. Neither activity is restrained by compulsory voting. Of course, one might object to the fact that compelling people to vote is an infringement of their freedom, but the question remains: assuming that voting can be made no more than a minor hindrance to other activities and freedoms one wants to pursue, what can be the value of the freedom *not* to vote? One way to make sense of the idea that—whatever one might think of the overall balance of reasons for and against making voting mandatory—something does get lost when people have that freedom taken away is to think of it in terms of an abridgment of the power to exercise citizens' prudence. In fact, when people are left to decide whether or not to show up at the polls, they are given the freedom to ponder the circumstances of their action: whether it is worthwhile, whether they should contribute to a high turnout or should instead signal a disaffection for the issues at stake, and how this responds to their specific political commitments and goals (Lever 2010). Of course, even when the vote is mandatory people still have a way to manifest their dissent and their opinion; however, they lose an important dimension of their power to decide how to engage with electoral politics at a given time, which is one of the ways in which political prudence is exercised.

Another less evident, but even more important, example of how democratic institutions can fail to support—or can short-circuit—political prudence is to be found in some proposals to institute randomly selected deliberative bodies of "lay citizens" as a substitute or guidance for the electoral powers of the democratic public (Fung 2003; Gastil and Richards 2013; Smith and Ryan 2014). Such "mini-publics" can take many forms and play various functions. In some popular versions, they are supposed to enhance the deliberative competence of ordinary citizens by shielding them from the undue influences of political rhetoric, social power, cultural biases, and money, by creating a safe haven in which the reason of the

---

[7] The literature on political intersectionality, for example, reports many cases in which the mobilisation of minorities may harm the cause of sub-minorities or other social groups; for recent overviews, see Verloo 2013 and Cole 2008.

people can calmly operate (Smith and Ryan 2014, 21). In doing so, how-ever, these institutional devices also excuse the "ordinary citizens" involved from the strategic, consequentialist, and contextual considerations that per-tain to the everyday exercise of politics. Therefore, to the extent that they are supposed to serve as a model and guidance for how ordinary citizens at large should engage with democratic decision making, these proposals shrink the space for the exercise of citizens' prudence, and may be seen as a way in which institutions can fail that important democratic virtue.[8]

These examples of how institutions can fail to support citizens' pru-dence might raise a fundamental objection, especially if considered along with the examples of how citizens can fail in exercising the same virtue. In fact, both mandatory voting and mini-publics can be taken to be extreme remedies against the systematic ill use of political prudence by the demo-cratic public. We know that in many countries it is not careful consideration of the political circumstances but social and economic determinants, such as education and age, that keep people away from polls (Lijphart 1997; Schlozman, Verba, and Brady 2012). We also know that the democratic public is very far from cultivating an adequate deliberative competence, and this is due not to an astute calculation of the pros and cons of public delib-eration in selected circumstances but to structural failures within the public sphere, which make citizens fall prey to meaningless catchphrases, sound bites, and slogans (Habermas 1989 and 2006; Fishkin 1995). So, what is really lost when the institutional space for the exercise of citizens' prudence is curbed?

In reply to this objection, and by way of a general conclusion to our discussion, we need to consider three points. First, our perception of the failures of citizens' prudence is likely to be exaggerated. As a matter of fact, citizens *do* exercise their political prudence, and there are plenty of examples of prudent behaviour in the recent history of our democracies, participating in elections being just the most obvious instance. Focusing on the failures of citizens' prudence should help us see how important it is that this virtue be recognized and cultivated; existing failures should not make us lose sight of the many silent, but important, ways in which this virtue is exercised in the everyday life of our democracies.

Secondly, the fact that citizens can fail to exercise political prudence does not mean that they should not enjoy the freedom to exercise it. The possibility of failure, in fact, is constitutive of all freedom and autonomy rights: the value of their exercise lies exactly in the fact that they allow us to choose between good and bad courses of action; this is how they establish us as competent moral agents. To the extent that democratic political rights

[8] This is not necessarily the case. Indeed, in some interpretations of the role of mini-publics, they can also be used strategically by some sections of the public (Lafont 2017); in others, ordinary citizens at large are called to judge whether and when to trust these devices (MacKenzie and Warren 2012). In both cases, mini-publics provide further opportunities for the use of citizens' prudence, rather than curbing it.

establish citizens as competent political agents, we need to take failures as evidence of the importance and value of the activities at stake, rather than as grounds for withdrawing the rights that enable such activities.

Finally, and relatedly, once we see the importance and value of the exercise of citizens' prudence, we should also see that when the appropriate conditions for its exercise are not in place, as when people lack relevant information or adequate education, the suppression of the institutional room for its exercise should be a remedy of last resort, to be applied only when all other plausible remedies have failed. The exercise of citizens' prudence should be feasible under the normal conditions of a representative regime. This does not require radical changes in existing rights and institutions, but it requires that the social and economic conditions needed for the full enjoyment of political rights be secured.

Acknowledgments

I am extremely grateful to Mikael M. Karlsson for his detailed and insightful comments and for invaluable conversations on the topic of citizens' political prudence. I also wish to thank Enrico Biale, Federico Zuolo, and the two editors of this collection for their very helpful suggestions on previous versions of this essay.

References

Ackerman, Bruce. 1991. *We the People, Volume 1: Foundations.* Cambridge, Mass.: Harvard University Press.

Aikin, Scott F., and J. Caleb Clanton. 2010. "Developing Group-Deliberative Virtues." *Journal of Applied Philosophy* 27, no. 4:409–24.

Allegretti, Aubrey. 2016. "The Brexit-Backers Who Regret Not Voting Remain after the EU Referendum Results." *Huffington Post,* 24 June 2016. Available at http://www.huffingtonpost.co.uk/entry/brexit-backers -change-vote-remain-eu-referendum_uk_576d37f9e4b0d25711498bb5 (last accessed 16 October 2017).

Bonotti, M. 2017. *Partisanship and Political Liberalism in Diverse Societies.* Oxford: Oxford University Press.

Boxill, Bernard. 1976. "Self-Respect and Protest." *Philosophy and Public Affairs* 6, no. 1:58–69.

Breiner, Peter. 1996. *Max Weber and Democratic Politics.* Ithaca, N.Y.: Cornell University Press.

Brennan, Geoffrey, and Loren E. Lomasky. 1989. *Politics and Process.* Cambridge: Cambridge University Press.

Cherniss, Joshua L. 2016. "An Ethos of Politics Between Realism and Idealism." *Journal of Politics* 78, no. 3:705–18.

Cole, Elizabeth R. 2008. "Coalitions as a Model for Intersectionality: From Practice to Theory." *Sex Roles* 59, nos. 5–6:443–53.

Coll, Alberto R. 1991. "Normative Prudence as a Tradition of Statecraft." *Ethics and International Affairs 5*, no. 1:33–51.

Cox, Gary W. 1997. *Making Votes Count*. Cambridge: Cambridge University Press.

Cuzzocrea, Annalisa. 2015. "Femministe contro la maternità surrogata: Non è un diritto." *La Repubblica*, 4 December 2015. Available at http://www.repubblica.it/cronaca/2015/12/04/news/femministe_contro_l_utero_in_affitto_non_e_un_diritto_-128746486/ (last accessed 14 October 2016).

Dahl, Robert A. 1989. *Democracy and Its Critics*. New Haven: Yale University Press.

Dearden, Lizzie. 2016. "Anger over 'Bregret.'" *Independent*, 25 June 2016. Available at http://www.independent.co.uk/news/uk/politics/brexit-anger-bregret-leave-voters-protest-vote-thought-uk-stay-in-eu-remain-win-a7102516.html (last accessed 14 October 2017).

Dewan, Torun, and Myatt David P. 2007. "Leading the Party: Coordination, Direction and Communication." *American Political Science Review* 101, no. 4:827–45.

Dobel, J. Patrick. 1998. "Political Prudence and the Ethics of Leadership." *Public Administration Review* 58, no. 1:74–81.

Dryzek, John. 1994. *Discursive Democracy*. Cambridge: Cambridge University Press.

Elliott, Kevin J. 2017. "Aid for Our Purposes: Mandatory Voting as Precommitment and Nudge." *Journal of Politics* 79, no. 2:656–69.

Fishkin, James S. 1995. *The Voice of the People*. New Haven: Yale University Press.

Fung, Archon. 2003. "Recipes for Public Spheres: Eight Institutional Design Choices and Their Consequences." *Journal of Political Philosophy* 11, no. 3:338–67.

Gastil, John, and Robert Richards. 2013. "Making Direct Democracy Deliberative Through Random Assemblies." *Politics and Society* 41, no. 2:253–81.

Grönlund, Kimmo, Maija Setäla, and Kaisa Herne. 2010. "Deliberation and Civic Virtue: Lessons from a Citizen Deliberation Experiment." *European Political Science Review* 2, no. 1:95–117.

Habermas, Jürgen. 1989. *The Structural Transformation of the Public Sphere*. Cambridge: Polity Press.

——. 2006. "Political Communication in Media Society." *Communication Theory* 16, no. 4:411–26.

Hill, Lisa. 2011. "Increasing Turnout Using Compulsory Voting." *Politics* 31, no. 1:27–36.

Kingston, Rebecca. 2011. *Public Passion*. Montreal: McGill-Queen's University Press.

Klein, Steven. 2017. "Between Charisma and Domination." *Journal of Politics* 79, no. 1:179–92.

Lafont, Cristina. 2017. "Can Democracy Be Deliberative and Partic-
ipatory? The Democratic Case for Political Uses of Mini-Publics."
Daedalus 146, no. 3:85–105.
LaVaque-Manty, Mika. 2002. *Arguments and Fists.* London: Routledge.
Lever, Annabelle. 2010. "Compulsory Voting: A Critical Perspective."
British Journal of Political Science 40, no. 4:897–915.
Leydet, Dominique. 2015. "Partisan Legislatures and Democratic Deliber-
ation." *Journal of Political Philosophy* 23, no. 3:235–60.
Lijphart, Arend. 1997. "Unequal Participation: Democracy's Unresolved
Dilemma." *American Political Science Review* 91, no. 1:1–14.
MacKenzie, Michael, and Mark Warren. 2012. "Two Trust-Based Uses of
Minipublics in Democratic Systems." In *Deliberative Systems,* edited by
John Parkinson and Jane Mansbridge, 95–124. Cambridge: Cambridge
University Press.
Manin, Bernard. 2011. "Comment promouvoir la délibération démo-
cratique?" *Raisons politiques* 42, no. 2:83–113.
Muirhead, Russell. 2006. "A Defense of Party Spirit." *Perspectives on
Politics* 4, no. 4:713–27.
Nelson, Eric Sean. 2004. "Moral and Political Prudence in Kant." *Interna-
tional Philosophical Quarterly* 44, no. 3:305–19.
Overeem, Patrick, and Femke E. Bakker. 2016. "Statesmanship Beyond
the Modern State." *Perspectives on Political Science.* DOI: 10.1080/
10457097.2016.1229563.
Philp, Mark. 2007. *Political Conduct.* Cambridge, Mass.: Harvard Univer-
sity Press.
Piggott, Mark. 2016. "Brexit Regrets? Yes, I Wish I Had Voted 'Leave.'"
Spectator, 5 July 2016. Available at https://blogs.spectator.co.uk/2016/
07/brexit-regrets-yes-wish-id-voted-leave/ (last accessed 16 October
2017).
Rawls, John. 1999. *The Law of Peoples.* Cambridge, Mass.: Harvard Uni-
versity Press.
Richardson, Henry S. 2002 *Democratic Autonomy.* Oxford: Oxford Univer-
sity Press.
Rosenblum, Nancy L. 2008. *On the Side of the Angels: An Appreciation of
Parties and Partisanship.* Princeton: Princeton University Press.
———. 2014. "Partisanship and Independence: The Peculiar Moralism of
American Politics." *Critical Review of International Social and Political
Philosophy* 17, no. 3:267–88.
Ruderman, Richard S. 1997a. "Aristotle and the Recovery of Political
Judgment." *American Political Science Review* 91, no. 2:409–20.
———. 1997b. "Democracy and the Problem of Statesmanship." *Review of
Politics* 59, no. 4:759–88.
Satkunanandan, Shalini. 2014. "Max Weber and the Ethos of Politics
Beyond Calculation." *American Political Science Review* 108, no. 1:
169–81.

Schlozman, Kay Lehman, Sidney Verba, and Henry E. Brady. 2012. *The Unheavenly Chorus: Unequal Political Voice and the Broken Promise of American Democracy*. Princeton: Princeton University Press.

Shaw, Tamsin. 2008. "Max Weber on Democracy: Can the People Have Power in Modern States?" *Constellations* 15, no. 1:34–45.

Smith, Graham, and Matthew Ryan. 2014. "Defining Mini-Publics: Making Sense of Existing Conceptions." In *Deliberative Mini-Publics: Involving Citizens in the Democratic Process*, edited by Kimmo Grönlund, André Bächtiger, and Maija Setälä, 9–26. Colchester: ECPR Press.

Talisse, Robert B. 2007. "Why Democrats Need the Virtues." In *Aristotle's Politics Today*, edited by Lenn E. Goodman and Robert B. Talisse, 45–52. Albany: State University of New York Press.

Verloo, Mieke. 2013. "Intersectional and Cross-Movement Politics and Policies." *Signs* 38, no. 4:893–915.

Walzer, Michael. 2005. *Politics and Passion*. New Haven: Yale University Press.

Warren, Mark. 1988. "Max Weber's Liberalism for a Nietzschean World." *American Political Science Review* 82, no. 1:31–50.

Weber, Max. 2004. *The Vocation Lectures*. Indianapolis: Hackett.

White, Jonathan, and Lea Ypi. 2016. *The Meaning of Partisanship*. Oxford: Oxford University Press.

CHAPTER 11

HOPE AS A DEMOCRATIC CIVIC VIRTUE

NANCY E. SNOW

Introduction

As a framework for reflecting about hope as a civic virtue, the past ten years of American presidential politics have been, to say the least, interesting. Barack Obama published a book entitled *The Audacity of Hope: Thoughts on Reclaiming the American Dream* in 2006, and in 2008 he campaigned for president on the promise of hope. In his presidential campaign of 2016, Donald J. Trump reversed that vision, sowing chaos and despair. The front cover of the October 15–21, 2016, issue of the *Economist* (2016b) depicted a red, white, and blue elephant with a questioning look on its face at one end and the profile of Trump on the rump with the headline "The Debasing of American Politics." The front cover of the November 5–11, 2016, issue (*Economist* 2016a) depicted a hand with fingers crossed and a sketch of Hillary Clinton's face on one finger, accompanied by the headline "America's Best Hope." After the election, on the front cover of its March 2017 issue, the *Atlantic* featured a sketch of Trump addressing a crowd with the headline "How to Build an Autocracy."[1] Many people, in commentaries in the news and on social media, express the view that American democracy is imperiled by the Trump administration.

Fears for democracy in America have been accompanied by similar worries in other countries. Far-right political parties in the United Kingdom and Europe have gained traction, in part from Trump's ascendancy, and their clout has caused some mainstream political candidates to lean toward the right.[2] Russia's meddling in the U.S. election has given rise to qualms

---

[1] The *Atlantic*'s March 2017 cover took its title from a story in that issue by David Frum.
[2] See, for example, Marcus Walker (2017, A8), who discusses the Dutch prime minister Mark Rutte's populist pivot as he faces challenges from the far-right candidate Geert Wilders.

Connecting Virtues: Advances in Ethics, Epistemology, and Political Philosophy.
Edited by Michel Croce and Maria Silvia Vaccarezza.
Chapters and book compilation © 2018 Metaphilosophy LLC and John Wiley & Sons Ltd.

that it will interfere in elections in other nations, for example, in France.[3] As Alan Mittleman remarks: "A new dark ages may be in the offing" (2009, 269–70).[4]

Yet some bright spots are worth noting. Federal judges stopped both versions of Trump's travel ban, most recently on the grounds that it would likely not survive a challenge to its constitutionality (see Kendall and Lovett 2017, A1, A8; Kendall 2017, A4; Liptak 2017, A1, A13). The far-right One Nation party garnered less than 5 percent of the vote in elections in the state of Western Australia, contributing to a conservative party loss (see Pannett and Cherney 2017, A9). Geert Wilders, the far-right candidate in the Netherlands, did not prevail in the Dutch election (see Pop and Walker 2017, A10, and Rubin 2017b). Remarking on the victory of the center-right candidate, Prime Minister Mark Rutte, a Dutch citizen stated: "In Europe we all see the developments in the United States, and that's not where we want to go because we see it as chaos" (qtd. in Rubin 2017a, A4). A recent article in the *Wall Street Journal* takes the view that the populist approach on the European continent of riding the wave in the light of Trump's election and Brexit has backfired, and that far-right populist movements have faced "election defeats, recriminations, and self-doubt" (Meichtry, Troianovski, and Walker, A1).

Against this backdrop, I wish to argue for a conception of hope as a civic virtue, especially well suited to democracies, that is most valuable in times like the present, when democracy faces significant challenges. In section 1, I offer a general overview of hope and sketch an initial conception of hope as a democratic civic virtue. In section 2, the stage is set for further theorizing of this conception in the present American context. Drawing on the work of Ghassan Hage (2003), I make the point that the United States is in the process of becoming a nation of worriers in part because of the failure of the government to distribute social hope. In section 3, I flesh out what hope as a democratic civic virtue could look like in the United States today.[5] Section 4 concludes with brief comments about theorizing civic hope in the context of a modified pragmatism.

Before beginning, a caveat is in order. My concern here is with hope as a *democratic* civic virtue, by which I mean hope as a civic virtue in the context of democratic political systems, that is, systems that embrace the notion that citizens elect those who govern. Democracies can take many forms— for example, representative and direct—or can be combined with forms of socialism. I do not doubt that hope can be a civic virtue in other types

[3] See the Editorial Board, *New York Times*, https://www.nytimes.com/2017/02/17/opinion/keeping-the-kremlins-hands-off-frances-elections.html?_r=0. Accessed March 19, 2017.

[4] Mittleman's comment is made in the context of concerns about climate change. Eight years after the publication of this magisterial work, we have even more reason to fear the advent of "dark ages."

[5] I use the phrases "hope as a civic virtue" and "hope as a democratic civic virtue" interchangeably.

of political systems, such as pure socialism, Marxist societies, theocracies, or monarchies. Whether it can be a civic virtue in authoritarian fascist or communist societies is an interesting question here left aside.

1. Hope

A review of literature on hope from various disciplines gives rise to two kinds of theories of what hope is and how it is generated. The first have been called "agency" theories; I call the second "receptivity" theories. Common to both is what I call the "bare bones" conception or "belief-desire" model of hope.

The bare bones conception or belief-desire model can be gleaned from the work of philosophers as diverse as Thomas Aquinas (2008), Thomas Hobbes (1968), Victoria McGeer (2004), and Margaret Walker (2006). According to this account, hope, at its most basic, is the desire for an end or object and the belief that it is possible to attain it. The belief that the end or object is possible carves out a space for hope between certainty and impossibility. If a desired end is certain, it does not make sense to hope for it. If it is impossible, hoping for it is fruitless and can be self-destructive.

The belief-desire model has been enhanced in various ways. One way is through the development of agency theories of hope, which focus on personal agency as a pathway to attaining hoped-for ends, and on hope as enhancing the agency of the individuals who possess it. Walker (2006, 47–48), for example, stresses that hope is not simply a belief-desire complex but an emotional attitude consisting of a variety of hope phenomena—such as plans, imaginings, and expectations. Some of our hopes, of course, outstrip the reach of our agency. For example, we can hope for good news about a biopsy outcome, or pleasant weather for the afternoon ball game. Other hopes might engage our agency, yet the effects it has might be minimal, as when we hope for an end to war, animal abuse, or famine. McGeer (2004) and Walker (2006) as well as the psychologist C. R. Snyder (2000), however, emphasize the motivational force of hope and its connections with agency. Hope, in their view, can motivate us to rise to challenges and undertake tasks that are possible, even though not probable. In yet another expansion of the belief-desire model, Patrick Shade (2001, 136) writes of the virtue of hopefulness, which is an entrenched character state or disposition of energetic openness to future possibilities. This kind of disposition forms the basis of hope as a virtue, which according to some theorists, such as Aquinas (2008), lies between the extremes of presumption, which is the certainty that good things are to come, and despair, which is the certainty that they won't.[6]

---

[6] For Aquinas (2008), we hope to achieve unification with God at the eschaton. Presumption is the certainty that we will achieve this; despair, the conviction that we won't. Some philosophers question whether hope fits nicely as a mean between extremes in this way. Luc

Specific hopes can, but need not, arise from a hopeful disposition. That is, even if I am not a hopeful person, it is possible for me to have specific hopes, both on specific occasions and in more temporally enduring ways. This is possible because even unhopeful people can care about certain things. I might be generally unhopeful, for example, but have loyalty toward my alma mater's football team and take pleasure in watching it play. Because I care about the team, I can hope that it wins this afternoon, or that it has a good season, or that it maintains a strong coaching staff and player base into the indefinite future, even if I am generally unhopeful about other things. One might wonder how this is psychologically possible. The answer can be found in individual histories and life experiences. Our unhopeful person could be middle aged or older, and might have had some hard knocks in life that left him cynical, depressed, and generally lacking in hope. Perhaps he is a military veteran whose experiences of war have left him emotionally battered and scarred. Despite such negative experiences, it seems possible for such a person to care about something in the present. Perhaps what he cares about sparks some bright spot, or harks back to better days in the past. Caring about an alma mater's football team, for example, could conjure up memories of happier days. To be sure, such memories could be romanticized. Even so, they could form bright spots on a dark horizon, giving rise to a specific and narrow range of hopes in an otherwise bleak emotional landscape.

The second way in which the belief-desire model of hope has been enhanced is through receptivity theories of hope. Receptivity theories draw on literatures and traditions different from those the agency theories do, yet all incorporate the core notion that, at bottom, hope is a belief-desire complex. It is important to note that receptivity theories do not preclude the importance of roles for hope in promoting and sustaining effective agency. They provide larger theoretical frameworks than the agency theories I've mentioned, within which individual agency and hope's effects on it are theorized and contextualized. According to receptivity theories, hope is "received from" or "inspired by" external sources, and then empowers the agency of its possessor. Examples of receptivity theories include those of the French Christian existentialist Gabriel Marcel (1978), the East German Marxist Ernst Bloch (1986), and the conception of hope attributed to the Crow tribe by Jonathan Lear in his book *Radical Hope* (2006).

Marcel (1978), for example, argues that hope occurs most profoundly in situations of "captivity," in which the forces of individual agency have been stymied or brought to a halt. In such situations, an attitude of patient expectation allows us to receive inspiration in the form of God's grace, which gives us hope. Often, we receive insights into how we can move

---

Bovens, for example, suggests that fear, like despair, is a contrary of hope; personal conversation, December 28, 2014; see also Spinoza (in Wild 1958, 270), Hume (1978, 439–48), Day (1969, 89), and Miyazaki (2017, 3) for discussions of the complexities of hope.

forward, what to do, or how to respond in our difficult circumstances. We cannot act or abide with hope, however, without having been receptive to divine guidance.

Bloch (1986) and Lear (2006) write of similar dynamics. For Bloch (1986), hope, a drive akin to hunger, is inspired by the *noch nicht*—the "not yet." Our achieving the not yet is based upon our ability to cut through the deceptions of life in capitalist society and be inspired by an ever-developing vision of a Marxist utopia. We are pulled forward through and out of the capitalist miasma by our hope of attaining that vision. Similarly, Lear (2006) attributes "radical hope" to the Crow tribe through the dreams and visions of its chief, Plenty Coups. These dreams and visions allowed Plenty Coups to receive wisdom from the spirit world by interpreting the words and signs of the Chickadee Person. This wisdom enabled Plenty Coups to lead his tribe forward into a future, dominated by whites, that threatened to destroy traditional Crow ways of life and replace them with conventions, such as private property, that outstripped the tribe's conceptual repertoire. Interestingly, Allen Thompson (2010) has applied the idea of radical hope—a hope for a future that we cannot fully conceptualize—to the challenge of climate change.

I mention agency and receptivity theories because I seek to bring resources from both types of theory to bear on conceptualizing hope as a democratic civic virtue. Bloch's theory provides an interesting model of how to do this. Though a receptivity theory, it also has roles for agency. Marxist hope, for Bloch, is a kind of hunger that drives individuals to seek the way forward to the realization of the Marxist utopia, a classless society. Hope motivates them to act, but it is hope for a specific end that is conceptualized within the context of political theory. Receptivity in this context means drawing on inspiration from Marxist sources, and sometimes waiting for the occluding impediments of capitalist culture to be cleared away by sustained thinking about the shape the Marxist way forward might take.

Similarly, hope as a democratic civic virtue relies on the agency of individuals. Agency theories typically afford more detail and nuance about how hope motivates and empowers agency than receptivity theories do, and it is useful to draw upon these resources. Yet hope as a democratic civic virtue parallels Bloch's conception of Marxist hope in the sense that it is a disposition that is theorized and contextualized by democratic political traditions. These traditions function as grounds for receptivity in the sense that hopeful citizens draw knowledge as well as motivation from them and are able to conceptualize, review, and revise goals by placing them within the context of specific democratic institutions, processes, and traditions. These democratic institutions, processes, and traditions are specific to different countries. Even within a country, different variants of the traditions can be in play. For example, the American political tradition is informed by pragmatists as diverse as Walt Whitman, John Dewey, Richard Rorty, and, arguably, Barack Obama.[7] Yet pragmatist readings of American democracy differ from those that view it as a form of civic religion rooted in the Puritan era (see Gorski 2017; Westbrook 2008, 141).

Writing of hope in a different context, Hirokazu Miyazaki notes: "Hope suggests a willingness to embrace uncertainty and also serves as a concrete method for keeping knowledge moving in conditions of uncertainty" (2017, 8). Part of the method of hope is the ability to draw on institutions, processes, and traditions in the sense of being receptive to the knowledge and tools they offer that can aid in the pursuit of hoped-for goals. Consistently with both Miyazaki's view of hope as a method and with Snyder's agentic conception of the skills of high hopers, flexibility is required to be able to adapt those resources effectively.

I revisit these themes in section 4. For now, we can draw upon the foregoing remarks to sketch an initial conception of hope as a democratic civic virtue:

> Hope as a democratic civic virtue is the entrenched disposition of openness to the political possibilities a democratic government can provide. It includes a desire to promote or attain the legitimate ends of democracy, and the belief that such ends are possible. To be a democratic civic virtue, the disposition of hope must include a commitment to democracy and democratic processes. Hope is fully theorized and contextualized within specific political traditions, which function as the grounds for receptivity to hope and inspiration for hope-motivated agency.

2. Worriers and Carers

To frame the discussion of hope as a democratic civic virtue in the present American context, we need an analysis of the current political situation. *Against Paranoid Nationalism* (2003), by Ghassan Hage, a Lebanese Australian anthropologist and social theorist, provides a useful framework. A brilliant indictment of immigration policies in John Howard's Australia, this book advances the thesis that societies, by distributing or failing to distribute what Hage calls "societal" hope, can create citizens who are worriers or carers. Societal hope refers to the fact that society distributes social routes by means of which people can envision and lead worthwhile lives. Such social routes include the provision of goods that meet basic needs, such as health care, safety, and security, and infrastructure, without which people will be unable to attain the minimum needed to lead worthwhile lives. Most important, perhaps, is that such routes include education, which enables people to imagine the kinds of futures they want to have and empowers them with the knowledge and skills to turn those dreams into realities. Strong, vibrant economies with opportunities for employment and

---

[7] See Whitman 2002, 2004; Westbrook 2008; Deneen 1999; Rorty 1989, 1999; and Kloppenberg 2011. For a different reading of Obama, see Miyazaki 2017, 181–86.

advancement are also routes by means of which society distributes social hope, for they enable people to put their educations to use to fulfill dreams of having careers and families. In these and other ways, society provides conditions conducive to the development of dispositional hope.

Part of Hage's analysis focuses on how collective national identities— national senses of "we"—can sustain or undermine hope in society (2003, 12–18). Hage gives a homely but apt illustration of how a collective "we" can sustain hope and inspire uplift. He confesses that he is hopeless at cricket; yet, through identification with the Australian national cricket team, he vicariously participates in their triumphs and experiences a sense of hope (2003, 13). The "we" has many uses. For one thing, it can be used comparatively: we are generally more educated than the people of Afghanistan. Another effect is aspirational: "The child uttering 'we are good at football' sets himself or herself on the road of 'trying to be good at football.' The imagined 'we'... actually becomes causal in influencing the capacity of the person who is trying to be what 'we' all are" (Hage 2003, 13).[8] By supporting the aspirations of citizens to improve themselves in specific ways, the imagined we—a collective identity—fosters conditions under which the disposition of hope is nurtured.

More can be said about Hage's complex analysis. Here let us note his thesis that societies, by distributing or failing to distribute hope, can create citizens who are worriers or carers. Hage draws on attachment theory from psychoanalysis to explain this (2003, 26ff.). He sees the nation-state as analogous to a parent; the language of "motherland" and "fatherland" reflects this role. According to him, we form attachments to our homeland, just as we do to our parents. As with parental attachments, the nature of our bonds to our homeland affects whether we are worriers or carers. Worriers are those whose attachments are insecure; they have not been sufficiently nurtured, nor given a sense of security and mastery over their own agency. A scarcity of hope, according to Hage, creates a society of worriers (2003, 20). Lacking hope, a citizenry sees threats at every turn and lacks the wherewithal to see how to overcome the problems that beset it. Failures of imagination and of cognitive openness to new possibilities form part of the worrier's mentality. The worrier's horizons are closed instead of expansive. The worrier, insecure from the start in her attachment to her homeland, sees novelty as a threat. Instead of seeing problems as challenges, the worrier takes a defensive posture, circling her wagons against innovation and change. Fear is the worrier's best friend; the fear of losing her nation causes the worrier to retreat to a mental landscape of nationalistic fantasies. Here, too, psychoanalysis informs Hage's analysis: the fantasies of the paranoid

---

[8] Of course, it is not always true that assertions such as "we are good at football" have the causal roles that Hage attributes to them. Such utterances could be self-deceptive, or mere wishful thinking lacking in causal force. I take it that Hage's claim is not that such statements always or necessarily have causal efficacy but that they sometimes do, and can thereby shape conceptions of the self and influence action.

nationalist are akin to those of persons who suffer from borderline personality disorders. In both kinds of case, the lines distinguishing fantasy from reality become blurred.

Paranoid nationalism results from a scarcity of hope. This is not to say that hope is completely absent from the paranoid nationalist's emotional landscape. Worriers can have hope, for example, hope that antiimmigration laws will be put in place, hope that a homeland they perceive as weakened will become great again, and so on. Such hopes, however, seem to be linked with and driven by fear. Paranoid nationalism is a kind of defensive nationalism that sees external or alien factors as threats—to cherished traditions, national integrity, indeed, to the very survival of the nation. For many nations today, immigration issues are focal points for paranoid nationalism.

By contrast, carers are those who have benefited from secure attachments to their homeland. They are confident in their agency and in their capacity to solve problems and meet challenges. Characterized by cognitive openness, the ability to use imagination, and the ability to deploy resources creatively, they are not afraid to experiment with new programs and policies. They are secure enough in their national self-identity to extend the benefits of their homeland to immigrants who seek to share them. Hage (2003) believes that the strength of carers resides in hope. Their hope results from a strong sense of identity and agency that has been nurtured through healthy attachments to their country. Here I can only note that Hage (2003), joined by other commentators, sees the forces of global capitalism as undermining the power of the nation-state and thus eroding its ability to inculcate hope (see, e.g., Tremonti 2008; Moïsi 2009; and Prideaux 2011).

Hage's analysis, published fifteen years ago, offers prescient yet chilling insights into the rise of far-right political parties and anti-immigrant populism in Europe and the United States today.[9] A spate of recent books examines deep social, cultural, and political divisions in the United States, focusing mostly on multiple schisms between affluence and liberalism in urban America and poverty and populism in rural areas.[10] In one of the most eloquent analyses, J. D. Vance's *Hillbilly Elegy: A Memoir of a Family and Culture in Crisis* (2016), the author tells the story of his family's migration from rural Kentucky to Ohio. Though the author and his sister eventually escape the cycle of poverty and despair, his grandparents and parents were trapped in substance abuse, addiction, poverty, and family violence. Believing themselves abandoned by both political parties, his family and those in the circles in which he moved in his early life experienced a

[9] For an analysis of the rise of globalism on the emergence of far-right nationalism, see Ip 2017.

[10] See, for example, Packer 2013, Cramer 2016, Hochschild 2016, Isenberg 2016, and Vance 2016. See also Coontz (2016), "The Shell-Shocked White Working Class," http://www.cnn.com/2016/09/23/opinions/shell-shocked-white-working-class-opinion-coontz/. Accessed March 16, 2017.

sense of hopelessness and despair, often coupled with a deep mistrust of and skepticism about the effectiveness of "systems," such as health care, education, and social services, to provide them with the means to become economically self-sufficient.

For these people, the American government failed to distribute societal hope. They and others in similar situations across the nation fueled the populism that elected Donald Trump.[11] In their view, the collective we with which they identify has been abandoned and disrespected, if not victimized, by government. Feeling alienated from the political mainstream, they sought a candidate whom they believed would promote their interests and take their concerns seriously, who would "drain the swamp" and create policies that would integrate them into the life of the nation. Trump's campaign preyed upon their hopelessness, their frustration with government, and their fears and mistaken beliefs about immigration—that all Muslim immigrants are prospective terrorists and that all immigrants take jobs that would otherwise be held by white Americans. Trump's campaign also legitimated hatred and violence based on racism, sexism, and homophobia. In short, Trump tapped into the biases, hatreds, and fears of a preexisting nation of worriers who had become devoid of hope in the government, whipping them into a visible and voluble crowd of paranoid nationalists.

This is one side of the current political story. On the other lies a range of reactions from liberals. Some, for example those who purchase and read books such as those previously mentioned, seek to understand what happened. Some look for ways to unify and move forward. Those of this ilk are potential carers who might seek to bind the wounds of the nation. On the other side are those who, like Garrison Keillor (2016), are critical of Trump's claims to champion a forsaken working class and criticize members of that class for irresponsible choices. He predicts that the disasters of a Trump presidency will fall mainly on Trump's working-class supporters, and does not lament that. He advises liberals, not responsible for electing Trump, to retire to private life and wait until the disaster of his presidency is over.

In the midst of this fractured landscape, what might hope as a democratic civic virtue look like?

3. Hope as a Democratic Civic Virtue

An inspirational example is found in the work of educational scholar Amanda LaShaw (2008), who studied a movement for small, equitable schools in Oakland, California. The movement began at the grassroots level in response to the need to provide better schooling for black and Latino working-class children. Eventually, it garnered support from

---

[11] For a different analysis of Trump's victory, see Coates (2017), who argues that white racism spanning socioeconomic classes fueled Trump's rise.

Oakland city agencies and beyond, attracting a $350-million bond from Oakland to build and improve schools, as well as a $9.5-million donation from the Bill and Melinda Gates Foundation. In such cases, I would say that citizens display hope as a civic virtue. Even when government fails, citizens are still free—and might have good reason—to initiate hope-based movements. Of course, civic hope is also displayed in grassroots initiatives that dovetail with or support government policy. Hope as a civic virtue of citizens need not, however, depend on the acquiescence of government in citizens' projects and goals. Witness how hope as a civic virtue has been displayed in acts of civil disobedience, such as occurred during the civil rights movement or in actions protesting the Vietnam War.

Civic hope is also displayed in the actions of individual citizens who do not band together for a common cause. Individual acts such as running for a position on a school board, attending a school board meeting, or voting can express the civic virtue of hope, provided they are done from the appropriate motivation of promoting a democratic end. The question of motivation is interesting, for it seems unduly stringent to insist that hope is a civic virtue only if citizéns' hopeful dispositions and actions spring from a purely disinterested commitment to democratic ends and processes. In LaShaw's example, we can see how odd it would be to think that the parents of black and Latino children in Oakland were moved only by a commitment to the generic end of providing better schooling because of the disinterested desire to enhance the ends of democracy and democratic processes. They legitimately wanted higher quality schools for their children, and worked for this within political constraints. This suggests that the appropriate motivations for hope as a civic virtue can include not only commitments to the ends of democracy and democratic processes but also legitimate self-interest.

The inclusion of legitimate self-interest as a possible motivation for civically hopeful dispositions and actions is not arbitrary but premised on the principle that democracy exists to further the interests of citizens within certain parameters. This principle can be traced to ideas espoused by the earliest exponents of liberal democracy. It is, for example, foreshadowed in the Lockean proviso stating that denizens of the state of nature may appropriate resources so long as they put them to good use and leave as much and as good for others (see Locke 1980, chap. 5). This provides a foundation for democratic institutions that recognize the legitimacy of promoting self-interests provided they do not impinge on the legitimate interests of others. Similar sentiments find expression in another exponent of liberal democracy, John Stuart Mill, who advanced the harm principle as a guide for democratic government. It affords the individual the freedom to live as she sees fit, provided that she does not harm others (see Mill 1869, chap. 4). The scope and nature of legitimate interest is difficult to specify and has clearly changed since the days when Locke wrote. Mill's harm principle, too, raises questions about what counts as harm, its scope, and how to distinguish harm from offense. So how are we to identify the kinds of motives that can work with hope as a civic virtue?

Elsewhere I have argued that virtues can be "impure" (Snow forthcoming).[12] A virtue is impure if the motives it includes are not all morally worthy but mixed. A set of mixed motives consists of morally worthy and morally neutral motives. The presence of morally vicious motives in a set renders the set not mixed but vicious, and can render the trait that includes the set a vice.

To illustrate how this works with civic hope, consider that parents of black and Latino children in the Oakland example likely acted from legitimate self-interest. We could call this a morally benign or worthy motive, since they acted on behalf of their children, or we could call it morally neutral. The point is that neither the desire to promote or attain the legitimate ends of democracy nor a commitment to democracy and democratic processes is intrinsic to the desire to obtain better schools for one's children. That is, the desire for better schooling is not part of the desires required to appropriately motivate civic hope. Yet, appropriately constrained, it can work in conjunction with the desires required for hope. Civic hope in such cases would count as an impure virtue.

Introducing the distinction between pure and impure virtues allows us to accommodate the notion that many citizens do not act from pure love of democracy but take advantage of democratic processes to legitimately advance their interests. The Oakland parents were probably not motivated by the pure desire to improve schooling in a democratic society but instead wanted something much nearer to the ground: better schools for their own children. If that was their primary motivation for acting, they cannot be said to have acted from a purely virtuous motive in a robust Aristotelian sense, according to which people do what is hopeful, generous, brave, and so on, from the selfless desire to act virtuously. Yet, because of this, I do not want to deny that the parents displayed hope or that their hope was a civic virtue.

When is a legitimate self-interest appropriately constrained so that it can function as a morally neutral motive alongside those required for civic hope? The answer is that self-interest is rendered "legitimate" when it is not morally tainted. If I seek to advance my self-interest by harming you or wronging you, my self-interest is morally tainted. If the Oakland parents had sought to provide better schools for their children by harming others, say, by redirecting vital funds for a program for disabled children and thereby denying them crucial care, that would have been a morally tainted, and consequently illegitimate, exercise of self-interest. Alternatively, if the parents had used nefarious means to advance their cause—for example, by bribing school board officials to support their project—this, too, would have rendered their motives and actions morally vicious.

---

[12] I draw upon Snow forthcoming in the paragraphs that follow.

A measure of unavoidable imprecision attends the question of when morally bad motives render a trait a vice that would otherwise be considered an impure virtue. How many morally bad motives are required to taint or outweigh the morally good and neutral motives that a trait displays, thereby rendering our evaluation of that trait morally negative? How strong does a single morally bad motive have to be for it to do this? Are there some morally bad motives, such as the desire to control another rational adult for one's own gain, which if it is the only bad motive in a set of otherwise morally good and neutral motives would render an otherwise seemingly benign trait, such as impure generosity, vicious? Such cases seem to me best judged on a case-by-case basis using practical wisdom, but they speak to the complexity of evaluations of traits and actions in real-world situations. One can imagine people whose hope is a pure civic virtue, who are motivated purely by love of their country and its democracy. For many others, I suspect that civic hope is an impure virtue in the sense described above. In other cases, I suspect that civic hope is tainted by malevolent ambition or other immoral motives, as when a person seeks political office from love of power or the desire to enact questionable policies, such as a ban on Muslim immigrants and visitors. Such individuals might have civic hope, in the sense that they could seek to advance the ends of democracy (as construed by their lights) and be committed to democracy and democratic processes, yet their hope would not be a virtue because their disposition and actions are mixed with immoral motives.

Given this discussion of motivation, we can amend our initial sketch of hope as a civic virtue as follows:

> Hope as a democratic civic virtue is the entrenched disposition of openness to the political possibilities a democratic government can provide. Hope must include the belief that the ends of democracy are possible. Hope is a pure civic virtue when it is motivated solely by the desire to promote or attain the legitimate ends of democracy, and includes a commitment to democracy and democratic processes.[13] If, in addition to these motives, hope includes motives of legitimate self-interest, it is an impure virtue. Hope is fully theorized and contextualized within specific political traditions, which function as the grounds for receptivity to hope and inspiration for hope-motivated agency.

4. Theorizing Hope: A Modified Pragmatism

The Oakland parents were unlikely to have had a theory to contextualize their hope, though they might have been inspired by democratic ideals from American history. Yet if we wish to promote activities like theirs, and

---

[13] What of someone who is lacking a commitment to democracy and to democratic processes? I believe such a person might have hope, even civic hope, but she would not have hope as a democratic civic virtue. What of someone whose commitment is weak, perhaps because of multiple political disappointments and setbacks? In that case, I would say that her democratic civic virtue of hope is also weak.

hope as a civic virtue more generally, we would do well to theorize hope in the context of American political traditions.[14] Articulating a background theory for civic hope can enable actors in the public realm to deliberately draw upon established democratic traditions, values, and ideals for inspiration and guidance, thereby expanding their knowledge base so as to explain and justify civic action to would-be participants as well as critics. As I mentioned earlier, two traditions of American democracy could furnish a background theory: American pragmatism and the tradition of democracy as a civic religion that traces its roots to the Puritans. Let me briefly sketch a modified pragmatism as a background theory for the conception of hope as a civic virtue offered here.

Richard Rorty draws on the pragmatism of John Dewey and Walt Whitman for his vision of social hope and maintains that both figures substitute hope for knowledge (1989, 106–7). Hope, as defined by Rorty and attributed to Whitman, Dewey, and the American transcendentalist Ralph Waldo Emerson, is "the ability to believe that the future will be unspecifiably different from, and unspecifiably freer than, the past"; hope is "the condition of all growth" (1999, 120). Rorty's idea of social hope is cast in an American idiom and directed to a distinctively American end: it is a hope that motivates us to "achieve our country" (1999, 34; 1998, 106–7; see also Westbrook 2008, 140–41). The foundations of American pragmatic hope lay in the "stuff" of America—its history, its social, political, and economic institutions, its distinctive spirit, and its emerging culture and national character (see Westbrook 2008, 141). I believe that Walt Whitman best gives the flavor of the hope that Rorty commends.

Whitman's poetry is a love affair with a nation in its adolescence— an America that has survived its infancy and is emerging, in the mid-nineteenth century, into the robustness of youth. Whitman's work conveys identification with the fullness of being in America and pays homage to any and everything that America can or has produced. Ebullient in its tone, the poetry brims with hope for the present and the future. "Song of Myself," first published in *Leaves of Grass* in 1855, is especially instructive in this regard (see Whitman 2004, xxi, 63–124). The poem is an extended identification with all that Whitman encounters. He sees himself in all, and all in him, and he loves all with force and fullness of being. The poem illustrates Rorty's claim that moral progress is "a matter of increasing *sensitivity*, increasing responsiveness to the needs of a larger and larger variety

---

[14] Michael Lamb (2016, 320) makes a similar point when he suggests using democratic traditions as a motivational resource to make democratic hope concrete for citizens. Doing so, he believes, could help motivate them to action in pursuit of goods that are difficult to obtain, thereby overcoming an abstract faith in democratic systems that are dominated by political elites. Lamb offers an interesting account of democratic hope that draws on Aquinas's account of hope as a theological virtue. For an account of hope as a political virtue from a Kantian-inspired perspective, see Moellendorf 2006. For a Deweyan theory of hope in dialogue with Snyder's hope theory, see Fishman and McCarthy 2005.

of people and things" (1999, 81; Rorty's italics). The poem expresses an ideal of social democracy—seeing equal value for all, having equal respect for all, and most important, loving all and seeing all as engaged in a common life. This Whitmanesque ideal is further developed in the philosophy of John Dewey in the early twentieth century and taken up again by Rorty later in the same century.

Leaves of Grass, published in 1855, predated the Civil War. Did the slaughter and horror of a nation turned against itself sour Whitman, causing him to abandon his hopeful vision? It did not. Arguably, the horrors of the war and the superficiality of the age that followed it tempered and fortified Whitman's hope. In *Democratic Vistas*, printed in 1888, Whitman shares his own experience of the Civil War. In addition, he registers dismay, indeed, revulsion, at what Mark Twain called America's "gilded age"—an age in which Whitman believed superficiality reigned in intellectual life, greed prevailed in business, vulgarity characterized manners, and hypocrisy infected morals (Whitman 2002, 11–14). Whitman is well aware of the trauma the young nation has endured, as well as the ills that beset it. Yet he finds in his experiences, especially his Civil War time in army hospitals, reasons for hope. Underlying the carnage of the war he sees the nobility of brave soldiers who fight and die for cherished causes. Beneath the superficial veneer of mediocrity and evidence of moral decay he sees strength and the ability to overcome temptation and weakness. He notes that the justification of American democracy ultimately lies in the future, specifically, in the ability of the new nation to produce people of good moral character and religious disposition (2002, 2, 40). The foundation needed to support American democracy, he contends, has yet to emerge. This foundation is a truly national imaginative literature—one that points the way for the people with stories of worthy role models (2002, 70–71). According to Whitman (2002, 8), this literature will shape the nation's moral identity. Here we find adumbrations of Hage's collective we.

Rorty and Whitman share a vision of American social democracy, yet both were aware of the failures of American political life. Failures in American political life beset us today. In light of the turmoil of our times, I suggest that we not follow the pragmatists in substituting hope for knowledge but instead buttress hope with knowledge. Recall the passage, quoted earlier, from Miyazaki: "Hope suggests a willingness to embrace uncertainty and also serves as a concrete method for keeping knowledge moving in conditions of uncertainty" (2017, 8). Recall, too, Snyder's view that high hopers display flexibility in pursuing their ends and the means to them. The work of psychologist Gabrielle Oettingen (2014) furnishes resources for a method of hoping that incorporates knowledge into the process of hoping, allows for flexibility, and fits well with the pragmatist vision of civic hope as involving imaginative possibilities.[15] Oettingen summarizes decades of

---

[15] I draw on Snow 2015, 214, in describing Oettingen's work.

studies that support her view that dreaming, indeed, many kinds of positive imaginative thinking, do not help people to achieve their goals but lead them to become frustrated and unhappy. Dreams and imaginings, she argues, must be supplemented. Elsewhere I've characterized her work as follows: "Her findings indicate that those who engage in what she calls 'mental contrasting' are happier and more successful. Mental contrasting involves tethering one's positive outlook to reality, that is, combining one's dreams with visualizing the obstacles that stand in the way" (Snow 2015, 214). Visualizing obstacles enables one to anticipate and overcome them in the actual pursuit of goals. This is integral to Snyder's "agency-pathways" theory of hope: the hoper must not only be able to imagine attaining the hoped-for end but also be able to adopt effective means to achieving it. This requires cognitive flexibility and emotional resilience. High hopers are cognitively flexible; they are able to adjust their ends as well as means when obstacles are encountered or the circumstances of pursuing goals change. Mental contrasting, I suggest, provides a promising method for hopers to employ.

The modified pragmatism briefly outlined here serves as a kind of receptivity theory or resource for hopers to better understand the content, forms, and functions of civic hope within the American democratic framework. Hopers can look to that resource for guidance and inspiration, and through reflection on it might come to discern the contours of ways forward through difficult political times, much as Bloch urged for Marxists, Lear thought of Plenty Coups, and Marcel thought of those who were stuck in agentic "captivity." Unlike Marcel and the case of Plenty Coups, I am not arguing that divine grace or guidance from a spirit world is part of the story. As I noted earlier, my view is more akin to Bloch's insofar as Bloch thought that Marxists could draw upon a political tradition for the cultivation of hope. By enlarging the access of civic hopers to the rich trove of ideas and experiences that have contributed to the American democratic tradition and using mental contrasting as a method for formulating ends, obstacles, and means, the agency of civic hopers can be empowered.

Before concluding, I should address a worry. How does the grassroots hope of the Oakland parents relate, if at all, to the hope of the likes of Whitman, Dewey, and Rorty? How can we connect, if at all, hope on the ground as displayed by ordinary citizens with that of intellectuals in the pragmatist tradition?

I have three responses to this concern. The first is to think of theorized democratic hope as occupying a continuum from conceptually thin to conceptually thick. Many ordinary hopers likely have conceptually thin hopes, in the sense that such hopes are not richly informed by democratic theory or political traditions. Oakland hopers likely did not know of the American pragmatist tradition, but, thanks to community organizers, they knew they could take action through democratic processes to achieve their goals. They might well have been inspired by aspects of American history more familiar to them than pragmatism. On the thicker end of the continuum, democratic hope can be well informed by American pragmatism and inspired by the vision of Whitman and others for our nation. The second response is that some individuals, such as community organizers, bridge the gap between ordinary folk and intellectuals by bringing knowledge of democratic processes and traditions to otherwise disempowered groups. A notable example is Barack Obama, who, as an intellectual, was also a community organizer. As a presidential candidate and later as president, he made empowering through hope an important part of his agenda. Finally, the worry about the disconnect between action on the ground and rich conceptualizations of ideas points to a need that academics should take seriously: the need to get out of the ivory tower and bring the resources of our shared intellectual traditions to bear on life today. In a separate project, I will argue that philosophers have a responsibility to bring their expertise to bear on the social issues our nation is facing.[16]

Conclusion

I have argued here for a conception of hope as a democratic civic virtue and have suggested that, in the American context, it is best theorized by adopting a modified pragmatism. Modified pragmatism embraces the spirit and flexibility of Whitman and Rorty but insists that hope should not supplant knowledge. Instead, modified pragmatism looks to empirical psychology for advice on how best to achieve hoped-for ends. In short, today we can draw upon the tradition of American pragmatism, with its emphasis on vision and inspiration despite setbacks and hardship, yet fortify it with empirical research that highlights roles for knowledge, strategy, and planning in efforts to achieve the goals we set for ourselves through civic imagination.

Acknowledgments

I am grateful to fellow participants in "The Nature and Norms of Hope" conference at Cornell University, April 27–29, 2017, and to the audience at the Institute for the Study of Human Flourishing Colloquium Series, August 30, 2017, for helpful comments on earlier versions of this essay. Research for the essay was supported by a grant from the Science of Virtues initiative, funded by The John Templeton Foundation.

References

Aquinas, Thomas. 2008. *Summa Theologica: Secunda Secundae Partis*. Question 17. http://www.newadvent.org/summa/3017.htm. Accessed March 19, 2017.

[16] This project is tentatively entitled *Out of the Ivory Tower: Public Philosophy in the Twenty-First Century*.

Bloch, Ernst. 1986. *The Principle of Hope*. 3 vols. Trans. Neville Plaice, Stephen Plaice, and Paul Knight. Cambridge, Mass.: MIT Press.
Coates, Ta-Nehisi. 2017. "The First White President." *Atlantic* 320, no. 3 (October): 74–87.
Coontz, Stephanie. 2016. "The Shell-Shocked White Working Class." http://www.cnn.com/2016/09/23/opinions/shell-shocked-white-working-class-opinion-coontz/. Accessed March 16, 2017.
Cramer, Katherine J. 2016. *The Politics of Resentment: Rural Consciousness in Wisconsin and the Rise of Scott Walker*. Chicago: University of Chicago Press.
Day, J. P. 1969. "Hope." *American Philosophical Quarterly* 6, no. 2: 89–102.
Deneen, Patrick J. 1999. "The Politics of Hope and Optimism: Rorty, Havel, and the Democratic Faith of John Dewey." *Social Research* 66, no. 2:577–606.
Economist. 2016a. "America's Best Hope." November 5–11.
———. 2016b. "The Debasing of American Politics." October 5–21.
Editorial Board, *New York Times*. 2017. "Keeping the Kremlin's Hands Off France's Elections." https://www.nytimes.com/2017/02/17/opinion/keeping-the-kremlins-hands-off-frances-elections.html?_r=0. Accessed March 19, 2017.
Fishman, Stanley M., and Lucille McCarthy. 2005. "The Morality and Politics of Hope: John Dewey and Positive Psychology in Dialogue." *Transactions of the Charles S. Pierce Society: A Quarterly Journal in American Philosophy* 41, no. 3:675–701.
Frum, David. 2017. "How to Build an Autocracy." *Atlantic* 319, no. 2 (March): 49–59.
Gorski, Philip. 2017. *American Covenant: A History of Civil Religion from the Puritans to the Present*. Princeton: Princeton University Press.
Hage, Ghassan. 2003. *Against Paranoid Nationalism: Searching for Hope in a Shrinking Society*. Annandale, Australia: Pluto Press.
Hobbes, Thomas. 1968. *Leviathan*. Ed. C. B. MacPherson. Harmondsworth, U.K.: Penguin.
Hochschild, Arlie Russell. 2016. *Strangers in Their Own Land: Anger and Mourning on the American Right*. New York: New Press.
Hume, David. 1978. *A Treatise of Human Nature*. Ed. P. H. Nidditch. Oxford: Clarendon Press.
Ip, Greg. 2017. "We Are Not the World." https://www.wsj.com/articles/we-arent-the-world-1483728161. Accessed March 19, 2017.
Isenberg, Nancy. 2016. *White Trash: The 400-Year Untold History of Class in America*. New York: Viking.
Lamb, Michael. 2016. "Aquinas and the Virtues of Hope: Theological and Democratic." *Journal of Religious Ethics* 44, no. 2:300–332.
Locke, John. 1980. *Second Treatise of Government*. Ed. C. B. Macpherson. Indianapolis: Hackett.

Keillor, Garrison. 2016. "Trump Voters Will Not Like What Happens Next." https://www.washingtonpost.com/opinions/trump-voters-will-not-like-what-happens-next/2016/11/09/e346ffc2-a67f-11e6-8fc0-7be8f848c492_story.html?utm_term=.67fa92ef6d8a. Accessed March 16, 2017.

Kendall, Brent. 2017. "Travel Ban Heads to Court in Transition." *Wall Street Journal*, March 17, A4.

Kendall, Brent, and Ian Lovett. 2017. "Judge Blocks Travel Ban." *Wall Street Journal*, March 16, A1, A8.

Kloppenberg, James T. 2011. *Reading Obama: Dreams, Hope, and the American Political Tradition*. Princeton: Princeton University Press.

LaShaw, Amanda. 2008. "Experiencing Imminent Justice: The Presence of Hope in a Movement for Equitable Schooling." *Space and Culture* 11, no. 2:109–24.

Lear, Jonathan. 2006. *Radical Hope: Ethics in the Face of Cultural Devastation*. Cambridge, Mass.: Harvard University Press.

Liptak, Adam. 2017. "Campaign Pledge of Muslim Ban Haunts the President in Court." *New York Times*, March 17, A1, A13.

Marcel, Gabriel. 1978. *Homo Viator: Introduction to a Metaphysic of Hope*. Trans. Peter Smith. Chicago: Gateway.

McGeer, Victoria. 2004. "The Art of Good Hope." *Annals of the American Academy of Political and Social Science* 592:100–127.

Meichtry, Stacy, Anton Troianovski, and Marcus Walker. 2017. "Europe's Populists Rethink Approach." *Wall Street Journal*, August 22, A1, A8.

Mill, John Stuart. 1869. *On Liberty*. http://www.bartleby.com/130/4.html. Accessed March 19, 2017.

Mittleman, Alan. 2009. *Hope in a Democratic Age: Philosophy, Religion, and Political Theory*. New York: Oxford University Press.

Miyazaki, Hirokazu. 2004. *The Method of Hope: Anthropology, Philosophy, and Fijian Knowledge*. Stanford: Stanford University Press.

———. 2017. "Obama's Hope: An Economy of Belief and Substance." In *The Economy of Hope*, ed. Hirokazu Miyazaki and Richard Swedberg, 172–89. Philadelphia: University of Pennsylvania Press.

Moellendorf, Darrel. 2006. "Hope as a Political Virtue." *Philosophical Papers* 35, no. 3:413–33.

Moïsi, Dominique. 2009. *The Geopolitics of Emotion: How Cultures of Fear, Humiliation, and Hope Are Reshaping the World*. New York: Anchor Books.

Obama, Barack. 2006. *The Audacity of Hope: Thoughts on Reclaiming the American Dream*. New York: Broadway Paperbacks.

Oettingen, Gabriele. 2014. *Rethinking Positive Thinking: Inside the New Science of Motivation*. New York: Current (Penguin).

Packer, George. 2013. *The Unwinding: An Inner History of the New America*. New York: Farrar, Straus and Giroux.

Pannett, Rachel, and Mike Cherney. 2017. "Australia Nationalists Lose." *Wall Street Journal*, March 14, A9.

Pettigrove, Glen, ed. Forthcoming. *Neglected Virtues*.

Prideaux, John. 2011. "Special Report Italy: Oh for a New Risorgimento." *Economist* 399, no. 8737 (June 11–17): 3–16.

Pop, Valentina, and Marcus Walker. 2017. "Dutch Leader Retains Power, Exit Polls Say." *Wall Street Journal*, March 16, A10.

Rorty, Richard. 1989. *Achieving Our Country: Leftist Thought in Twentieth-Century America*. Cambridge, Mass.: Harvard University Press.

——. 1999. *Philosophy and Social Hope*. New York: Penguin.

Rubin, Alissa J. 2017a. "Trump May Have Pushed Dutch Voters Away from Populism." *New York Times*, March 17, A4.

——. 2017b. "Geert Wilders Falls Short in Election, as Wary Dutch Scatter Their Votes." https://www.nytimes.com/2017/03/15/world/europe/geert-wilders-netherlands-far-right-vote.html. Accessed March 16, 2017.

Shade, Patrick. 2001. *Habits of Hope: A Pragmatic Theory*. Nashville, Tenn.: Vanderbilt University Press.

Snow, Nancy E. 2015. "Comments on Badhwar, Well-Being: Happiness in a Worthwhile Life." *Journal of Value Inquiry* 50, no. 1:209–17.

——. Forthcoming. "The Perils of Magnificence." In Pettigrove forthcoming.

——. 2000. "Hypothesis: There Is Hope." In *Handbook of Hope: Theory, Measures, and Applications*, ed. C. R. Snyder, 3–21. San Diego: Academic Press.

Thompson, Allen. 2010. "Radical Hope for Living Well in a Warmer World." *Journal of Agricultural and Environmental Ethics* 23:43–59.

Tremonti, Giulio. 2008. *La paura e la speranza*. Milan: Arnoldo Mondadori.

Vance, J. D. 2016. *Hillbilly Elegy: A Memoir of a Family and Culture in Crisis*. New York: HarperCollins.

Walker, Marcus. 2017. "Facing Vote, Dutch Leader Pivots." *Wall Street Journal*, March 13, A8.

Walker, Margaret Urban. 2006. *Moral Repair: Reconstructing Moral Relations After Wrongdoing*. New York: Cambridge University Press.

Westbrook, Robert B. 2008. *Democratic Hope: Pragmatism and the Politics of Truth*. Ithaca, N.Y.: Cornell University Press.

Whitman, Walt. 2002. *Democratic Vistas and Other Papers*. Amsterdam: Fredonia Books.

——. 2004. *The Complete Poems*. Ed. Francis Murphy. London: Penguin Books.

Wild, John, ed. 1958. *Spinoza Selections*. New York: Charles Scribner's Sons.

INDEX

Page numbers in *italics* refer to figures

Connecting Virtues: Advances in Ethics, Epistemology, and Political Philosophy.
Edited by Michel Croce and Maria Silvia Vaccarezza.
Chapters and book compilation © 2018 Metaphilosophy LLC and John Wiley & Sons Ltd.

228 INDEX